THESE WERE THE

WOMEN

U.S.A. 1776–1860

May we ever seek truth for authority,

never take authority for truth.

LUCRETIA MOTT

THESE WERE THE

WOMEN

U.S.A. 1776-1860

By

Mary Ormsbee Whitton

HASTINGS HOUSE, PUBLISHERS

NEW YORK

TO HELEN ORMSBEE

FOR CRITICISM AND ENCOURAGEMENT

INTRODUCTION

A PHASE of our American heritage that is passed over lightly in political history is the story of the women of the new republic. To present them where they lived and as they lived is the object of this study. Some notable figures will appear, but the accent will be on the average woman in a period when she was publicly inarticulate.

The panorama starts with the Revolution and carries to the dark days of the Civil War when women swarmed into Washington to staff the hospitals and to furnish clerical help for mushrooming government departments. After that, no one need be too deeply concerned for the weaker sex. Typewriter and vote were still to come, but once women became officially something more than females, they would never be forced back into a domesticity from which there was no economic escape. Today's women who go far in arts and industry were foreshadowed by those Civil War clerks, lifting their hoop skirts high above the mud of Washington, in a morning rush to reach their desks on time.

To a historian of the more inarticulate period, a problem is paucity of authentic source material. In the opening decades of independence, this country's best minds were centered on government and theology. Practical men were building up commerce and expanding boundaries. Very few observers stopped to notice the women or to make mention of them in the new scheme of things.

But the women were there, wives, mothers, daughters, genteel ladies and underpaid workers. Caught in the journals of travelers, in local histories, in letters and diaries, one can find them. Like a mosaic, the picture must be built up of many little glimpses, most convincing when the testimony was unintentional.

Many women will make up this pageant, but there will be no full-length portraiture. Instead there will be candid shots of all kinds of women against all kinds of backgrounds. In these pages laundresses receiving sixpence per diem plus rations from British commanders are as valid to the picture as a *grande dame* importing her cap gauze from Europe.

One factor must be continually reckoned with—the enormous variety of early American life. There were differences of geography besides wide divergencies of custom and financial standing. There were women of the farms and of the cities; ladies of fine mansions, both North and South, and their rougher sisters in frontier cabins.

The author has no axe to grind, no thesis to propound. Her object is to let these women tell their own stories as much as possible. In our time, museums and collectors have set about preserving the physical relics of the past—houses, furnishings, costumes, tools. Here I purpose showing the women who wore those satin slippers and handled the dainty teacups; also the women who wove their own linsey-woolsey and carried water up from the spring in wooden buckets.

Sometimes the record as found will clash with tradition, since tradition is often more romantic than the facts. But in these cases, the author will stand by the record. In earlier decades one also discovers considerable variation in dates. Wherever possible, these have been checked, but the interest here is not antiquarian. The goal is to find the real woman, the living woman.

Deliberately the author has avoided repeating material used four years ago in her *First First Ladies,* sketches of the few women of this period whose husbands reached the White House. Rather than duplicate these portraits, it was decided to illustrate the backgrounds from which these first ladies came, by lives of other women still unchronicled. Consequently, in these pages there will be scant reference to Dolly Madison or Sarah Polk or Abigail Fillmore whose stories have already been told in *First First Ladies.* Where in the opening chapters of this present study, one encounters Martha Washington and Abigail Adams, fresh sources have been drawn upon, some of them not available when the previous book was written.

Here I offer a final word of gratitude to librarians from Berkeley, California, to New Canaan, Connecticut, who have helped me in my search.

M.O.W.

CONTENTS

THESE WERE THE

WOMEN

U.S.A. 1776–1860

CHAPTER ONE

Daughters of the Revolution

*T*HE starting point of this survey of American women and how they lived will be the American Revolution. That initial date gives the benefit of ample war annals to draw upon. Because of the Revolution—one of the most significant events of the eighteenth century—people kept journals, wrote letters and recorded anecdotes which reveal, sometimes unintentionally, the activities of the country's female citizens.

When one sets out on a pilgrimage into the past, the temptation is to shorten the journey by seizing on some outstanding figure, and presenting her as typical of her time. However, even in the days of ancient simplicities, there was no such thing as a typical American woman. There were women of many racial strains, rich and poor, able and slack, sick and well, domestic and intellectual, bond and free. Homes in New England differed from those of New York and New Jersey. Customs prevailing in Virginia could not be predicated of the Carolinas or Pennsylvania. Even within the same geographical unit startling variations can be unearthed by shifting from city to country, or from the aristocracy to the downtrodden.

Thus, in the Revolutionary decade, Mercy Warren of Plymouth turned a lettered pen to plays in blank verse, at the same time that Deborah Samson, a bound orphan from the same township, was

1

enlisting as a man to fight in the Revolutionary armies and finding military service no more rugged than farm labor. Or take Martha Wilson of New Jersey, who managed widely scattered landed properties, handling legal affairs in several colonies. Contrast her with Mrs. Peter Coffin of Boscawen, N.H., wife of a small farmer and mother of a month-old infant. She arose from childbed and, with the help of a fourteen-year-old boy, harvested the farm's wheat because all the men of the neighborhood were off with Stark at Bennington.

Kitty Livingston, daughter of Governor Livingston of New York, ordered quantities of silk stockings, cap wire, kid gloves and other feminine luxuries, imported from France. Margaret Shippen of Philadelphia, who married Benedict Arnold, was "young, gay, frivolous, fond of display and admiration . . . utterly unfitted for the duties and privations of a poor man's wife." And Ann Eliza Bleecker, one of the earliest American women poets, died of hardships as a war refugee.

Farther south in a rougher country, an eighteen-year-old bride, Mary Slocumb, took entire charge of a North Carolina plantation in her husband's absence, even splitting rails. Frances Slocumb (no relation to Mary of North Carolina) was carried off by Indians in the Wyoming Valley massacre in Pennsylvania, married an Indian chief and lived happily ever afterwards.

Meanwhile Dorothy Hancock, wife of the notable John, through war and rumor of war entertained profusely and kept her own carriage. But for every mansion boasting the dining tables and sideboards so impressively preserved as museum pieces, there were hundreds of farm households like those noted in Crèvecoeur's American journals. In his pages farm children ate their suppers— bowls of hot samp—held in their laps, sitting around the fireplace, while "the industrious mother is rattling at her loom." This farmhouse supper without benefit of any table Crèvecoeur accepts without comment as the custom of the country. A copious annalist, he had little to remark about American women except to lament "the allurements of fineries so powerful with our young girls." But he did exclaim: "What a useful acquisition a good wife is to an American farmer. . . . How small is his chance of prosperity if he draws a blank in that lottery."

Once more warned against the pursuit of type, let the search for the individual take over. Each woman selected is an item in a social whole. Through her personal experience we can sense the tone of a group or a region. Thus, woman by woman, we construct a composite portrait of time and place.

THE WASHINGTONS, MARY AND MARTHA

For personality as well as her place in history, the first example is Mary Ball Washington, mother of the immortal George, who lived just long enough to see her son elected President. In spite of her prominence, it is amazing to note how small is the residuum of fact concerning her after conventional adulation has been deleted. Traditional accounts of her stem from 1840–50, the period of the glorification of motherhood. Authors then seized upon the mother of Washington and remade her according to their notions of what she should have been. Historians of our own era (notably Douglas Freeman) have reconstructed from the records a far less flattering picture—a domineering woman who insisted on managing her own affairs in her own way and didn't do it very well.

Truth probably lies somewhere between these two extremes. For there is an old family letter dated from Williamsburg in 1722, which describes "sweet Molly . . . about sixteen years old . . . very sensible, modest and loving. Her hair is like unto flax . . . and her cheeks are like May blossoms."

Born around 1704–06, Mary Ball enters history as a slightly mature second wife who added five children to her husband's household, and survived him. There was never the slightest hint of her remarrying, as did so many plantation widows. "The home in which Mrs. Washington presided was a sanctuary of domestic virtues," proclaimed Elizabeth Ellet, a fashionable writer of 1850 (Chapter Note 1). The widow was "remarkable for vigour of intellect, strength of resolution and inflexible firmness wherever principle was concerned." Intellect or no, this inflexible firmness kept her young son George from becoming a midshipman in the British navy.

From contemporary appraisals Mary Washington emerges as a formidable product of her age. Take this account from Lawrence Washington's recollections: "I was often there (Ferry Farm) with

George. Of the mother I was ten times more afraid than I ever was of my own parents. She awed me in the midst of her kindness, for she was indeed truly kind. Even now when time has whitened my locks, and I am a grandparent of a second generation, I could not behold that majestic woman without feelings it is impossible to describe." Lafayette once observed that the mother of George Washington belonged to the age of Sparta or Rome.

Before Washington took command of the newly raised American armies, his mother had left Ferry Farm for the nearby village of Fredericksburg. There, on Charles Street, she had a small house within walking distance of the home of her daughter Betty, wife of Fielding Lewis. That was the famous house later known as Kenmore. One of the Kenmore bedrooms is designated as that of Mary Washington, but the fact seems to be that, until her last years, she maintained her own independence in her own house.

Inhabitants of Fredericksburg "long remembered the matron seated in an old-fashioned chaise," visiting her farm, giving her orders, and seeing that they were followed. When, on one occasion, an overseer departed from her instructions, she reproved him. "I command you," she announced. "There is nothing left for you but to obey." That went much better in 1780 than it would have in 1950, and it may explain those items of cash borrowed from her son George who proved to be a better agriculturist than his mother.

It should also be noted that although George always signed himself her obedient son, he did not invite his mother to come and live at Mount Vernon. There is a letter in which he tells her plainly that she would not enjoy it there. She would have to be dressed for company at all hours, he explains, and could not do as she liked. Obviously, though George never failed in his duty, he preferred to have his mother under another roof. From the volumes of Washington's later correspondence, it becomes evident that the family confidante of his mature years was his sister Betty, the wife of Fielding Lewis, and the mistress of Kenmore. For Washington, the warmth of family feeling had been deflected from mother to sister.

On the General's final victorious return to Virginia, his neighbors gave a ball in his honor, to which Madam Washington was especially invited. She replied that her dancing days were "pretty much over," but agreed to attend. She was then nearing eighty.

From this period stem most of the Mary Washington traditions, her walks along the river with her grandchildren, and the gingerbread that she baked for them, source of that famous recipe. More than tradition was her covering her own small Bible in homespun of buff and blue, the colors of the official Continental uniform, when the Continentals had any.

Letters from the hand of Mary Washington are rare. One such, dating from the months of the Yorktown campaign, is quoted here by permission of the trustees of the Morgan library. This letter, with spelling and punctuation characteristic of her generation of Virginia women, was one of the last she ever wrote. It shows clearly the ravages of years and sickness.

1782 March the 13th

My dear Georg
> *I was truly uneasy by Not being at hom when you went thru fredericksburg it was a unlucky thing for me now I am afraid I Never Shall have that pleasure agin I am soe very unwell this trip of the Mountains has almost kill'd me I got the 2 ginnes you was soe kind to send me iam greatly obliged to you for I was greatly shoct [line missing here] ever to be driven up this way agin but will goe in some little hous of my one if it is only twelve foot squar Benjamin Hardesty has four hinderd akers of Land of yours jis by Georg Le if you will let me goe there if I should be obliged to come over the Mountain again I shall be Very Much obliged to you pray give my kind love to Mrs. Washington & am My Dear Georg your Loveing and affectionat Mother*

Mary Washington

Mr. Nur desired me to Mention his Son to you he writs in the Treasurs Office of Congress MW

The end, though, in 1789, was grim. When Washington, recently elected the first President, came to visit his mother before journeying north, she was bedridden in a large corner room of the Charles Street cottage, and a victim of cancer.

In July Mrs. Lewis wrote to her brother: "I am sorry to inform you my mother's breast still continues bad. God only knows how it will end . . . she is sensible of it and perfectly resigned—wishes for nothing more than to keep it easy." The sister then asks Washington to send some drug that the doctors could not obtain locally. When the invalid died, August 25, her famous son was himself too weak from recent illness to attend her funeral.

When Mary Washington's son George married, the woman of his choice was very different from Mary Ball who had remained the Widow Washington. The Dandridges, Martha's family, were Tidewater gentry. Martha had been taught to embroider, to dance and to play the spinet. At seventeen she had been pledged to Daniel Parke Custis, wealthy, aristocratic and nearly twenty years her senior. It seemed a good match to the families, and Martha did not demur.

But when ten years later she was left "splendidly endowed with worldly benefits,"—a widow with two young children—she married Colonel Washington despite black looks from certain male Dandridges. The Colonel had made a name for himself in the recent Duquesne campaign, even if he did come from the unfashionable upper reaches of the Potomac. "Nor does it appear," says an old chronicler, "that she was a very notable housewife, but rather inclined to leave the matter under her husband's control." That, one suspects, was just what George Washington liked. He could certainly manage for both of them.

Of their life at Mount Vernon, many descriptions remain. But our interest here centers on Martha Washington as a woman of the Revolution. Her little daughter Patsy had died at thirteen. Jacky Custis, Martha's son, was married and established nearby. This left her free, if she so chose, to become an army wife.

She did so choose. Every winter from 1776 till the signing of the peace found the General's Lady with the troops. The places she visited, the people she encountered were far beyond the restricted world of the plantation lady. The first winter was spent in Craigie House, one of the famous mansions of Tory Row in Cambridge. But over succeeding years her quarters were far less genteel. Wherever cold weather stopped the army, there Martha Washington drove up from Virginia, her coach completely filled with cooked food from Mount Vernon. "Her arrival at camp," says an old journal, "was an event much anticipated." Soon came the Valley Forge winter, with officers and men in huts "tolerable comfortable," she wrote to Mercy Warren. No complaints came from one of the country's richest women.

An anecdote of Martha's campaigning dates from the little village of Manchester, Massachusetts, when Washington had temporary quarters there. The place was so small that it boasted only two frame houses, neither with a finished upper story. One of the upper stories the General ordered ceiled and made ready for his lady. The only carpenters to be had were two apprentices, for grown men were in the army. Long afterwards, as a man of 92 years, one of these apprentices told his story to Elizabeth Ellet.

"We went to work with all our might. Every morning about eleven Mrs. Washington came upstairs with a glass of spirits for each of us, [the temperature in that unheated upper story must have been frigid] and after she and the General had dined, we were called down to eat at their table. We studied to do everything to please so pleasant a lady." By the fourth day, they had finished their work. Shelves had been made, pegs put up on the walls. Mrs. Washington came up to inspect. This woman whose own home was furnished with imported luxuries, turned to the sixteen-year-old apprentices, and told them they had "done master work."

This was the Martha Washington who dressed so plainly on her campaigning that she was sometimes mistaken for her own traveling maid. But Abigail Adams of Boston would never make such a blunder. "That plainness," the observant Abigail set down, "is the best of every article." Another person who understood was Martha Wilson of Hunterton, New Jersey. While stopping overnight at Mrs. Wilson's mansion, the General's wife exhibited two cotton dresses, striped with silk, the product of Mount Vernon where sixteen spinning wheels were kept constantly at work. The silk stripes had been made by raveling old silk stockings and crimson damask chair cushions. Mrs. Washington's coachman, footman and waiting maid were all "habited in domestic cloth," though the coachman's scarlet cuffs "must have been imported." In Philadelphia Mrs. Washington had paid six shillings for her own handkerchiefs, but stretched it to seven shillings for the General's. So two landed ladies, North and South, met and chatted easily about clothes.

Even the Yorktown victory, which cost Martha Washington her only son, did not bring her release from life with the army. Until a peace could be signed, unwilling troops must be kept together. That meant nearly two more years of exile for Martha. She must have been badly homesick for Mount Vernon, for, at Newburgh, she tried to have a Dutch gardener make her a flower bed, like the one she had at home. Not till Christmas of 1783 did the General return to Mount Vernon. Martha straightway gave a party for him. "The gen'l," wrote a visiting young lady, "seemed very happy and Mistress Washington was from daybrake making everything as agreeable as possible for everyone."

MERCY WARREN AND HER CIRCLE

For a complete contrast to Martha Washington, Massachusetts provides Mercy Warren, authoress, and one of the few women of her period included in present college textbooks of early American writers. It would be easy to make game of her today merely by quoting from her compositions, which were written in the pompous literary fashion of the hour. The longer the phrase, the more exalted the writer. By that standard, Mercy Warren ranked high. Her political satires, apart from their original setting, now fall flat.

There was nothing in either heredity or environment to give Mercy Warren a lighter touch. She was born in 1728, daughter of Colonel James Otis of Barnstable, and sister of the notable James Otis. It was "a family of high respectability." Since no schooling was wasted on females, she had only such teaching as she could get from their clergyman and from her brother. At twenty-six (not too young in those days) she married James Warren, a Plymouth merchant, and began to write poetry. She had several children, all boys. Encompassed thus by complete masculinity, she either had to assert herself or give up the battle. "Attached as she was to literary pursuits, she never permitted them to interfere with her household duties." Quite the correct attitude.

The poetess early took the side of the colonists, devoting her pen to the cause in a series of political plays. John Adams praised them, but when she shifted to formal tragedies in blank verse, even her friends found it hard going.

All the while, Mrs. Warren was carrying on an active correspondence with the leading personages of the revolt, including Samuel and John Adams, Jefferson, Knox, Hamilton and even George Washington. Exchange of long letters dealing with public issues was an important medium in the propagation of eighteenth-century ideas. The novelty was in a woman's participating. Mercy Warren kept all these letters. Then twenty years later, with surprising modernity, she used them as a basis for the first history of the American Revolution. It was published in 1805.

In Mrs. Warren's select circle, a lady's letter was a literary effort, mingling classical allusions with patriotic sentiment. The composition was signed with a *nom de plume*. Hannah Winthrop of Cambridge became "Honoria." Abigail Smith began as "Diana," but on marrying John Adams, she shifted her signature to "Portia." To Mrs. Winthrop, Mercy Warren was "Philomela," while that lady addressed Mrs. Winthrop as "Narcissa." It seems a safe guess that Philomela, Narcissa and Honoria expressed personality cravings not compatible with the stern workaday environment of New England. These select ladies were creating their own escape literature.

More human than Mercy Warren was her young friend Abigail Smith Adams of Weymouth, whose forbears had been clergymen of learning for three generations. So they cultivated the mind as well as the conscience, in the parsonage where she was born in 1744. Destined to be the wife of our second President, and mother of the sixth, Abigail was never sent to school. But she was encouraged to educate herself in her father's library.

Just past nineteen (the year was 1764) she married the son of a Braintree farmer who had been to Harvard and was already a rising young lawyer. It is family tradition that, on the afternoon before the birth of her first child, she scrubbed the floor of her own bedroom.

Since Abigail had helped manage the farm while her husband was off circuit riding, she was ready to take charge at home when he went to sit with the First Continental Congress in Philadelphia. Deadly fighting around Boston soon followed. Writing to the absent John, Abigail recounted the war diseases that were sweeping their countryside. Her youngest boy was very sick, and the housemaid, Patty, was like to die. Her own mother did die.

Later Abigail witnessed the bombardment of Boston from Dorchester Heights. To John in Philadelphia, she described the people of Braintree boiling down cornstalks for sugar because the West India trade had been cut off by the war. "Coffee and sugar I use only as a rarety. There are none of these things but I could renounce," wrote the daughter of the parsonage.

While Abigail Adams might abjure luxuries, food shortages in and around Boston had provoked violence at the hands of less high-minded females. In the summer of 1777 a mob of some hundred women descended on a store reputed to be hoarding. Tossing the shop owner bodily into a cart, they obtained his keys and cleared his shelves of both sugar and coffee. A little later a similar mob of women seized two hogsheads of sugar from a Beverly merchant, forcing him to sell it at the legal price. Nor was Massachusetts alone in its possession of mob-minded females. Dutch hausfraus of Kinderhook, up the Hudson, also obtained their tea by force. A clergyman's daughter would not applaud such acts of violence.

When John Adams was sent to France, taking ten-year-old Johnny with him as copyist, that cut close to the quick. Fighting had swept away from New England, but Abigail's private war of separation continued through the making of the peace. Then, since John could not return, after Yorktown she crossed the ocean to join him.

These war letters of Abigail Adams, edited by her grandson, have remained a classic for more than a century. But today research raises another question: how much were those famous letters revised before publication? Unedited letters of Abigail's, recently made public by the American Antiquarian Society, show clearly the gaps in her self-conducted education. These untouched messages to her favorite sister, Mary Cranch, were "first thoughts without correction" set down when she was "too laizy to coppy. [sic]" Her first-thought spelling is so faulty that we can now picture her, dictionary in hand, making corrected copies to send abroad to her college-educated husband.

Of all the daughters of that Weymouth parsonage, Abigail only seems to have inherited a share of her father's wit. The others took themselves much more ponderously. Elizabeth, the youngest, was noted for her ability to quote long passages of Shakespeare and Dryden. She was twice married, both times to clergymen, and her

Haverhill parsonage became "the center of an elegant little circle of society." Even when visiting, she carried improving literature with her. Thus she read aloud "Zulima the Coquette" and "Virtue and Constancy Rewarded" to the three pretty daughters of her host, while they bent their young heads over the quilting frame. We are told that the young ladies liked it and asked for more.

THE FASHIONABLE HANCOCKS

Surviving memorials of the Revolutionary period present their long dead subjects as examples of all virtues, devoted to their children, their churches and their pantries. Never was there the slightest breath of domestic infelicity. Amid such a welter of unmitigated propriety, it is almost a relief to learn that John Hancock of the impeccable signature was not completely impeccable indoors. One early biographer even goes so far as to imply that Mrs. Hancock was sometimes put to it to soothe and calm her liege lord.

John Hancock with his Dorothy might walk out of the pages of a novel today. Born a Quincy, she had for her background the luxuries of that small group who composed the upper-upper of Boston colonial society. The Quincys lived on an estate out Braintree way where cards were played and wine was freely drunk. There the seven Quincy daughters made life gay and carefree, always within the bounds of ladylike convention.

When Dorothy, the youngest, was growing up, the fourth Edmund Quincy, her father, had lost most of his fortune, but her older sisters had already made advantageous marriages. Soon it was known that Dorothy—Dolly in the old journals—had found favor with John Hancock, nephew and heir of Thomas Hancock, reckoned the wealthiest Bostonian of his day. Like John Hancock, Dolly is a well-documented personality. Several portraits of her remain, one as a young girl, slight, blond and pretty. The last portrait, a Copley, shows an old lady, still surprisingly slight and alert for her eighty years. This Dorothy, however, is not that Dorothy Q. of Holmes's poem, who was a younger member of the clan.

" 'Tis said John Hancock courts Dolly Quincy," wrote a gossip in 1771. At this point the story goes modern. Although Aunt Lydia Hancock encouraged the match, Dolly was reluctant. Onlookers

11

called her coy. There were quarrels, reconciliations, and quarrels again. Not till the summer after the battle of Lexington did Aunt Lydia finally persuade Dolly into marrying John Hancock. She was then in her twenty-eighth year, a ripe old age for an eighteenth-century belle.

Research can supply a possible answer. John Hancock had a mistress, a widow named Dorcas Griffiths. Apparently Dorothy did not accept the situation with genteel meekness. Fate and the American Revolution were on Dolly's side. When, in 1774, incoming British troops took over Hancock's wharf, Dorcas "had at her home Captain David Johnstone of the British marines." Dorcas followed this new protector back to London. In August, 1775, Dorothy Quincy married John Hancock.

Their wedding journey was a trip by coach, over bad roads, to Philadelphia. There John, the patriot, functioned as President of the First Continental Congress, while the giddy belle was transformed into a proper matron. "Among a hundred men at this house," John Adams informed his absent Abigail, "she lives and behaves with modesty, decency, dignity and discretion . . . Her behavior is easy and genteel. She avoids talking upon politics. In large and mixed companies, she is totally silent, as a lady ought to be."

It was after the loss of Philadelphia to the British that the Hancocks had their first child. Friends, relatives and lawyers were all set to welcome an heir to the Hancock fortune. But alas, the baby was a girl, no great matter to anyone except her mother. This infant, greeted by her father with a silver teething ring, lived less than a year. Then in May, 1778, came the great event, the birth of a son named John George Washington Hancock.

The family meanwhile had returned to Boston where John was to become the almost perennial Governor of Massachusetts, with Dolly as that region's most notable hostess. Her entertaining was not all frivolous. There was, for example, a banquet given for the officers of the French fleet after two of their number had perished in a street riot. Likewise a breakfast for the French seamen, en masse, the famous occasion for which Mistress Hancock sent out her servants to milk all the cows pastured on Boston Common.

Within the Hancock mansion, famed for its good eating, Madeira flowed almost like water, in addition to liberal consumption of less aristocratic strong drink. Hancock, never robust, became disabled by gout. In 1787 a devastating blow fell on the merchant dynasty. The one son, an accomplished little boy (at nine he could walk the minuet), died of a fall on the ice. Dorothy Hancock was left alone in the great house to face John's failing health and rising temper. He died in 1797. Unfortunately for his widow, he died with a will unsigned that would have made her heir to the Hancock estate. Instead, she received dower rights.

This fall in fortune may have urged her remarriage, three years later, when she was 49. To the scandal of select Boston, her second choice was that Captain Scott who had commanded the best of the Hancock fleet. The bride left Boston to make her home "in the seclusion of Portsmouth [N.H.] . . . content with a less brilliant yet not less happy life." The Scott household must also have set a lavish table for when the Captain died, in 1819, his chief asset (willed to his wife) was his wine cellar, including 300 gallons of "London Particular Madiera."

Twice widowed and with a diminished income, Dorothy returned to Boston where she was forgiven and accepted as the town's first lady for the rest of her life. Somewhere along the years there was a mysterious disappearance of letters known to have been written by her. Possibly they were too revealing. She died in her home on Federal Street in 1830.

AND SOME UNFASHIONABLE WOMEN

Attention now turns to Dorcas Griffiths the woman whom John Hancock did not marry. She represents a type not usually included in clerical memorials, but she was a real person.

A widow when we first pick up her story, she kept a shop on the famous Hancock wharf where ocean-going ships came in. Over the counter she sold tea, groceries, linen and also liquor, since colonial Massachusetts doled out liquor licenses to widows almost like a pension. She was considerably older than her wealthy lover, and had a full grown daughter. Some antiquarians have reckoned her as nearing fifty when she left Boston.

But Dorcas was enterprising. Arrived in England, she put in a compensation claim to the British government for property lost through loyalty to the crown, and was awarded an allowance. After Yorktown, government agents began weeding out questionable items on the King's list, and among them was Dorcas Griffiths. In 1784 there was a hearing. According to the record, she "was a common prostitute and bred up her daughter in the same way. She was kept by the famous Hancock."

To her credit, though, Dorcas had started out as a shopkeeper, a favorite means of self-support for indigent females in early American cities. A more elegant shopkeeper on Hancock's wharf was Mrs. Hiller who made and displayed waxworks, figures of regally costumed kings and queens in the days when royalty was popular in Boston. To eke out a living, Mrs. Hiller also taught young ladies "the art of feathers, quilt work and embroidery." Lace making as a trade for women developed after the war cut off the European supply.

By colonial laws widows of skilled craftsmen were permitted to take over the management of a deceased husband's shop, as did the mother of Paul Revere. This custom undoubtedly accounts for the dozen women printers of the old colonies. Benjamin Franklin noted favorably doing business with a woman who was carrying on her husband's printshop after his death. Similarly, records of pre-Revolutionary Philadelphia list "Ann Penrose, shipwright," she being a widow in that shipbuilding family.

But the usual recourse for female self-support was domestic service. Pay was desperately small. The first warning received in Boston of the British advance towards Lexington came from "a Mrs. Stedman . . . housemaid to the wife of one of the British soldiers." A bit later on a "sailor's washerwoman" named Spencer started a yellow fever epidemic in Brooklyn. She lived over a grogshop on Sands Street near the docks, and went aboard a ship in from Havana to get the captain's laundry. The ship had just discharged a passenger who died the next day of yellow fever. The sailor's washerwoman also died, together with four other groghouse tenants, the first victims of a lethal outbreak of the dreaded scourge.

DEBORAH SAMSON AND "MOLLY PITCHER"

It is a far cry from the Hancock mansion or Mercy Warren's select circle to the case of Deborah Samson. Like Mrs. Warren, Deborah came from Plymouth, but there the resemblance ceases. Her story furnishes a sociological study, and possibly a psychological one as well. Deborah belonged to the section of society seldom noted except in jail records. Her earliest home was bad enough to cause the town authorities to remove the children. This half-grown girl was placed "in the house of a respectable farmer whose wife bestowed on her as much attention as is common in such cases." That apparently was not much. She was never sent to school. She taught herself to read by borrowing books from other children. At eighteen, when the law terminated her indenture, she could not write. She then put herself through grade school by hiring out, part time, to a farmer.

In brief, eighteenth-century New England made Deborah into a farm laborer. She was big and strong, tall for a woman and probably lonely. A bound girl from a dissolute home would have no standing in her community.

Her becoming a soldier was not an impulse. She taught district school for an entire summer term to obtain the twelve dollars that she needed to outfit herself as a man. "Working at intervals when she could be secure from observation, she made up a suit of men's clothing." Had crude farm tailoring been one of her tasks as a bound girl? When her outfit was ready, she announced that she was leaving Plymouth to look for better wages. Then she disappeared into a nearby wood, to emerge as Robert Shirtliffe, on his way to enlist. This was in October 1778.

As Robert Shirtliffe she joined the company of Captain Nathan Thayer of Medway, Massachusetts. There she made an error that might have led to discovery, for, when a uniform was allotted to her, she cut it over to make it fit better. This feminine reaction Private Shirtliffe explained by saying that "he" had been apprenticed to a tailor. The story was good enough to pass. For three years Deborah Samson was a common soldier. She was twice wounded, the first time a head injury. The second wound, a severe one, was to prove her undoing, for she was sent to an army hospital, supposedly dying. The surgeon, a Dr. Binney of Philadelphia, discovered that his patient was a woman.

Knowing that the young woman would be disgraced if her secret became public, Dr. Binney consulted Shirtliffe's commanding officer, who devised a plan to rid the army of this female without blasting her reputation. When the patient recovered, she was given a letter to deliver to General Washington. "He said not a word, but in silence handed her a discharge." He also provided "sufficient money to take her home." Later tradition says that after Washington became President, he invited Deborah Samson to visit him.

Today it is easy to write off Deborah Samson as a pathological case. But before consigning her to that category, her postwar life must also be considered. That was completely prosaic. She married Benjamin Gannett of Sharon, Massachusetts, described as "a good sort of man . . . of small force in business." By 1795 Deborah had become the mother of three children, and family finances were in poor shape. Probably assisted in the writing, in 1797 she published a romanticised version of her story for the *Female Review*.

By 1804 Paul Revere in his prosperous old age became acquainted with Mrs. Gannett. He appealed to their Massachusetts congressman for a pension for the ex-soldier, recommending her as "a woman of handsome talents, good morals, a dutiful wife and an affectionate parent." Deborah was then 44 years old. She was awarded a modest pension, but in 1806 was writing Revere for a loan of "ten dollars for a short time." Both she and her son were ill. We don't know whether Revere sent the money, but in 1818 Congress doubled Deborah's four dollars a month. She died in 1827.

The story ends on a sour note. In 1837 Benjamin Gannett, the widower, was 83 years old, infirm and without property. He then recalled that he had formerly expended some 600 dollars on medical attention for his deceased soldier-wife, and applied to Congress for reimbursement. He was granted 80 dollars a month for the rest of his life. Considering that Deborah herself had never rated more than eight dollars, this generosity might well have stunned him. He died not long afterwards.

There are also records of women who saw brief fighting along with their soldier husbands. Best known is "Molly Pitcher" who went on serving her husband's gun on the field of Monmouth after the artilleryman was disabled. But the life of this woman, whose real name was not Molly Pitcher, is more significant than any fanciful rendering of her exploit.

She was born Ludwig in 1754 of German immigrant stock. Her

parents had a dairy near Trenton, New Jersey, not too prosperous, since the girl was placed in her early teens as a servant in the home of Dr. William Irvine of Carlisle, Pennsylvania. At fifteen she married John Casper Hays. When Hays enlisted (1777) in a Pennsylvania artillery regiment, his wife returned to the family farm. She was a short, stocky, rough-looking woman, who cooked and washed for the soldiers of a nearby army camp. The day of the Monmouth battle, June 28, 1778, was one of the hottest known. Carrying water to the wounded, Mary Hays won her *nom de guerre,* Molly Pitcher.

But never in her entire life did Mary-Molly attain comfort. A second marriage didn't turn out well. In 1822, when she was 68, the state of Pennsylvania remembered its heroine to the extent of 40 dollars per annum. She lived ten years longer. A hundred years after her death, the city of Carlisle named its best hotel for this woman who had had one hour of glory in a life of heavy cleaning.

The authenticated record of Margaret Corbin closely parallels that of the better known Molly Pitcher. Margaret's husband, also an artilleryman, was stationed at Fort Washington following the Battle of Long Island. When he fell, she too went on serving his gun.

In July 1799 a resolution in Congress referred to her as disabled by wounds. It voted her a pension "for her natural life or continuance of said disability." The allotment was "one-half the monthly pay drawn by a soldier" and "out of the public stores, one suit of clothes or the value thereof in money." As Congress was then very short of currency, one hopes that Mrs. Margaret got her value thereof.

IN THE PROSPEROUS REGIONS

Yet to present a fair picture, more prosperous strata must not be omitted. In the region of which Philadelphia and Baltimore were the centers, frontiering was long since over. Ease and abundance prevailed among the gentry. Witness, for example, the dinner served by Mrs. Bingham of Philadelphia at Christmas, 1779, and the New Year's feast set out by the Chew mansion there that same season.

The Christmas dinner began with lobster, followed by a soup made of fresh shrimp, ham-bone and green peas. Then came wild turkey and plover eggs in wine, and a "salada" made from fruit prepared in sweet wine vinegar, flavored with rosemary and green thyme. There followed pumpkin pie, plum pudding and "orange smash," whatever that was. Mrs. Chew's New Year's dinner began with a bouillion of clams, cold lobster knuckles, pickled frost fish and a soup made from "blackeyed peas, ham-bones and Potomac oysters." A suckling pig was stuffed with corn pone, blanched in cider, and served with fried apples and candied sweet potatoes. Then there was jugged hare with "Mithyglen, and spices served on Dough cake." The mince pie for this occasion was said to have been in preparation for five months.

Yet in this same year (1779) and in this same city Sarah Franklin Bache and her friend Esther Reed were struggling to raise money for the care of the wounded. The two women gathered 7,000 dollars, much of it in cash, then especially hard come by. Writing to her father Benjamin in Paris, Sarah recounted their struggles, begging "Poor Richard" not to reproach her for buying a little finery for herself. She wanted to look right to pay a call on Madam Washington.

It was an opulent background that furnished the most enigmatic woman of the Revolution—Margaret Shippen, the Philadelphia-born second wife of Benedict Arnold whose name remains a symbol of treason for Americans. About him, there is no doubt; as to his young wife, the question mark rises, with biographers ranged for and against.

At the time of Arnold's intended betrayal of West Point (prevented, school books remind us, by the accidental capture of Major André) the thesis of Mrs. Arnold's complete innocence was launched by Alexander Hamilton. He was one of Washington's aides on the scene when Arnold fled. Older members of the staff were less impressed by Peggy's hysterical delirium on being informed of her husband's treason. Washington himself never voiced a judgment. After the manner of eighteenth-century gentility, he ordered Mrs. Arnold returned to her father's house under escort of a military aide. Incidentally, that trip was made largely by back roads to spare Peggy and her baby the threat of mobbing. Later on Peggy, with her child, left the parental roof to rejoin Arnold when he was a British commander operating against his own countrymen.

That was public knowledge. But Philadelphians also knew that from the beginning of the conflict, the Shippen elders had maintained a resolute neutrality, never identifying themselves with either camp. But Margaret, young and beautiful, had been prominent in the theatricals arranged by British officers when Howe held Philadelphia. After the Continentals regained their capital, Peggy had met and married General Arnold, the dashing hero of Saratoga. Nothing but romantic love can explain her choice of a bridegroom twice her age, a widower with grown sons.

Such a girl, wrapped up in a new baby, might easily have been ignorant of Arnold's maneuvers. Yet when, a few years ago, old and secret British military files were opened, Arnold's wife appears as a point of contact between him and active loyalists. She may have listened to a siren-song of reconciliation with England, romantically visualizing her husband as the great negotiator. It has yet to be proved that she was concerned with the ugly realities of military betrayal.

For the rest of her story, we have only bare facts. When British troops were evacuated, Margaret Shippen followed her husband to England. Had her earlier return to Arnold been her free choice, or had she been under pressure from a family anxious to dissociate itself from Arnold's disgrace? No one knows. The fact remains that she shared Arnold's after-life. Once only, and that when her mother was seriously ill, did she return to the country her husband had betrayed. Then she was so coldly received in Philadelphia that she seldom left the house, and she never again visited the United States (Chapter Note 2).

On leaving the mercantile North and entering the world of the plantation, a traveler found contrasts in living greatly sharpened. Hemmed in physically by bad roads and mentally by a scanty education, the plantation lady expected to brighten her domestic corner with imported luxuries. Before the war, the Virginia Gazette of February 1767 announced the arrival from London of "Catherine Randall, milliner . . . with the best flowered and plain satins . . . a great variety of ribands . . . silk and leather gloves and mitts, Persians flowered and striped, and plain English gauze. Gentlemen's laced ruffles . . . a variety of silver buckles, bags for wigs. She also makes all sorts of millinery in the best and newest taste."

In this agricultural economy the middle class, powerful in the

North, was represented chiefly by a small group of shopkeepers, whose wives were expected to serve behind the counter. One struggling schoolmaster, advertising for private tutoring, added that his wife was prepared to do dressmaking. Among the clothes-loving Virginians, a skilled traveling seamstress could earn a living. Such was Nancy West, employed by the Fairfax family where she also made shirts for George Washington.

A few mansions prided themselves on fine classical libraries, but the average plantation house seldom offered anything beyond a Bible, a prayer book and a handy "Every Man His Own Physician." Daughters were taught to dance elegantly, but their book learning remained meager. Apparently most of the ladies liked it that way. A woman of property, Mrs. Ann Beckman, had this set down in her will: "My daughter's education is to be able to read, write and cipher, and the use of her needle" (Chapter Note 3).

Outside the charmed circle of plantation ladies, women wore cheap homespun, linen in summer, and coarse wool for winter. Sometimes these garments were neither new nor clean. An advertisement for the return of a runaway indentured woman servant describes her as wearing an old striped cotton gown, the front breadth of which had been replaced with something else. Another runaway took with her several pairs of "imported shoes with red heels," besides other bits of family finery. This method of financing flight suggests a ready market, probably illegal, for used luxury clothing.

Travelers who left the Tidewater counties to follow the rivers to their mountain sources soon encountered crude living. Young George Washington paused in his surveying trips to jot down some uncomplimentary phrases in his journals. The frontier people were a parcel of barbarians, an uncouth set. In their cabins man, wife and children were stowed at night "like a parcel of cats and dogs, and happy's he who gets the berth nearest the fire."

WOMEN OF THE CAROLINAS

South of Virginia's Tidewater and western frontier lay the Carolinas. South Carolina's rich plantation districts supported a culture more advanced than that of her neighbors. In Charleston where the British strain had been leavened by a touch of French, the first opera in the old colonies was performed, not to forget some early Shakespearian productions. Back from the seaport were notable plantations which boasted the first gardens mentioned in American annals.

This, too, was the territory of the great lady, accustomed to command and to be obeyed. She might also be capable, if need arose, of managing her own landholdings. Such a woman was Eliza Lucas Pinckney who experimented with indigo and silk and whose letters are to Charleston what those of Abigail Adams are to Boston. However, she cannot be claimed as an American. Her father was a British army officer in the West Indies. Threatened with slave insurrections there, he had removed his daughter to South Carolina for safety. Later Eliza became the second wife of Chief Justice Pinckney. When the Revolution broke out, the widowed Eliza sided with the colonies.

More strictly American was Rebecca Motte, another wealthy widow and the mother of six children, who agreed to the destruction of her own seaside mansion to facilitate the recapture of Fort Motte. This incident is preserved in many school histories. Admirable as was her patriotism, one notes that this dwelling was but one of several in the Motte landholdings. Besides a fine house in Charleston itself, she owned at least two plantations along the Santee. It was the men slaves from these estates whom she had transported to Charleston for work on the fortifications there, she paying for their maintenance.

What the schoolbooks do not tell is that the end of hostilities left Mrs. Motte deeply in debt. Nothing daunted, she purchased on credit some uncleared swamp acres on the Santee, which she believed would make good rice land. It was uphill work, but she persisted against the advice of her best friends. At length the new lands proved fruitful, debts were paid off, and, in the end, the widow left a large estate for her descendants.

The great plantations were self-sustaining units with their own manufactures. There is record of a young widow, Sabina Elliott, who at twenty-eight found herself responsible for large holdings where they made both wool and cotton cloth and manufactured salt. With such lady proprietors the sense of authority often ran high. The daughter of Margaret Gaston of New Berne "could venture but stolen glances in a mirror; nor did she or any of her juvenile companions ever allow their shoulders to rest on the back of a chair in Mrs. Gaston's presence."

In the Carolinas and Georgia the Revolutionary struggle took on a tinge of ferocity. Isolated plantations on lonely creeks invited bloody reprisals on both sides. This entire region is the background for some extraordinary feats of endurance credited to women. There was Jane Thomas, mother of nine grown children, whose husband and two sons had already been captured by the British. Learning that a third son was in danger, she rode 60 miles to bring him warning. On another occasion, Mrs. Thomas, with two sons and two daughters helping her, stood off a raid of Tories on her log house, in which was stored the gunpowder for Sumter's troops.

Jane Thomas, certainly well past youth, was not unique in hardihood. Near Moor's Creek in North Carolina Mary Slocumb had a bad dream about her husband. Worried, she saddled a horse and rode overnight more than 30 miles in the general direction of the American forces. By morning she came upon the battle of Moor's Creek. She found her husband safe, assisted with the wounded and that night rode all the way home again. The champion horsewoman, however, seems to have been Esther Wake, sister-in-law of Governor Tryon of North Carolina, who rode 80 miles one day on a visit, and returned the next day. Such were the figures set down a generation later, suggesting to the skeptical a possible elasticity in mileage.

These Southern women all belonged to families of local standing; their menfolk were officers in the army. Their sons became judges and officials.

FRONTIER AMAZONS

Quite different were those women in territories exposed to Indian depredations. Frontier annals show that, in this country, as in medieval Europe, chivalry was the flower of comparative peace and security. The genuine frontiersmen were realists and their women accepted them as such.

Take the siege of Bryant's station near what is now Lexington, Kentucky, in August 1782. Here the foe was the redskin, not the redcoat. The garrison drew its water from a certain spring, near which the main body of Indians was believed to be waiting in ambush. A smaller body in plain sight, it was argued, was a decoy force to tempt the white men out of their fortifications. There was dire need of water, but who should go and get it? The men decided to have the women do it in a body, each one bringing her own bucket.

Of the women thus elected "some as was natural, had no relish for it . . . they were not bullet-proof and Indians made no distinction between male and female scalps." But the strategists maintained that the women were in the habit of bringing water every morning . . . if the Indians saw them proceeding as usual, they would believe that their ambush still remained undiscovered. They would not unmask their position to fire at a few women.

"A few of the boldest women declared their readiness," says an old manuscript. "The younger and more timid rallying in the rear of these veterans, they all marched down . . . to the spring, within point blank shot of five hundred Indian warriors. Some of the girls could not help betraying symptoms of terror, but the married women moved with a steadiness . . . that completely deceived the Indians. Not a shot was fired." The buckets were filled, and very little was spilled on the return trip which the women made with their backs to the Indians. Here the story ends, a mere item in the defense of a long forgotten barricade (Chapter Note 4).

THE WHITE WOMAN OF GENESSEE

The reverse side of frontier adventure is embodied in Mary Jemison, captured as a girl of fourteen in an Indian raid on the west Pennsylvania settlements (1750). When the rest of her family—father, mother, brothers and sisters—were massacred, she was spared and adopted into a Seneca tribe. She lived as a contented Seneca for the rest of her 90 years. Most important for the historian, is the fact that at 80, and still living in Genessee, N.Y., she encountered an interested white man to whom she told her story (Chapter Note 5).

It opens with the family's seven prosperous years as frontier settlers in Marsh Creek. The Jemisons had been emigrants from northern Ireland, and Mary herself had been born on the sailing voyage to Philadelphia. Before the fatal raid she had been taught to read a little in the Bible, and had memorized her catechism. When she had been marked for captivity and her family for slaughter, her mother's parting injunction had been to remember her name and the English language. Many many years later Mary's biographer was to note that she spoke English with the Irish accent of her childhood.

After a fearsome death march through the wilderness, the captive had been brought to a Seneca settlement on the Ohio where she was adopted by two Indian squaws, "kind, goodnatured women," whom she always called her sisters. Two years went by, with the Indians planting corn in summer and hunting in the winter. Then Mary was bade to "go live in the house of" a visiting Delaware of rank, the tribal equivalent of marriage.

She came near dying at the birth of a short-lived first child, but four years later successfully bore a son. Meanwhile Mary's Indian husband whom she had come to love, decided to join the Senecas at Genessee Flats in New York. He died on the journey. Following his death, she married another Indian, half-brother of a famous Seneca chief. By him she had six more children. To all of them she gave the "white" names of her own lost family. Yet again she counted this a happy marriage. Twice during her many decades as a squaw she was offered re-patriation to Pennsylvania, but both times she preferred to remain an Indian. In times of peace, she assured her biographer, "No people live more happy than the Indians."

Other pages detail the Indian's barbarous code of war, to which she seems to have become callous, accepting it as she did the lawless life of white traders within Indian territory. She recounts bloody feuding, and polygamous families, sometimes with white wives, sometimes with red, and sometimes with mates of both colors. In one case, a white trader found it necessary to keep a fifth wife, white, away from the dwelling that housed her four red rivals.

Finally the Senecas of Genessee sold their land and went West, alotting to Mary and her children some 18,000 acres of land to support her widowhood. Much of the later narrative concerns the machinations of the whites to get Mary's land away from her. Her biographer in 1823 describes her, then 80, as short, erect, walking nimbly, her hair gray, her eyes a light blue. She had never known comb nor cap. She was then losing vision, but she still had her own front teeth. A still later remove took Mary Jemison, when nearing 90, to the Buffalo reservation. There, in the summer of 1833, she was "converted" by a white missionary a few months before her death.

OTHER FRONTIER WOMEN

Most women of the outposts both North and South were of a tough and valorous fibre. But there were exceptions, such as an anonymous woman going by boat from Louisville, Ky., to Bullett's Lick in 1788. When the boat was attacked by Indians, the men aboard urged her to flee to the woods. "But" says the record, "she sat with her face buried in her hands." She was carried to Canada by the Indians, where she was ransomed years later by an Indian trader. She finally returned to Kentucky in 1798.

Surprising especially is the bravery of Elizabeth Zane, of the family for whom Zanesville, Ohio, was named. She was no frontier product, raised and hardened in a log cabin. In 1777, she was just a schoolgirl from Philadelphia, on a visit to her brothers near Fort Fincastle, in the region that is now West Virginia.

Successive attacks on the Fort had reduced its garrison of forty men to twelve. All were resolved to fight to the last, although their powder was running low. There was another keg hidden in the house of Ebenezer Zane, about 60 yards from the Fort. The commander was trying to decide which man he could best spare to risk the chance of getting it, when Elizabeth volunteered. She was the most useless person there, she declared, and so could be most readily spared. "Her request was granted," says the chronicle.

She reached the house, wrapped the powder in a tablecloth and returned unharmed through bullet fire. The story belongs to the early records of Wheeling, West Virginia.

These incidents also bear witness to the everyday lives of the women there. Thus Elizabeth Zane's sister-in-law owned a large tablecloth, the first to be mentioned in frontier annals. The first imported carpet west of the Alleghenies was a rug, twelve feet by fifteen, the treasured possession of Catherine Sevier, wife of the only governor of the short-lived state of Frankland-Franklin which was to become Tennessee. When company was expected, the carpet was literally rolled out, once more to be stowed away after the guests' departure.

The first mirror mentioned west of the Ohio belonged to a family of transplanted New Englanders named Moultin, members of the early Marietta settlement. When Indians attacked in 1791, people from surrounding farms came rushing back to the block-house, bearing with them their most precious household goods—a family Bible, a china teapot. But Mrs. Moultin was not among these first arrivals. She lingered to put her cabin to rights. Then, having justified her reputation for neat housekeeping, "mother" finally appeared, carrying the family looking glass.

THE TALE OF NANCY HART

But for complete frontier drama, there is Nancy Hart of Wilks County, Georgia, a two-gun woman who drank and swore, admittedly ignorant of all niceties of living. In this region a deadly guerilla warfare was being carried on by the Liberty Boys and the Tories. Nancy's husband was rated locally as a poor stick, with small stomach for throat cutting, content to let Nancy earn the family honors for patriotism.

When a group of five Tory guerillas crossed the Broad River to charge Nancy with participation in a recent raid, she boldly owned her part, though the admission might easily have caused her instant execution. The Tories, however, compromised by threatening her, and ordering her to make dinner for them, shooting one of Nancy's turkeys for her to clean and cook. With Nancy in her one-room cabin was a daughter of ten or twelve years. So skilled had this child become in border warfare that when her mother sent her to the spring for water, she rightly interpreted the order to include warning her father and the nearby neighbors. Near the spring hung a conch shell. By primitive signal code certain calls told the men to stay in hiding, while another call meant a summons to come running. Young Sukey now blew the notes which told the men to lie low and let mother perform.

Meanwhile, within the cabin, Nancy was preparing a turkey stew. The raiders had stacked their muskets while they enjoyed the contents of the frontier hip-flask. Nancy joined in the drinking but kept a cool head. When she saw the men grow befuddled, she forced out some of the pine "chinking" between the logs, and began slipping the raiders' guns out through the opening. Sukey was then sent to the spring for more water, the sagacious child recognizing in this an order to sound a call for quick action.

Nancy had disposed of two muskets and was reaching for a third when the raiders caught her at it. The whole party sprang at her. As one man advanced, she shot him dead, and seized another gun. The four survivors started in a rush. Nancy shot a second man dead in his tracks, while Sukey on a hard run back from the spring, handed the last gun to her mama. Mrs. Hart blocked the doorway with it, calling on the three to surrender what a nicer historian set down later as "their d—— Tory carcasses." Capitulation was delayed till Nancy's husband and the neighbors appeared. The "poor stick" was about to shoot the captives, but Nancy protested that that was too good for them. The survivors, including one wounded man, were then dragged out to a more lingering hanging.

It is not a pretty story, but it illustrates a type of life that created callous hardihood of mind and body. That movable thing, the American frontier, had no use for imagination or fine feeling. A truly gentle woman could not have survived the living conditions, much less answered the demand to flourish and multiply.

That pressure of frontier hardness was better understood by our ancestors who were closer to it. Thus, in 1838, Elizabeth Ellet— the first historian of American women—visited Nancy Hart's cabin, talked to people who had known her, and was shown the tree where the men had been hanged. Mrs. Ellet who was later to purvey elegant literature to New York's fashionables, felt obliged to represent Nancy's good round oaths in delicate abbreviations. But she was ready to accept her services in the cause of liberty, as did Nancy's neighbors. "Poor Nancy," she quotes one of them, "she was a honey of a patriot, but a devil of a wife."

1 The background for these pages comes from travelers' journals, most of them slightly post-Revolutionary, records made by early foreign visitors who came to check on commercial openings and political ideas. But women's activities had scant notice in these manuscripts.

The first account of women in the Revolution was written by a woman, Elizabeth F. L. Ellet, who did not publish her *Women of the American Revolution* till 1850. The work had been a personal hobby carried on for many years while she and her husband were living in South Carolina, but not printed till their return to New York much later.

In 1852, she added her *Pioneer Women*. Mrs. Ellet herself had had a pioneering background. Her father had left New Jersey for the early settlements along Lake Ontario. Elizabeth, born at Sodus in 1818, went to school in Aurora. At seventeen, she married W. H. Ellet, a professor of chemistry who left Columbia to teach at South Carolina College. While he experimented with guncotton, his wife busied herself tracing the course of Revolutionary fighting in the Carolinas and Georgia. This part of her book is the most valuable.

After the success of these two volumes, Mrs. Ellet degenerated into a fashionable member of New York's "literati." The most discreditable episode in her career is her part in the harassment of Poe, 1847–48. Her later work is distinctly inferior. *Queens of American Society* (1867) and *Court Circles of the New Republic* show plainly the hand of a "ghost." But she had been a genuine pioneer in the history of American women.

2 No final judgment should be passed on Peggy Shippen without weighing the letters that she wrote home in the later years of her exile, after Arnold's ventures in the West India trade had gone sour. Apparently there had been some sort of reconciliation with her father, now one of the leading lights of the Pennsylvania bar. He sent her money, and she responded with a portrait of herself which is still preserved.

Both tone and content of her letters suggest a mature woman with an intelligent interest in public affairs, and greatly concerned with the up-bringing of her children. It is to be noted that she trained them to the strictest notions of honor. Her sons, placed in military schools for the sons of British officers, went on to highly creditable careers. Infatuated with Arnold she certainly was. Duped she may have been. It becomes difficult to see the writer of these letters as a conscious betrayer of public trust.

3   A striking instance of the helplessness of Virginia ladies under colonial laws is recounted in one of George Washington's pre-Revolutionary journals. He, along with other neighboring gentlemen, intervened vainly to prevent a lady's being stripped of her own property by a spendthrift husband. This husband had married one heiress, and had then run her estate into bankruptcy. As a widower, he had again secured an amply dowered bride, this time from the eastern shore of Maryland where his previous misdoing was not known. (No railways, telegraphs or telephones in 1750.) With this second wife's dowry, the husband purchased a new set of slaves for the estate, and once more began running through a wife's fortune.

When creditors began closing in, the squire sailed off to the West Indies taking with him a shipload of plantation hands who would fetch a good price from island sugar-growers. The Virginia gentlemen nearby tried to help the deserted wife, whose property had become legally her husband's. In the end, she returned penniless to her family. What happened to the luckless Virginia blacks sold into West India heat, no one knows.

4   This episode is found in Mc Clung's *Sketches of Western Adventures,* one of the earliest regional records. Within the last few years several of Mc Clung's accounts have been re-appearing made into short stories.

5   The "Narrative of Mary Jemison" was made public by her biographer, James E. Seaver, in a pamphlet printed in 1829 in Canandaigua, N.Y. Later it went through many editions. A 29th reprint was done in 1929 by Random House. A statue to Mary Jemison can be seen in Letchworth State Park, New York, near the site of Mary's lost acres, in Genessee.

CHAPTER TWO

Female Citizens of the New Republic

*B*Y the decade between 1800 and 1810, the new United States had had twenty years in which to recover from the ravages of war and to initiate a march of progress under the very new Constitution. That was adopted, every school child knows, in a desperate effort to emerge from the financial chaos which beset the fledgling republic, only too loosely held together by the earlier Articles of Confederation. In these pages the governmental theories and political practices involved, about which whole libraries have been written, will be passed over. The object of search will be to see the people themselves, and more especially to discover how women citizens were faring.

Even by 1800 certain lasting characteristics of American life had appeared. With the stabilization of public finances, commerce in the seaport cities had sprung to life. Their population had increased fabulously, giving rise to intense land speculation in and around market centers. Speculation in the newer frontier lands soon followed. Fortunes were made and lost in that early time, quite without benefit of any stock market.

The most dramatic ventures were maritime. Mighty profitable they were for those who survived sailing voyages to the West Indies,

South America and points much farther east, with fever, pirates and privateering added to the perils of the deep. As soon as the war restrictions had ended the entire North Atlantic sea coast began to lift canvas wings from ports large and small. Venture shares in a ship and its cargo were subdivided till even the cabin boy might have his stake in the voyage. And so might his land-abiding neighbors, down to his cousins and his aunts.

Losses of ships and crews were savage, but the profit of a single success was dazzling. Easy money and plenty of it began pouring back into the seaport towns. Stately mansions were built for rough and ready captains. Similarly, their wives were transformed into ladies who would replace their pewter porringers with fine china. It was this mushrooming of wealth that introduced the chaperon to the early American scene, to refine the conduct of the rising generation. Old wealth in the new world had known its manners. New wealth would learn.

That was boom. Bust meant financial difficulties to the new states plagued with the uncertainties of depreciated local currencies. The country's industries still remained in the cottage stage, leaving agriculture to carry the load. Taxation fell heaviest on land, because land couldn't run away. Neither could the farmer, with the threat of imprisonment for debt held over him. In spite of the noble sentiments of Revolutionary oratory, the poor man had gained little political power, rarely even a vote. Suffrage remained hedged about with property and church qualifications. Jail for debt was accepted legal procedure, and mortgage rates soared. To sell their tax-burdened farms, if sale was possible, and to set out for frontier lands became the recourse of distress. The tax collector and the mortgage usurer more than the spirit of adventure urged many a family to try its luck in newly opened sections of Maine, Vermont, western New York or even across the Alleghenies. Where their men folk went, the women had to go.

In the South as well, great estates felt the squeeze. Country squires who had loaned good sound money to Virginia or the Carolinas under enemy attack, now found themselves repaid belatedly with doubtful currency. Again taxes forced large landowners to sell off their extended estates. Sons and daughters no longer had profitable farms waiting to support their marriages (Chapter Note 1).

THESE WERE THE WOMEN

Foremost in the ranks of discontent both North and South were Revolutionary soldiers who had served largely for promises of pay. Years later they were still holding only promises. The earliest Ohio ventures were undertaken to right this wrong. Such then were the pressures that formed the background of the first decade of the nineteenth century in the United States.

Now, what of the women who lived through these times?

WE SEE BY THE PAPERS

The modern instinct turns to the newspapers of the period, assuming that such printed matter will reveal the activities of women readers. The columns between 1800 and 1810 were fairly plentiful but they tell nothing directly of how American women were living. Reports are masculine and commercial, registering the arrival of ships and auctioning of cargoes, with an occasional political piece from Philadelphia or London or Washington.

Paging through the yellowing files of *The New York Evening Post* for this decade, one can find vestigial traces of possible women readers. There is a recurrent advertisement of Mr. Lalliat's dancing school, where ladies will be taught in the afternoon, and gentlemen in the evening. There is a legal notice of one Jane Shorter who has left her husband's bed and board. Another legal notice concerns the sale of certain properties on Pearl Street in an estate settlement. It bears the name of "Margaret Tierce, her mark." Property owner or no, this widow could not write her own name. A bookstore recommends the "Devotional Works of Mrs. Ann Steel." One A. J. Young is about to "form a class of a select number of ladies for the study of polite literature," while Miss Woofendale's school announces its removal from Brooklyn to Maiden Lane.

The presence of a "Juvenile Book Store at 357 Pearl Street" as well as the sale of a "remedy for whooping cough" seem to be the only printed evidence in these columns of the city's children. Ladies are also urged to buy "Lily Lotion for the secret infirmities that delicacy forbids them to disclose." Piano makers from London can now be found at 63 Barclay Street, and Christian Loss, late of Albany, offers to teach the harp.

Farther down in the social scale, Rebecca M'Hinch, of 58 Wall

Street, sells Irish linen. Hers is the only woman's name appearing in a decade of business cards. An anonymous householder advertises for "a cook that can be recommended" and a country girl seeks kitchen work "in a small respectable family."

A more frequent domestic item was the buying and selling of Negro houseworkers. For 60 pounds one might purchase a strong and healthy Negro wench "perfectly honest and not given to drink or running out at night." Also for sale was another stout and healthy Negress "about twenty-four . . . capable of doing all kinds of work, country or city. She has a male child of two years whose time of service may be had if it bests suits the purchaser." Mulatto boys from twelve years up were frequently in demand "to wait on table." (The use of pounds in these advertisements suggests that the discarded British monetary unit was still more stable in value than the new American dollar.) There was also an "African School" where "masters of families" could have their servants taught the three R's.

LITTLE OLD NEW YORK

New York even then had a metropolitan flavor, although it had lost to Philadelphia its brief rank as the nation's capital. New York boasted paved footways with a curb separating them from the road. Trade was booming and houses were beautiful. Windows and sidewalks were washed every Saturday though "no one removes dead dogs, cats and rats from the streets," a visiting foreigner noted.

New York's hostelries rated well. There was the Tontine Tavern, which also served informally as a stock exchange, where room and board was ten shillings a day, as against the accepted five shilling rate in Boston. There was also Loring's, near the Battery, with a common room 50 feet by 30, and ceilings 20 feet high. This enterprise was Mrs. Loring's, who should rank high on the roster of early American women of business, but for the fact that she was a relict of the losing side of the Revolution. Her husband had been the British quartermaster general.

New York, too, had its poorhouse and its hospital which also cared for some two hundred foundlings. These were brought up at city expense and did not wear "any particular dress" because the early City Fathers "wished to spare them humiliation." The children in blue uniforms at Trinity church belonged to the respectable poor, clothed and educated by the parish. In summer, boats were provided for cold-water bathing, with some reserved for women. But the morals of the city had a seaport tone. "Whole sections of streets are given over to street-walkers . . . of every color . . . proudly flaunting their licentiousness." Nevertheless, New Yorkers were in general "refined and amiable," and their city "the pleasantest of all places in the U.S. in which to live."

All urban rents were high—the usual post-war housing shortage. In New York a modest shop-keeper had to pay 500 dollars a year to house his family. In Boston a good dwelling cost double that amount. This, no doubt, accounts for the rise of the boarding house, an American domestic innovation which met with strong disapproval from transatlantic visitors.

PHILADELPHIA STORY

Philadelphia, though, was the first city of the land. Although it ceased to be the capital in 1801, it still led in population, commerce and science. Its wharves were busy and its streets paved as far as Fifth Street, and all lighted at night. After 1795 no wooden buildings were permitted below Tenth Street, and after 1805 water was piped in the streets. Approaching the former capital, travelers noted an increased air of wealth and activity. There would be carriages on the roads, cabriolets and phaetons, sometimes driven by women. Women on horseback were also a frequent sight.

In 1800 the town was reckoned to have 9,000 houses, mostly of clapboards, with ground floor, first floor and attic. Narrow doorways were of brick with white trim, and, by custom, doors, sidewalks and window ledges were scrubbed every Wednesday and Saturday morning, even in freezing weather. But the servant who did the scrubbing went barefoot, "making no point of cleanliness."

For its women and how they lived, we shall use the observations of a refugee Frenchman. In this period Frenchmen who had fled either the Terror or the rise of Napoleon were numerous enough to have a small magazine of their own, *Le Petit Censeur*. But most notable and most concerned with Philadelphia and its womenfolk was Moreau de St. Méry, who had established a bookshop and printing business there. He had also clerked in Norfolk, Virginia, checked ships' stores in New York, and inspected the intervening territory.

"American women are pretty," the Frenchman states forthrightly, "and those of Philadelphia are prettiest of all." But that praise was only for the very young, girls from fourteen to eighteen. Beauty was soon lost. The young women grew pale, they lost their hair and their teeth. "Charming and adorable at fifteen, they are faded at twenty-three, old at thirty, decrepit at forty." The young Quaker women, he thought, combined a pretended simplicity with extremely worldly tastes.

When it came to buying ribbons, shoes and lawn, Philadelphia women were remarkably extravagant, but could not capture the elegance of a French lady. There was also their American habit of letting the men pay for what they bought in the shops, and forgetting to repay. Everyone, excepting ladies of the highest rank, went to market on Thursday and Friday evenings "dressed as for dancing." This complaint of St. Méry's is borne out by the earlier stricture of the Marquis de Chastellux. "The rage for dress among the women in America . . . was beyond all bound." Even Martha Lamb, herself a New Yorker, declared that "the expense of women causes matrimony to be dreaded by men."

But house furnishings were of the simplest. At least so the exiled Frenchman found as a lodger among Philadelphia's plain people. There might be several pieces of mahogany with chairs to match in the homes of the wealthy. "Other classes" used walnut furniture with wooden chairs, usually painted green. There were no hangings, no upholstery, no mirrors, though there might be carpets imported from England. Even such modest decoration was limited to "rooms the visitor is likely to see . . . everything out of sight is ugly and little cared for."

Americans today are surprised to find that our ancestors were considered dirty by visiting foreigners of the upper classes. St. Méry detailed his strictures with startling frankness. American women did not wash their underwear as did the women of France. As for chemises, American women had few and changed them seldom. They washed their faces and hands carefully, but not their mouths, rarely their feet and still more rarely their bodies. "Bastards are extremely common in Philadelphia," the critic continued, "where, after one year, the mother might farm out her child for twenty-one years." "Abortion" he added, "is seldom resorted to."

As to food, Philadelphians lived well. They breakfasted at nine on ham or salt fish with coffee or tea, and bread spread with Philadelphia butter, which already ranked as a superior article. Dinner came at two, with broth, an English roast surrounded by potatoes and green peas. This would be followed by baked or fried eggs or fish, a salad, usually of thinly sliced cabbage, and pastries. Americans were especially partial to sweets. For dessert there would be fruit, cheese and pudding, "the entire meal washed down with cider." "Men who never sit down to table without three courses," was *Le Petit Censeur's* phrase for the gentlemen of Philadelphia.

This description of domesticity in Philadelphia agrees with the observations of Abigail Adams in those chatty, ill spelled letters that she dashed off to her sister, Mary Cranch, for private consumption. The First Lady had her housekeeping troubles. In 1797, they had three domestics, a sad set of creatures. "This city is becoming as vile and debauched as London—nay more so—for in the lower classes, much more respect is had to character there."

Later on she had had seven new servants in eighteen months and "not a virtuous woman amongst them all." Her little housemaid Celia would be led astray if not strictly guarded. Mrs. Adams soon announced triumphantly that she had "a cleaver [sic] sober, honest & Neat black woman" as her daily cook. Of course, she always hired extra for company. "Politics," she concluded briefly, "they begin to grow pretty warm."

Like a good New Englander, Abigail blamed all the discredit on the "foreigners" who had been flocking into both New York and Philadelphia. St. Méry was much more sympathetic toward these immigrants driven by poverty into the fever-ridden holds of sailing ships. As indentured servants, they were usually unhappy. The girls could not marry without their masters' consent. Once having served out their time, few female servants were willing to continue. "As a rule, they are immoral, and can be had for very little money . . . ordinarily they have but one chemise and some not even that . . . masters treat servants with haughtiness that verges on contempt . . ."

Yet when these despised houseworkers were dressed for their Sunday evening promenade, St. Méry found it difficult to distinguish mistresses from servants. After a freed, indentured man married, wrote the Frenchman, "he then expects his wife to serve him." Hard as was their lot, in 1798, alone, 13,000 men and women entered the new republic as indentured servants.

THE FIRST FASHION WAR

Such then was the world of Philadelphia that was to face its first war of fashion. For the government of France had become the directorate, and directoire gowns had crossed the Atlantic, and were about to invade the Presidential drawing-room.

"A sattin peticoat of not more than three breadths gored at the top, nothing beneath but a chemise. Over this a thin coat, a Muslin sometimes . . . made so strait before as perfectly to show the whole form. The arm naked almost to the shoulder and without stays or Bodice. A tight girdle round the waist . . . and the rich Luxuriance of nature's Charms, without a handkerchief, fully displayed. The face, á la mode de Paris, Red as a Brick hearth." That is Abigail Adams' description.

When a lady so clad was led up to make her formal curtsy to the President, Abigail could literally see through her, she complained. The new fashion plate then danced, without regard to splitting her scanty coat. Most of the ladies presented wore their clothes too scant upon the body and too full upon the bosom, so that, to Mrs. Adams, they looked "like Nursing Mothers." But the First Lady was not impervious to the changes of fashion herself. She would not affect the directoire, but she began looking about for red broadcloth, since "red cloth Cloaks are all the Mode, trim'd with white fur," she told Mrs. Cranch.

Later on directoire fashions scandalized the country's new capital, Washington. There the tempest swirled around the attractive person of Mrs. Jerome Bonaparte, formerly Miss Patterson of Baltimore. But the reaction of conservatives was equally sharp.

"She has made a great noise here," wrote Margaret Bayard Smith, whose husband was an ardent Jeffersonian. Mobs of boys crowded around her carriage to see "what I hope will not often be seen in this country, an almost naked woman." The elegant and select party given for the noted couple was thrown into confusion . . . "no one dared look at her but by stealth," while outside unshuttered windows, a crowd assembled. "Her dress was the thinnest sarcenet . . . there was scarcely any waist to it and no sleeves; her back, her bosom, part of her waist and her arms were uncovered and the rest of her form visible." Several Washington ladies warned the bride that "she must promise to have more clothes on" at the entertainment scheduled for the following evening.

Domestic handicaps of official Washington appear in many of Margaret Smith's letters. Servant trouble was constant in households where no slaves were kept. Members of the diplomatic corps were obliged to take on almost anyone who would consent to wear livery, while even President Monroe's White House staff was "out of livery." Margaret Smith could hire servants, but the servants could not cook. It was the lady of the house who prepared the open-hearth meals. An item astounding to us today is her acquiring a "bound girl," aged six, to guard her own toddlers from getting into the fireplace. Apparently there was no other local provision for orphans than to "bind them out," even at six.

FROM A DOWN EAST PARSONAGE

So much then for women's life in New York, Philadelphia and Washington in this first decade of the nineteenth century. But then, more than now, city life did not speak for the entire country. By letters and journals a rough circuit can be made of the new republic's farming regions.

The start will be in Maine, twenty years before it became a separate state. The postwar period had seen the opening up of the Massachusetts Down East District through the spread of shipbuilding to Maine seaports, supported by farms in the magnificent river valleys back from salt water. Accepting what was almost a missionary post, the Reverend Jonathan Fisher came fresh from Harvard to the harsh realities of a country parsonage in Blue Hill.

From his arrival in 1794 the parson kept a private diary in a shorthand of his own invention. In this, safe from prying eyes, he entered the doings of his family and his parish, a record recently

translated by historians. A true scholar was Fisher, who read scrip-
ture to his household in French, Hebrew, Latin and Greek. Yet for
all his learning, incessant toil was the lot of the preacher, his wife
and daughters.

Come with his bride from Dedham, Fisher found that his house
was still to be built, though they were given a cow, "much good beef,
a quarter of lamb and a large cheese" as well as wool for his wife to
knit into stockings. In return for these gifts the clergyman helped
clear the winter roads, repaired clocks, re-bottomed chairs and made
274 book labels for a newly established town library, pasting them
"upon the books therein."

Farm, workshop, pulpit—that was the routine, and the family
shared it. As the children grew up they all helped make buttons from
the bones of slaughtered farm animals, painting them to sell at 25
cents per dozen. They braided an incredible number of straw hats,
wove baskets, made brooms. Father's workshop also provided toys
for his children, a wagon, a cage for their pet squirrel, a little red
sleigh on runners for "my seven children to take to school with
them," besides "a little bookcase" for their library.

The diary makes no mention of these children before their
arrival in this world. Then "Mrs. Fisher sent for help about 10
o'clock A.M. at 7 hrs 30 minutes, she was through kind Providence,
delivered of a fine son after severe labor, God be praised." For none
of her nine children was there ever a doctor, only some neighbor
woman called in. Three times, after weeks of fever following childbirth, a doctor was finally summoned.

Yet it was a happy marriage, though in his diary the parson
never called her anything but Mrs. Fisher. On their fifteenth anniversary he noted: "Blessed be God in respect to my connection with
Mrs. Fisher, to a good measure free from altercation and strife."
There were also thanks for "eight pleasant children." All these years
it was the dominie who arose at five in the morning to lay the fires
and start breakfast.

Part of the family pattern was the grandmother. When nearly
80, during one summer, she wove "20 yds. of checked shirting, 18
yds. linen, 20 yds. of heavy Thersy for blankets and 31 yds. of carpet." Indolence and sloth, the old lady warned her grandchildren,
were weapons of Satan to snare and deceive. Accordingly, grand-

daughter Sally at the age of eleven "wove 23 yds. of woolen cloth." In 1813 Mrs. Fisher and her daughters "in 6 months wove 56 yards of cloth." An advanced thinker, though, was this parson, for his children were paid for their household labor. Finally, in 1822, "Mrs. F" inherited a legacy of 50 dollars. Whereupon, by her wish, the parson bought a colt and himself built a sleigh. Until that momentous year the Fisher family had walked.

In contrast to this well ordered, affectionate family, we have the record of Fisher's parishoners, for the church also sat as a morals court. Charges tried there included "sinful anger, extreme intemperance . . . abuse of wives by husbands and of husbands by wives, adultery, propagation of scandal, lewd behavior and contention with a mother-in-law." Despite hard living and hellfire, the most frequent charge on the clergyman's judgment book was fornication, usually confessed by the defendants. Occasionally some girl who had falsely accused another girl was sentenced to eat her words in public.

In one instance the Blue Hill church caught a tartar. The matron in question confessed to the sins of anger, falsehood, arrogance and pride. But when charged with marital infidelity, she made a staunch denial, even though her own child was made to testify against her. At this point the husband sprang to his wife's defense, protesting the proceedings as based on hearsay. Nevertheless, both husband and wife were excommunicated from the Blue Hill church.

Nevertheless, the husband prospered, becoming a prominent citizen. Finally they joined the nearby church at Bucksport. The old charges were sent up to a regional council, and the Blue Hill church was ordered to "annul its past votes expressing suspicions of Mrs. Ray's modesty." This reversal Parson Fisher noted down in his shorthand without comment except to commend himself once more to prayer.

The only self-supporting women found in the Fisher journals were teachers imported from Massachusetts for the Blue Hill school at a wage of two dollars a week. Boys and girls were taught separately in the Academy, the girls under strict supervision by a very superior "female assistant" who received all of three dollars a week, plus board. By 1805, Blue Hill had a teacher "in the art of sacred music." Painting was not added till 1820, and then only as an extra.

At length, as an old man, Parson Fisher retired from his Maine pastorate to the family farm in Massachusetts, with a final word of advice to the young men of Blue Hill. It was: "When connected, live joyfully with your partner."

THE JOURNAL OF TRYPHENA WHITE

From the secret records of Parson Fisher we turn to the simple pages of Tryphena White, whose family moved from Massachusetts to new lands being opened in western New York. In 1805 the father, Joseph White, set out from Springfield for Camillus in Onondaga County, to build a mill on Nine Mile Creek. This site was some three miles beyond what is now Syracuse, but in June 1805, the last two miles took the White family an entire day because there was no road. The newcomers were crudely accommodated in a neighboring farmhouse till their own dwelling should be ready.

There, among strangers, Tryphena began her journal in a small book that she made out of scraps of paper sewed together. It is all very plain, the work and days in this near wilderness. There were no Indians threatening, but . . . "helped Polly kill a rattlesnake . . . got drinking water from woods spring . . . weed in the garden . . . tried to catch trout." Mother and daughters joined in washing clothes and making soap, but the water wasn't right, and for all their labor, the soap didn't turn out well. Days later they were still struggling with the soap. "Tis poor stuff yet," said Tryphena. By August, the new house and the mill were nearing completion, but there had been nine workmen to feed. Tryphena had baked "towards a bushel of cake."

The real heartbreak for the girl, one can guess, was isolation. On July 4th there had been an Independence Ball at the nearest settlement, with "19 gentlemen and 14 ladies but Polly and I stayed home." Also, there was no church. Once in July there was a "meeting" but on other Sundays "our joiner exhorted and pray'd." Still, she was proud of their new house, though the cooking pot still hung outdoors. Wash, iron, bake. That was the weekly round. "Greens are a very scarce article here," so she had been out into the fields to gather "pusley."

In the fall the journal sounded a modest note of triumph. She and Polly had actually been visiting to the nearest town and have met "2 young ladies as accomplished . . . as any in W. Springfield, almost." Tryphena, a well bred girl from a settled town had at last found people of her own sort, not like the rough farmer-workmen around her father's new mill. And right here the journal stops.

A few years later Tryphena married, had one child and then died "of a rapid decline." Her family saved the little homemade book to keep for her boy when he should grow up, as a memorial of his mother. By this accident of fate Tryphena's journal was preserved to become a small, authentic document of her time and place.

In the older regions of New England life was still based on the small landholding. Of course, there were a few rural magnates. Near Newport, Rhode Island, for instance, was an estate of 12,000 acres, which supported 4,000 sheep and kept twelve dairy maids at work providing the great quantities of cheese consumed daily. With a pre-Gilbert-and-Sullivan touch, each of these twelve maids had another girl to wait on her. This rural luxury, though, was not for the plain farmer's wife, such as the mother of Lucy Stone, who milked eight cows the night before the rebellious Lucy entered the world.

Nor was the lot of the self-supporting woman much easier. Wages for housework were microscopic and demands were heavy. Take for instance the Mrs. Mallery who kept house for Eli Whitney in 1812 when he was making rifles for the government. (The cotton gin had brought him more lawsuits than profit.) Whitney had his factory outside of New Haven, together with a large house in which lived the proprietor, two young nephews and nine apprentice lads for the mill. Washing, cooking and cleaning for this establishment brought Mrs. Mallery "one Dollar per Week." To assist her, she had her daughter Betsy who was to have schooling for three months, "in which time she is to work mornings and evenings." Betsy's food was provided, but she had no other compensation. "Mrs. M. is also to have the privelege of doing her husband's washing here," the inventor's account book states.

Shortly after this Whitney married "Miss Henrietta F. Edwards, daughter of the Hon. Pierpont E." Of this union came four children, including one son "born on the 24th Nov. Eli Whitney jr." This was in 1821. But nowhere does the father record the birthdates of any of his three daughters.

THE EARLY SCHOOLS

But, for women, the great event in the first decade of 1800 was the rise of schools for girls. Boston took the lead in offering a public grammar school. Other communities followed, but taxpayers' bounty stopped at the three R's, and, only too often, before that. In 1788 authorities at Northampton, Massachusetts, (later the site of Smith College) voted down a money grant for a girls' school as a needless waste of public funds.

Soon, however, New England was spotted with private schools for young ladies whose parents would pay the fees—Bradford Academy in Massachusetts was speedily joined by academies at Byfield, Pittsfield and Saugus, and the Down East academies at Blue Hill and Bath, Maine. A little later came Adams Academy at Derry, New Hampshire, the first school endowed, though modestly, for the education of young women. In 1803 Bradford Academy in Pennsylvania opened its doors.

Strictly speaking, the palm for priority goes much farther south, to the Ursuline nuns of New Orleans, sent out from France, who began their teaching fully 75 years before the Louisiana Purchase. Next came the Moravians of Pennsylvania who had a pre-Revolutionary school at Allentown where girls were taught "needlework, silk, silver and gold, and manufacture in flax and cotton," singing as they wove. One visitor thought the misses "took too little exercise and fresh air to be healthy." In 1802 these same Moravians started a girls' school at Salem, North Carolina, one that was to become famous, and that has survived to this day.

Even more restricted were the women of the Rappite colony, founded in 1805 at Harmony, Butler County, Pennsylvania. There wool raising was the chief industry, the men providing the raw product, the women carrying on its manufacture. They were taught the necessary sorting, carding, spinning and weaving, and again the girls at the loom sang "church music, most melodiously." In the evenings, when the community assembled for divine service, the women sat at one end of the room, the men at the other. The men had what their crude neighbors called a "band," really a small orchestra of strings, wood winds and brass, the first to be maintained

43

in this new world. Women, however, were not among the instru-
mentalists, though at church services they were permitted to join in
the chorus.

Compared with these establishments, the early Quaker schools
seem marvels of progress. For wherever there were Friends, girls
were welcome at their schools, since that inner light was admitted
to shine regardless of sex. These schools, open to both brothers and
sisters, undoubtedly accounted for the notable Quaker women who
will be found leading the reforms of the next generation.

But the Quakers did not go too far in this business of freedom.
At a Dutchess County, New York, boarding school which Lucretia
Mott entered in 1806, boys and girls were kept in separate classes
with separate teachers. Boys and girls, except near relatives, were
not permitted to speak to each other. On certain set occasions near
relatives might talk to each other over a designated corner of the
solid fence that separated the boys' yard from that of the girls.
Naughty boys who looked through knotholes at the girls were
promptly punished.

There were always a few exceptions, where some one girl received thorough schooling. Such a girl was little Lucinda Foote of
New Haven, who was tutored by no less a person than Ezra Stiles,
the president of Yale. When Lucinda was only twelve, Dr. Stiles
attested to her proficiency in reading Virgil, Cicero and the Greek
Testament. "She is fully qualified," he certified, "except in regard
to sex," to be received as an entering pupil at Yale. Later Lucinda
pursued the entire college course under Dr. Stiles, including Hebrew.
After which she married, had ten children and disappeared from
the annals of erudition.

By this time fashionable schools in the new republic had the
services of well-born French emigrés. French women of standing
either opened schools of their own, or taught in others'. Madame
Capron at Newark, for instance, provided French, geography, drawing and "embroidery of all kinds" at $136. per annum. It is best not
to inquire too closely into the type of learning dispensed to the select.
Miss Brenton of South Kingston, Rhode Island, offered "epistolary
style . . . temple work, paper work, fringing and netting." The
best New England schools in 1808 boasted of "music, geography,
parsing from Pope's *Essay on Man,* rhetoric and embroidery on

satin." A certain Charlestown finishing school promised, besides, "60 lace stitches." But European spectators considered American pupils spoiled, learning only what they wanted to learn.

TALES OF THE EARLY TRAVELERS

A partial eyewitness survey of American women can be had by way of travelers' journals. No sooner had the United States become a growing concern than visitors began taking notes. Some were intellectuals interested in theories of government. Others were commercial missionaries preparing to do business with the new republic. But they all came, pencils in hand.

Civilization was still a thin veneer laid on around the larger seaports. Even that finish had its cracks, and travelers found them. In the best hostelries guests were lodged "generally two in a room, and not very cleanly." Vermin were plentiful in Boston and Philadelphia. Special praise was given to Isaac Shiver's inn on the road to New York because the beds there had "truly clean sheets which is the rarest of all things in an American tavern." Nor were bed-lice restricted to inns and hotels. An etiquette book of the period bids visiting ladies who encounter night vermin, not to mention that unpleasantness to their hostess. Apparently the situation was common enough to warrant this caution.

Travel was still a hazardous combination of boat and stage with frequent change of horses and equally frequent quenching of thirst. Should there be ladies in a coach, they were gallantly served their drinks free. In the South, with its notoriously bad roads, private hospitality was unbounded, but public provision for the wayfarer was dubious. A foreign visitor in 1800 described a Carolina "ordinary" as a one-story affair, built of logs and marked as a place of entertainment by a wooden jug hung from a pole outside. Before the door, hogs wallowed in sun or mud. Within, there might be two rooms, but generally a Carolina inn was a one-room apartment, with the innkeeper's family bed in one corner. In another corner would stand a pine chest, the family clothespress and larder, while a third corner would be ruled off for a bar, furnished with a rum keg and one glass. In the open place stood a slab table and two chairs, all home-made.

On pulling up before such an establishment, wrote an Englishman, "you usually found the landlord gone to market, the landlady cutting wood in the swamp . . . If hunger and fatigue compelled you to remain, a little Indian corn for your horse, and a blanket for the hearth with your saddle for a pillow, were the most you could obtain. As to edibles, whether you called for breakfast, dinner or supper, the reply was eggs and bacon . . . Ten to one, you had to cook the meal yourself."

Although this was a shock to foreigners, cooking one's own meals at an inn was the accepted mode for American pioneers. When the wagons of the first settlers, pushing their perilous way across the Alleghenies, reached a stopping place for the night, the men expected to attend to their own cattle, the women to cook the food for the caravan. An inn was merely a place where, by the blessing of Providence, one might sleep dry for the night.

THE LAND OF PLENTY

Yet back of all this crudity, beyond these roads that to a European were no roads at all, was rich farming country. William Cobbett, later a stormy petrel in British politics, was impressed with this when he visited the country just before 1800, and revisited it in 1817. Speaking of Long Island, he wrote: "When I say a good farmhouse, I mean a great deal better than the general run of farmhouses in England, more neatly finished on the inside, more in the parlor style, though round about the house things do not look so neat and tight as in England."

He obtained from a farmer's wife what he called her "bill of fare for the year." This early food budget included "fourteen fat hogs, four beeves, and forty-six fat sheep, besides sucking pigs, lambs and the produce of seventy hen fowls, not to mention good parcels of geese, ducks, and turkeys." There was also the butter from ten cows, not an ounce of which was sold, and a kitchen-garden of three-quarters of an acre. Nor did this farmer's wife face a life of unremitting drudgery, for Cobbett noted that the maid servants received from 40 to 50 dollars a year.

This tale of fat living is borne out by the dinner party described in *The Pioneers,* in which James Fenimore Cooper recalled the pioneer days of Cooperstown, New York, as seen in his own boyhood. "Before Elizabeth was placed an enormous roasted turkey, and before Richard, one boiled. On the last platter was a venison steak. Between these dishes and the turkeys stood . . . a prodigious chine of roasted boar's meat and . . . a boiled leg of delicious mutton." The four corners of the table were likewise garnished with plates of cake and sweetmeats, "while at each place stood a complete but motley pie," composed of wedges of apple, mince, pumpkin, cranberry and custard. To wash down the food, there were decanters of brandy, rum, gin and wine, and pitchers of cider, beer and hot flip. In the good old days of the open fireplace, people ate to supply their own central heating.

Obviously cooking and serving at this rate called for many hands and feet, but before the rise of the factory, the country districts had no shortage of domestic help. The poor they also had with them, and many of them right in the kitchen. Brooklyn in 1808 had 1,400 inhabitants, 600 of whom were black servants, making it a very comfortable little town for the governing 800.

But early prosperity was not limited to the genteel. When John Melish, a textile manufacturer of Glasgow, came here in 1811 to inspect the infant industries of the new world, he wrote enthusiastically of good living prevailing in the backwoods of Pennsylvania. There a country landlady served him a breakfast of ham, fritters, bread, butter and tea, all for twenty-five cents. In western New York he noted the prosperity of the farmers, and the high wages paid to carpenters. A mechanic, he maintained, could earn as much in two days as would support a family for a week. Since Mr. Melish was a Scot, his journal pictures the mechanic "investing the surplus in a judicious manner."

FROM VIRGINIA TO "MULBERRY GROVE"

The ladies of Virginia had a literary champion in John Bernard, the noted English comedian, who was George Washington's favorite actor, and who was invited to Mount Vernon. Following a trip to Virginia in 1799, Bernard wrote:

"Of the planters' ladies, I must speak in terms of unqualified praise; they had an easy kindliness of manner . . . which being natural to them (for they mixed with no society) was the more admirable . . . The one thing I did not quite approve of was the juvenile period at which they bloomed and decayed. A lady here was in the habit of marrying nearly ten years earlier than a European, so that at twenty, if she had proved a fruitful olive, her husband's table was surrounded with tall shoots . . . At thirty—the glowing summer of an English dame—she has fallen into the sere leaf; and at forty, the autumn fullness of a royal taste, the bel age of St. James, the faces of these matrons . . . are cut up with as many lines as the map of Europe."

Of the women of Georgia, farthest south of the original thirteen states there is little record. From the start that colony represented a diversity of nationalities. When John Wesley of later Methodist fame was sent there as an Anglican clergyman, he read prayers in German, French and Italian for the different settlements. The Italians were Piedmontese brought to introduce the culture of the silkworm. Altogether, Wesley reckoned that fully a third of the colony was not of English birth.

Yet it was in this faraway spot that a most significant step was taken, and one in which a woman was an important factor. The woman was Catherine Greene, widow of General Nathaniel Greene, and the step was the invention and development of the cotton gin. Although both Greene and his wife were Rhode Islanders, Greene was the hero of the southern phase of the Revolution. In gratitude, the state of Georgia presented him with a plantation in the Savannah region. There, at Mulberry Grove, the Greenes made their new home, and there the sprightly Kitty chose to bring up her five children after the General's death.

Thither in 1792 came by chance a young graduate of Yale, who had supposed himself engaged as a tutor by some neighboring family. The Yankee youth found the position filled, and himself stranded, practically penniless. Learning of his plight, the widow of Mulberry Grove invited him to stay at her home until another position could be obtained. The young tutor was Eli Whitney.

Planters of the region were then discussing the possibilities of mechanical aid in ginning short-fibred cotton. The stranded tutor, who had been a mechanic before entering Yale, agreed to make a try, fitting up a workshop in the basement of Kitty Greene's house.

Tradition shows her standing beside him with a brush, clearing the metal prongs of Whitney's first model, an action that suggested a mechanical improvement to the young inventor, a second cylinder to prevent the massing of material.

So promising was the second attempt that a neighboring planter, Phineas Miller, (another transplanted New Englander from Yale) agreed to bear all the expense of "maturing" the invention, and to divide future profits with Whitney. As all the world knows, the result was the cotton gin which was to bring about a new era in American history. But not all the world knows that the Widow Greene thereupon married Mr. Miller.

IN THE DEEP SOUTH

New Orleans, still farther south, with its amazing contrasts of mud and splendor, is described in an old memoir in 1805. There ladies of wealth and fashion were forced to walk barefoot to their great balls, because streets were still unpaved (Chapter Note 2). The eyewitness in the case was a seventeen-year-old lad from Baltimore who kept a journal of his travels.

"Everything prepared," he wrote, "the order was given to march. When, to my horror and amazement, the young ladies doffed their shoes and stockings, which were carefully tied up in silk handkerchiefs, and took up the line of march barefooted, for the ballroom. After paddling through mud, lighted by lanterns carried by negro slaves, the young ladies halted before the door and shook one foot after another in a pool of water close by. After repeating this process some half dozen times, the feet were . . . in a proper state to be wiped dry by the slaves who had carried towels for the purpose. Then silk stockings and satin slippers were put on again, tucked up trains were let down, and the ladies entered the ballroom dryshod and lovely in the candlelight."

The young reporter was the son of the United States judge first appointed to Attakapas County after the Louisiana Purchase. Later pages of the journal describe the family's slow and painful journey thither, over roads so deep in mud and water that the last stages of the trip were made in oxcarts. Arrived finally on the banks of the beautiful Bayou Teche, the travelers found a whole cavalcade of

Creole gentlemen on horseback assembled to do honor to the family of the Grand Judge.

"We crossed the stream on a flatboat, and there before us was my father's house. But what a house! How shall I describe it?" It was the best house in the village, but so dilapidated that the ladies from Baltimore sat down and wept. "But not for long. By dint of washing, rubbing, and scrubbing, and with the aid of lime and paint, the house soon gained an air of snugness. Besides, the occupation diverted the minds of my mother and sister from pondering too long on the dark side of the question."

Another small historical item of particular interest concerns the trip of the first steamer to go from Pittsburgh to New Orleans. By special arrangement with Robert Fulton, "Mr. Roosevelt of New York" was to make the venture. No passengers were permitted, but Nicholas Roosevelt saw fit to take his "young wife and family" with him. The steamer required four days between Pittsburgh and Louisville, where they waited for the water to rise so that they might traverse certain rapids. While they waited, "the lady of the family, a delicate female," added another passenger to the list. Name and sex of the infant were omitted in this early record of the voyage, but the Rooseveltian flavor of the episode is unmistakable. The first steamer on the Mississippi reached Natchez in January, 1812.

IN THE NEW SETTLEMENTS

By 1806, when one Thomas Ashe traveled through what is now West Virginia, the Indians were gone, leaving behind them a life that to a European seemed totally barbaric. Hard drinking and horrible fighting were the amusements of a day when Charlestown had 250 houses. At the chief tavern there the young Englishman attended a banjo-ball, which ended in so bloody a brawl that the ladies and the music were forced to beat a precipitate retreat.

But already a new trek was on, one that swept its way past the mountains, and across the Ohio into the Northwest Territory. Of this migration which was to drain New England of only too many farmers, there is an eyewitness account set down by Henry Fearon. Beyond "M'connel's Ville," which contained 40 houses, he came upon immigrants all the way on foot from Massachusetts. Farther on he overtook a group of 20 small family wagons, with the women "walking before their wagons." Near a spot called Dry Ridge he encountered groups of farm settlers from Maine, who had already been 80 days upon the road. He found the women "most communicative."

Then he stopped to chat with a woman from New Jersey—"out thirty-two days," the phrase went—whom he found sitting on a log, which served her both for seat and fire. She had sat there all night. Their wagon had broken down the day before, and her husband had it at a distant blacksmith's. "I wish to God we had never left home," were her parting words to the diarist.

Yet still earlier than these voyagers were the families whom Judge Symmes of Morristown, New Jersey, had led out into the new Northwest Territory in 1789, to start their pioneer settlement near what is now Cincinnati, Ohio. Of the women in this group we know little, but Marietta, settled a year later, had church services and a Sunday School in its blockhouse. There, in unbroken wilderness, was the first school for white children, though Moravian schools for Indian converts antedated these pioneers.

Out in Marietta Mrs. Andrew Lake, a kind-hearted old lady from New York, taught twenty children their Westminster catechism. Fourteen miles farther down the river was Belprie, also settled in 1789, and likewise by New Englanders, who the very next year opened a school. The first schoolmarm in the Northwest Territory was Miss Bathsheba Rouse, from Rochester, Massachusetts.

Tradition says that the first woman to join her husband in the Marietta colony was awarded 100 acres of land for her temerity. To a comfort-loving generation, she does not seem to have been overpaid. Aside from bearing and raising a family, the settler's wife could be found lending a hand at everything from bullet making to chimney building. Frequently she was also a good shot and an excellent horsewoman. Records tell of one woman who made two trips back and forth between Connecticut and the Ohio settlements, on horseback all the way. "The logs I rolled in," wrote another woman, "would surprise anyone who has never been put to the test of necessity."

Inside a settler's cabin cooking arrangements were primitive, and in winter food was scarce. A family gathered round a common pot of mush and milk. There were no salad forks. If the cornmeal gave out, the men of the family took down their muskets and went after whatever game offered. Christian Schultz, traveling through this region in 1807, describes a frontier wife, busy with her spinning, who suddenly jumped up to seize the family rifle to shoot a deer which had bounded unexpectedly past the open cabin door.

The first child born in the Western Reserve died, and the mother came close to starvation because the father was delayed returning from a hunting trip. For those who escaped starving, smallpox and scarlet fever lay waiting. Yet in spite of everything, some pioneer women lived to a ripe old age. A further marvel is that some of them actually enjoyed it. When John Harper, first settler of Unionville, Ohio, died of fever, relatives back in Pennsylvania urged his widow to return to them. But she clung to her lakeside clearing, even when she was down to wild leeks before the Spring provisions came in. In the end, she persuaded her Pennsylvania kinfolk to come out to her.

Later on, when settling had been relieved of its perils, some of the frontier women resented it. Life had become just dull farming.

FRONTIER ETIQUETTE

In those new-West farm homes, the "linsey petticoat and the bedgown" was the universal dress of the women, with perhaps a small homemade handkerchief added as a touch of elegance. In warm weather women went barefoot, and in winter they could choose between moccasins and "shoepacks," a homemade cross between moccasins and sandals. All clothing, meager as it was, was displayed hung on wooden pegs around the cabin, as evidence of family prosperity. As for the women who made and wore it, they were expected to be handy with the distaff and the shuttle, the sickle and the hoe. Such as it was, all dressmaking and tailoring was women's work, including the men's hunting shirts, leggings and drawers.

Young people married young. They were all poor together, and a new home required little more than labor. Weddings were the most popular sort of frontier entertainment, possibly because all other forms, such as log rolling or cabin raising, called for work from the guests.

A log cabin wedding had its own etiquette. The ceremony must take place before dinner, and the bride had the right to choose the parson. Early in the day men guests gathered at the cabin of the bridegroom's father, and made their way in a party. When within a mile of the destination, two young men were selected to "run for the bottle." The one first to reach the bride's doorstep received the prize, which he was supposed to return to the men's party for general consumption, the groom being honored with the first swig. Then, whooping as they went, the men's party proceeded to the bride's cabin.

Here a backwoods feast was being made ready, with beef, pork, fowls and sometimes venison and bear meat, both roasted and boiled. For vegetables there were always potatoes and cabbage to start with. After the ceremony everyone sat down to the feast, a large slab of timber forming the table. There would be some pewter dishes and plates, with more wooden bowls and trenchers. Spoons were of pewter or horn, but men supplied their own cutlery in the form of the scalping knives that were carried, sheathed, under home-made linsey hunting jackets. Liquor flowed plentifully, "the greatest hilarity prevailing." Dancing followed, four-handed reels, square sets and jigs.

"At about nine or ten," says a chronicler, "a deputation of young ladies stole off the bride and put her to bed" in the cabin loft. Then the young men "stole off the groom and placed him snugly by the side of his bride. The dance still continued." Later, the bottle, called Black Betty, was carried to the young couple, who by etiquette were required to eat and drink whatever was brought them. Meanwhile the dancing went on, interrupted only for toasts. "Here's health to the bride, thumping luck and big children" was an accepted formula. Drinking, dancing and feasting would last till morning, and sometimes through the succeeding day. It usually required several days' rest before members of the wedding were fit to take up their daily labors once more.

In spite of crudity, moral standards were surprisingly high. "Seduction and bastardy did not frequently happen in our early times," wrote Doddridge, who in 1824 was looking back on his boyhood. "This crime could not take place without great personal danger" from brothers or other relatives of the victim.

Curiously enough, it was this region, with its rough and hearty manners, which was swept by a religious hysteria at the opening of the century. Participants in frontier revival services were seized with what was called "the jerks." The phenomenon spread like wildfire, regardless of denomination, though one analist noted that Methodist "jerks" seemed to be more powerful than Presbyterian ones. Both men and women, caught in the contagion, fell, jerked, rolled, danced and sometimes barked. Sometimes, too, the devotees saw visions or fell into trances which lasted from a few hours to two days. Sometimes congregations "jerked" from the elbows down, sometimes with the entire body. Some members were thrown into convulsions "like a live fish cast on the land," one old observer declared.

No one knew why it happened. The first recorded instance occurred in east Tennessee, but from there it spread into all the surrounding backwoods regions, where a seizure of jerks was accepted as a religious visitation. "It was like an epidemic," reported one more literate observer. Hysteria or blessing, it was some form of violent reaction to the harsh demands of frontier living.

And where, one may ask, in this survey, were the women of intellect? Or, if not intellect, of literate pursuits? Or as today's jargon has it, the career women?

The dozen women who had run pre-Revolutionary printshops, and published the official gazettes in half a dozen colonies, had gone to their reward. No woman stepped forth to take their place, nor were there to be any of note for nearly 50 years. For the publishing of a chronicle was no longer mere setting up of some royal governor's official pronouncement. Printing had become part of politics in the new system, and from politics women were barred.

UNA SED LEA

Throughout this rapidly expanding territory history records only one woman who in this early period wrote and published. That was Hannah Adams, of Boston, precursor of all American women students who later took pen in hand, or still later, worked for diplomas. Hannah Adams, in nowise related to those other notable Adamses, was a pioneer intellectual, and too much the pioneer for her own good. Throughout her long years of scholarship and industry she earned almost nothing from her writings. There was no copyright. There were no royalties. For her first book, a compendium of existing Christian denominations, the publisher rewarded her with 50 copies of her own work, to sell if she could. Uninviting as the subject sounds to modern ears, the compendium must have had readers, for Miss Adams was paid something for later editions, and she seems to have had no difficulty in securing a publisher for succeeding work.

This Hannah Adams, spinster, born in 1755, was the daughter of an early Boston bookshop keeper, who loved learning too well to prosper in his business. The family eked out a living by boarding theological students who came for training at Harvard. From these serious gentlemen Hannah Adams gained her own education, with always a bent toward the theological. In her turn she became so proficient in the ancient tongues that afterward she was able to tutor farm boys who lacked the Latin and Greek needed to begin their clerical studies.

But she was then no bluestocking. When learned boarders were scarce, she earned money for the household by spinning, sewing and knitting for hire. During the Revolution she had become a maker of bobbin lace. But learning was her love. Following her *View of Religions,* she produced a *History of New England,* and after that, a *History of the Jews.*

For these literary achievements she received no applause from her own sex. No woman in this post-Revolutionary decade could expect to be regarded as a lady after she had written a book. She was held up as a horrible example of what happened when a woman went in for learning. Any recognition she had came from men who like herself, worked with books. Hannah was the only woman admitted to the sacred precincts of the Boston Athenaeum (Chapter Note 3).

There she could be seen, queer looking, oldish, in gray clothes and a cap, working away at heavy tomes, or scribbling notes for her own use, blissfully unconscious of the hole in her stocking, which seems to have been clearly evident to gentlemen readers. Once, they said, she even walked down Beacon Street in this ghastly state of disarray. At 63 Miss Adams was still enough of a pioneer to found a woman's club in Boston.

Yet for all her industrious learning, Hannah Adams might have starved in her old age but for the stern gallantry of Boston merchants who raised a pension fund for her. As a young boy, Josiah Quincy remembered going around with his father, then Mayor of Boston, to collect the money. When Hannah died at 77, she was busy penning an autobiography. Her portrait, cap and all, still hangs in the Boston Athenaeum.

But in spite of a valiant pioneer like Hannah Adams, and in spite of that wonderful new Constitution, the women citizens were to remain publicly inarticulate for another generation.

Sources for this chapter are listed in the bibliography. Early travelers like Henry Wansey and John McClunn cover up to 1794. Christian Schultz's *Inland Voyage* is dated 1807–08. Henry Howe's *Great West* was reprinted in 1851.

Three books of recent scholarship have also been drawn upon: the translation of the *Journals of Moreau de Saint Méry,* by Kenneth and Anna Roberts; Mary Ellen Chase's study of Jonathan Fisher, *Maine Parson,* and the *New Letters of Abigail Adams,* edited by Stewart Mitchell for the American Antiquarian Society. Besides drawing on the files of period newspapers, numerous brief items about the women of this decade have been gleaned from old books, pamphlets and historical collections.

1　Two presidential families were involved in this early Western expansion. William Henry Harrison, son of Benjamin Harrison, a Tidewater planter, was forced by money pressure to quit his medical studies and take a commission in a regiment going to the western border. The father of Zachary Taylor sold his Virginia property to buy large tracts of new land in Kentucky. The adventures of these presidential couples in the frontier regions are told in the author's *First First Ladies.*

2　Going barefoot to the ball was not exclusively a New Orleans maneuver. When James Fenimore Cooper was a Navy midshipman, he attended the "grand military ball" given in 1810 in Oswego, to celebrate the launching of a Navy brig on Lake Ontario. On this formal occasion the ladies of Oswego combatted local mud by going, barefoot, to the dance.

3　Records of the Boston Athenaeum give a sidelight on the story of Hannah Adams. Several sources depict her working there, the only woman to be so honored, by special permission of William Smith Shaw, one of the founders. He died in 1826, but the formal vote of the trustees admitting Miss Adams did not come till 1829, when she was 76. (She died in 1832.) Obviously Hannah Adams did the bulk of her work at the Athenaeum long before this formal permission was granted. The trustees may have intended it as a gesture of scholastic recognition.

It did not mean, though, that other women readers were welcome. The Athenaeum remained a masculine stronghold. No woman was employed there till 1856, and there is no record of the year when women were admitted as readers. Their presence was opposed by Mr. Folsom, librarian, from 1847 to 1856. He argued that the steep staircases of the building would "cause a decent female to shrink." Nor was it desirable "that a modest young woman should have anything to do with the corrupter portions of polite literature."

CHAPTER THREE

Travelers' Tales of the 'Thirties

*T*HIS chapter will take a jaunt around the country to see how its women were faring between 1830 and 1840. The search will be by way of journals of the decade, accounts set down by several pens from varying motives.

The most striking change is the extent of territory now to be covered. The republic had been expanding rapidly. Since 1810 seven new states had been added—Louisiana, Indiana, Mississippi, Alabama, Maine and Missouri. During the '30's two others were admitted, Arkansas and Michigan. Florida, Texas, Iowa and Wisconsin were to attain statehood in the '40's. Far to the West, the Rocky Mountain region was being opened by widely spaced army posts and by trappers and hunters operating at their own risk beyond the forts.

Travelers, foreign and domestic, have left their records, some in forgotten journals, some in volumes of professional writers like Mrs. Trollope and Captain Marryat. Where these authors wrote for transatlantic consumption, their prejudices will be checked by other observations, made strictly in America.

WHAT ANN ROYALL SAW

The first witness will be a woman, Anne Newport Royall, pioneer traveling pamphleteer, whose pointed comment on her fellow Americans was rewarded with a sentence to the ducking stool as a "common scold." That was in 1829, but today she is ranked as the republic's first woman journalist. Certainly she was a personality. An untrained, penniless widow nearing 60, she began making a meager living selling her own travel booklets.

Anne Royall's life was enmeshed in her travels and provides the key to her writing. Born in Maryland in 1769, she was "raised" in that first frontier across the Alleghenies, in the present area of Pittsburgh. The family cabin measured eight feet by ten, complete with a bed and four homemade stools. Still, the Newports could hold up their heads in the settlement because they possessed six tin cups and a few pewter plates and spoons. Most of their neighbors used spoons made with mussel shells. Also, there must have been a book or two carted up from Maryland, for Anne's father taught her to read. In the early Indian raids the child was driven from home and soon lost her father. A step-father died shortly after the Indian raids of 1782. After that, mother and two children became wanderers on the road.

Record picks them up near Staunton, Virginia, at a plantation called Sweet Springs, squired by William Royall, formerly an officer in the Revolutionary army who came from Bermuda Hundred. Like many Tidewater planters of his time, he had opened fresh lands in the new counties. Royall was wealthy, elderly and rated eccentric by his neighbors—he read Voltaire and the French philosophers. He took in the wanderers, and, to the horror of his Tidewater relatives, married the eighteen-year-old daughter. Then he set about educating her out of his unorthodox library. At times he made over lesser pieces of property to Anne; dying, he willed her life use of his large estate. Whereupon the family brought suit, since Sweet Springs had been family land.

Considering herself wealthy, the widow, a bit past forty, began to travel for pleasure till the lawsuit should be settled. Never doubting a victory, she set out in style in her own carriage with two men slaves and a maid, also a courier. Her destination was northern Alabama which she called an earthly paradise. The Cherokee Indians had recently been ousted from some of the region's best farming land, but Anne, who had lost her childhood home to Indian warfare, had no tears to shed for the Cherokees.

She rested in Alabama for ten years with occasional tours through the western counties of Pennsylvania and Tennessee, writing voluminous descriptive letters to the lawyer who was handling her affairs. By the end of this decade she had lost both suit and an appeal. Sweet Springs went to Royall's nephew. In the interim Anne's own property had been consumed. Now she headed for Washington to lodge a pension claim for Royall's services in the Revolution. He was always General Royall in her journals, but his actual rank had been captain. Twenty years later Congress voted her a minimum pension.

To keep herself alive, she began turning her travel notes into books for sale. Without money, but backed by local Masons (Royall had been active in that order), she set out once more, writing and selling. Her farthest south was New Orleans. North she reached Burlington, Vermont, where an irate theologian pushed her down four icy steps. With homespun egotism she discarded the surgical splints and other aids of official medicine in favor of her own remedies. It was five weeks before she could enter a stagecoach, and nearly a year before she could walk again.

Obviously Anne Royall was biassed. Obviously, too, the women she now encountered were not gently mannered ladies in their homes. The women about whom she wrote were wives of innkeepers in the new regions, sharp tongued and unlettered, though prospering from their rough and ready establishments. One Pennsylvania hostess she called "a savage in petticoats." In Tennessee a self-righteous landlady refused shelter to a young woman with a baby. She'd seen too many "strumpits" following Jackson's men to the Cherokee war. Another hostess reproved a widower for his methods of wooing. He was too old-fashioned. " 'No one offers to touch a lady these days . . . when you court a girl, you must sit at a distance and talk to her.' " A belle of the Muscle Shoals region was just fourteen. A widow from Virginia was "ignorant and proud as Lucifer." On the streets of New Orleans she saw women "of every shade from snowy white to sooty." With women everywhere it was ignorance that prevailed. With men it was drink. "There is too much whiskey everywhere."

PRAISE AND BLAME

Heading north, Anne noted the ladies of Raleigh, North Carolina, dipping snuff. Charleston, for all its elegance, she found "the receptacle for the refuse of all nations on earth—the only reputable people were the Jews." In Virginia, "roads were as bad as its schools." The women of Washington and Baltimore were the worst dressed in the United States. Also, Baltimore was "illiterate, proud and ignorant," though Richmond, Virginia, was worse. In Baltimore, she charged, some of the finest dressed ladies could not read. Or if they did read, they restricted themselves to dream books.

Wherever she went, the complaint was the same. Females did not buy books. A widow who had a bookstore at Annapolis said so. A Pennsylvanian who kept a bookstore in prosperous Lancaster lamented that literature had few supporters there. Of all cities, Philadelphia was the "most unfeeling, inhospitable and uncharitable toward strangers . . . Philadelphia ladies the most insignificant of all our towns." Perhaps the fact that the woman doorkeeper at Peale's museum denied her free admittance there accentuated her dislike. Besides, Anne Royall was traveling alone, without introductions to Philadelphians of standing.

Her only words of praise were reserved for the new-come Germans and for the Moravian schools. From a stagecoach passing through an Allegheny valley she saw "cherry-cheeked damsels dressed in domestic woolsey" with red and blue stripes. Standing in mid-stream, washing her churns, was a German farmer's wife. Then there was a German landlady at Easton who slung the heavy kettles around "as boys would a pot," and who set a good table. At fair time in Reading, German girls danced in the barroom in couples or as solo performers, but had nothing to say for themselves. A bar patron told Mrs. Royall not to worry. The silent German misses would find their tongues after marriage.

The Moravian Academy at Bethlehem was declared to be "the best female seminary in the United States." Board and tuition she set down as $28 . . . plus an entrance fee of $6.00. For use of the library the charge was $2.00 and $3.00 extra per quarter covered music, French, drawing and fancy work.

On the northern trip that was to end so disastrously, Mrs. Royall noted the Yankee "taste for learning everywhere prevalent . . . a Boston chambermaid will read as correct as the most finished scholar." The young people of the upper Connecticut valley she found "rather uncouth, though innocent and modest." Uncouth or no, these young people performed what to her were amazing feats in mental arithmetic, an educational novelty.

THE DUCKING STOOL TRIAL

What brought Anne Royall into court was not complaints about greedy landladies and their sluttish maids, but savage denunciation of the traveling preachers sent as missionaries into new territories. For she was operating in an early Bible belt, a region greatly stirred by the first big revival crusade. Anne did not sympathize. On the contrary, like Voltaire attacking *l'Infame,* she poured frontier invective on the "Holy Willies" and the "Miss Dismals" who followed them. Finally two Presbyterian clergymen brought suit, digging up a long-forgotten statute for the purpose. Among the charges was that the widow had called Captain John Coyle "a damned old baldheaded son of a bitch." While carpenters at the Alexandria docks tried to reconstruct the equally forgotten ducking stool, the judge suspended sentence. But the notoriety of the trial ruined Anne Royall's road trade in pamphlets.

She cut short her travels, but continued the publication of her "black books" from Washington, together with *Paul Pry* her pioneering venture into political journalism, and her chief claim to fame. Always poor—"down to my last neckerchief" was her own phrase—only that much-belated pension kept her from starvation in her last years. She lived on till 1854.

THE CASE OF MRS. TROLLOPE

Anne Royall's sketches of the women of her time are a useful introduction to the pages of that more literate and successful annalist,

Frances Trollope. Mother of the much greater Anthony, her book on the domestic manners of Americans created almost an international episode. Chance had thrown rich material in her way. Bitter necessity forced her to use it.

The story of Frances Trollope and how she came to write her book is as strange a tale as can be found in fiction. Her husband, Thomas Anthony Trollope, had been playing the country squire on hopes of inheritance till the birth of a nearer heir set him looking for ways to repair his lost fortune. By supreme irony, he hit on the idea of emigrating to Cincinnati, then hardly more than a border town, there to open a select bazaar for the sale of imported articles. Profits, he believed, would not only support six children, but would also recoup his shattered capital. Since he could not leave England just then, Mrs. Trollope set out in November 1827, to start the business.

A crazier scheme was never concocted by supposedly sane people. Probably they were egged on by a woman quite as wide-eyed as themselves, who was destined to fill many pages of later American gossip. This was Miss Frances Wright, a young Scots woman of large fortune and a ward of Lafayette. Imbued with doctrinaire French thought, this early radical had decided to devote "her time, her talents and her all" to Africans in the United States. She took as her point of attack the thesis that colored people were intellectually equal to white, and with equal schooling, could prove it. In 1830 that was decidedly an advanced position. Even Anne Royall rated Miss Wright as "very independent."

Why fate should have thrown the Trollopes in the path of this enthusiast, only fate knows. The fact remains that Miss Wright, Mrs. Trollope and three small Trollope children embarked for the United States, the British matron with no business experience whatever, to start a department store; her companion, with no knowledge of actual conditions, to open an interracial school in Tennessee.

These babes in the philosophical woods landed at New Orleans on Christmas Day, 1827. From that moment, their re-education commenced. In three years all of the Trollope capital was gone. The store, still incomplete, was in bankruptcy. Mrs. Trollope was left stranded in a strange country. Then she began to write, and who can blame her if she wrote to sell? None of her own story, however, enters into *The Domestic Manners of the Americans*. An English lady would not admit to having kept a store. But she knew the reading class of England and aimed at it. Her book sold enormously and set up its author as a successful novelist. Many, many years later, her son Anthony's biographers unearthed the commercial background of his mother's famous book.

Frances Trollope entered the New World by its back door, up the Mississippi. Without acquaintance with the older regions, she was plunged into border territory. She had been promised a paradise. She found a frontier. Disillusion marked her for its own from the moment when she embarked upon a fine riverboat at New Orleans to discover that the carpet in the ladies' cabin had been liberally spat upon.

At Memphis, she alighted with Miss Wright, whose educational Utopia was situated at some little distance from that very new town. At the best hotel Mrs. Trollope's man-servant William presented a local problem, for Memphis in 1828 had no place for a white valet in its social code. Since the code could not be changed, William was promoted to a place at table opposite his mistress, a solution scarcely pleasing to either of them. Thereupon the lady noted acridly that it was the custom for all the male inhabitants of Memphis to dine and breakfast at the hotel on turkey and venison, while their wives "regaled themselves on mush and milk at home."

NASHOBA TO CINCINNATI

From Memphis, the travelers were driven out to Nashoba over a terrifying stump road. Arriving bruised and shaken, one glance at the high-minded experiment was sufficient for Mrs. Trollope. "Desolation," she recorded, "was the only word." Alas for Miss Wright's theories of *egalité!* The only white recruits at Nashoba were the reformer herself, her sister and her brother-in-law. Some thirty or forty slaves had been gathered, books had been collected and teachers engaged. But there it stopped. With unexpected charity the English visitor concludes, "I do not exactly know what was the cause for abandoning Nashoba." Records however are more enlightening. The founder of Nashoba did not linger in the stump-clearing. She returned to civilization leaving a disciple of Robert Owen's New Harmony in charge of her experiment. He shortly added free love to the curriculum. When reports of this reached the East, they cost Miss Wright the backing of more conservative philanthropists. Unwilling to abandon her helpless black pupils, in 1830 Miss Wright took them to Haiti and freed and resettled them there at the cost of half her fortune. Perhaps she remembered then that Nashoba was an old Indian word for wolf (Chapter Note 1).

The extreme contempt meted out to both Anne Royall and Frances Wright in the upper circles of contemporary American society is shown in a letter written by Horace Mann to his fiancée, Charlotte Messer. In 1829, Mann (later a champion of liberal education) demanded: "What museum of monsters . . . can exhibit such a horrid monstrosity as that two-fisted chap Miss Royall or Fanny Wright, esquire."

MRS. TROLLOPE DISCOVERS CINCINNATI

Meanwhile Frances Trollope had left Memphis to make her way by river-steamer to Cincinnati. Her travel journal praises pretty dwellings alternating with intervals of wild forest along the banks of the Ohio. Cincinnati she found finely situated on a hill sloping to the water's edge. The town was well paved and its busy wharves impressed even a visitor from overseas. On closer acquaintance, though, all was not so pleasing. The Trollope dwelling "looked neat and comfortable enough" but lacked pump, cistern or drain of any kind. Garbage was to be deposited in the street or left for the pigs. There was no "dustman's cart."

Soon the exiles were struggling with the servant problem. Our readers already know that even in New York or Philadelphia household service was often dubious. But this situation was a body blow to Mrs. Trollope, fresh from an England where each had his or her appointed place in the state of life to which God had called, and with a polite curtsy to one's betters. In Cincinnati "hundreds of half-naked girls were going into the paper mills rather than take domestic service." No engagements by the year (oh, good old English stability of life) could be made. At length a girl was found who "would consider $1.50 a week and her mother's slave Phyllis to come in and do the cleaning."

This independent specimen started work clad in a yellow dress, gay with red roses. When her startled employer suggested a house dress less violently colored, the "help" announced that 'twas her best and her worst, for she had no other. Whereupon the good-hearted Frances herself constructed a more suitable uniform. No whit abashed, the maid then tried to borrow her employer's apparel. At the end of two months Miss America left because Mrs. Trollope refused to advance wages for the purchase of a silk gown for a ball. The next domestic wept when she found she was not expected to eat with the family. As soon as she had saved enough to buy a few clothes, she left. A third, under plea of attending prayer-meetings was discovered to be conducting a night life of her own. Never did the New World offer the domestic peace of the Old.

TOWN AND COUNTRY

The visitors were soon included in Cincinnati's social gatherings. At parties, Mrs. Trollope wrote, "the women invariably herd together at one part of the room, and the men at the other," a practice by no means peculiar to the New World. In fact, it had taken the blue-stocking ladies of Dr. Johnson's time to open war against this social crudity. But in Cincinnati "the gentlemen spit, talk of elections, and spit again. . . . The ladies look at each other's dresses, talk of sermons and dyspepsia pills." Refreshments were overwhelming, including everything from hot breads to pickled oysters. Following a massive meal, the guests "return to the drawing room, rise *en masse*, cloak, bonnet, shawl and exit."

For foodstuffs early Ohio had advantages. "The market is wonderful for abundance and cheapness . . . beef excellent at 4 cents a pound; full-sized chicken ready for the table, 12 cents, much less if bought alive; turkeys and geese, fifty cents. Ohio river fish, butter, eggs, vegetables, tomatoes six pence the peck . . . watermelons abundant and cheap but the manner of devouring them extremely unpleasant." Cows were milked night and morning at the door, and then let wander through the streets.

Already the town was taking education seriously. Schools were plenty, and Mrs. Trollope commended "Dr. Lock's liberal ideas on female education." These ran to algebra, political economy, moral philosophy and quadratic equations. But, demanded the British matron with a touch of bitter truth, "what stock of these sciences would stand the wear and tear of half a score of children and one 'help'?"

Then there were the farms. Mrs. Trollope visited "a partial clearing in the very heart of the forest . . . The house was built of logs and consisted of two rooms, besides a little shanty used as a kitchen. Both rooms were comfortably furnished with good beds, drawers, etc. The farmer's wife and her sister were spinning and three little children were playing about." The two women spun and wove all the cotton and woolen garments, and knit all the stockings. The husband made the shoes. They manufactured their own soap and candles and prepared "sugar from sugar trees on the farm." Money was needed only for coffee, tea and whiskey. "Still the wife did not look in health . . . they had ague in the fall . . . but she seemed proud of her independence."

"The American poor," the Squire's lady reminded her readers, "are accustomed to eat meat three times a day . . . But if the conditions of the labourer be not superior to that of an English peasant, that of his wife and daughters is incomparably worse . . . It is they who are indeed the slaves of the soil."

A STRICTLY AMERICAN DIGRESSION

Mrs. Trollope's estimate of Ohio farm women can be weighed by reference to one of those new farms that later made its way into American literary annals. That was the Cary place in the Miami valley not far from Cincinnati. There lived the sisters Alice and Phoebe who were to become prominent among New York's "literati." At the time when Mrs. Trollope did not enjoy Cincinnati, the Cary farm was paying off its indebtedness.

Although Robert Cary was a direct descendant of the first Latin teacher of the Plymouth colony, his children had only irregular terms at the nearest district school. This scant instruction he supplemented by reading to them at night from the family's few treasured books, or reciting the poetry he had memorized in his own youth.

For the mother and five daughters life was a round of knitting, sewing, spinning, cooking and churning. To Alice, for fourteen years, "there was nothing in existence but work." When the farm had been cleared of debt, Robert Cary called in his neighbors to help in the building of a better house, while his wife and the girls boarded all the workers. The new house was completed in 1835, but the mother and two of the younger girls died. Ironically, the region had been named Mount Healthy. Ironically, also, it was a nostalgic picture of this Ohio farm that later formed the basis of the Carys' literary fortune. Proceeds from the *Clovernook Papers* in the '50's paid for Alice's "little house on Twentieth Street."

But back on the farm, in reality, life grew grimmer. In 1837 the father remarried. Ohio neighbors called the step-mother "a suitable widow." But New Yorkers remembered her as the "hard, uncultured, utilitarian woman" who denied the girls candles to study by at night when their day's work was done. Thus Alice and Pheobe began their long apprenticeship as unpaid contributors to any magazine that came their way. After years of effort they received an actual ten dollars for several months of prose and poetry sent to the *National Era* in Washington. The poems, reprinted in 1850, brought Alice Cary 100 dollars. That was her escape money. She fled the farm, first to Boston, then to New York. "Ignorance," she later noted, "stood me instead of courage."

Here is the toll that that early Ohio farm took of its daughters: one lived to 55; Alice to 51; Phoebe to 46, and a younger sister to 31. And they were the survivors. A final comment came from the father who visited Alice and Phoebe in New York at the height of their popularity. He was amazed to be told that a good-looking matron was the mother of a grown son. "Mothers of grown-up sons never looked as young as that in my day," exclaimed this pioneer of the Miami valley.

MRS. TROLLOPE SUMMARIZES

Although the Englishwoman's account was deeply resented by Americans at the time, perhaps her Ohio observations were fairly accurate. Town life for the women, she agreed was far less laborious, but was "frightfully dull . . . I never saw people who appeared to live so much without amusement as the Cincinnatians. Billiards are forbidden by law, so are cards. They have no public balls except during the Christmas holidays. They have no concerts . . . no dinner-parties." There was a theatre but ladies were rarely seen there. Church and chapel, however, brought them out "in full dress . . . I never read of any country where religion had so strong a hold on the women, or a slighter hold upon the men." Decidedly Frances Trollope did not like American men, though she had a fellow feeling for her own sex.

With a further decline in the Trollope income, the family rented a house in the country where they were startled by "the extraordinary familiarity of our poor neighbors." The Trollope children were called by their first names, and their mother found herself addressed as "honey." Still worse, she heard tradespersons refer to herself as "the old woman."

Chapter XII of *Domestic Manners* is headed "The Peasantry," a caption that speaks volumes for the author's point of view. It was rare, she said, to see a farm woman who had reached thirty without losing every trace of youth and beauty; "even the young girls, though often with lovely features, look thin, pale and haggard." The daughters were "domestic slaves . . . This condition is changed only for the still sadder burdens of a teeming wife. They marry very young. 'We shall get along' is the answer . . . for all the advice to a boy and girl who take it into their heads to go before a magistrate and 'get married.' They do get along, till sickness overtakes them."

One feature of this premature mating would escape such a visitor as Mrs. Trollope. That was the social pressure brought on girls, urging them to early marriages. Candace Thurber Wheeler, who was later a pioneer in American decorative art, and who herself was a mother at seventeen, recounts the forcing process. "In my youth, there were very few unmarried women. There was no place in American life for them. They were old maids . . . a subject of pity and derision . . . Did we stop to think about the responsibilities of marriage, or the possible habits of our prospective husbands? Not at all! Did we question the ability of the boy-man . . . to make proper opportunities for a growing family? Not in the least! . . . In those days, a girl *must* marry. There was nothing else for her to do, and the sooner the better."

Some of Mrs. Trollope's strictures were purely parochial. She was horrified by the religious diversity of the New World. "I knew a family where one was a Methodist, one a Presbyterian, and a third a Baptist." In another, one was a Quaker, "one a declared Atheist and another a Universalist. These are all females."

At a Washington's Birthday ball in Cincinnati the visitor saw the room filled with extremely well dressed company. Then she was Britishly scandalized to discover that the beaux "were the shopmen of town." These gentlemen "had a splendid entertainment set out for them in a separate room of the hotel; the ladies sat down by themselves, and were handed cakes, sweets and creams." This separation was not "an arrangement of economy, but because the gentlemen liked it better so." Except for dancing among the young and unmarried, American men dined, played cards, had musical evenings and suppers, "all without women." This social separation of the sexes prevailed throughout the new republic. It took the best of Boston and the most fashionable of New York to drive an entering wedge into this older tradition.

AN INDIANA CAMP MEETING

Then there is Mrs. Trollope's description of an Indiana camp meeting in "a spot chosen on the verge of an unbroken forest . . . with tents pitched in a circle around a clear space." At the four corners of the opening "frames like altars were piled high with burning hardwood." On a rude platform, fifteen preachers exhorted in rotation from Tuesday to Saturday, day and night, with brief intervals for "refreshment and private devotion." Tents were laid with straw on which the participants knelt, "one youth with his arm around the neck of a young girl," while they listened to an exhorter of "incredible vehemence . . . From all around came . . . sobs, groans and a sort of low howling incredibly painful to hear; the woeful and convulsive cries gave to each tent the air of a cell in Bedlam."

At midnight a horn summoned all from private to public worship. About two thousand people assembled, the Negroes having a special tent of their own; "the preachers came down from the platform . . . and led hymns. The voice of the whole multitude joined

71

in chorus. This was the only moment at which I perceived anything like the solemn and beautiful effect which I heard ascribed to this woodland worship."

The revival followed the singing. "Above a hundred persons, nearly all females, came forward uttering howlings and groans . . . Soon they were all lying on the ground in an indescribable confusion of heads and legs . . . The preachers moved about . . . at once exciting and soothing their agonies. I saw the insidious lips approach the cheeks of these unhappy girls . . . At length, the atrocious wickedness of this horrible scene increased to a grossness that drove us from our station. At daybreak, the horn again sounded and . . . afterward I saw the whole camp as joyously . . . employed in preparing their substantial breakfasts as if the night had been passed in dancing." Certainly the ecstasies and sorrows of a camp meeting were beyond the comprehension of the Squire's lady.

TROLLOPE VS. FRETAGOT

All the while the Trollopes had been growing poorer. In desperation the mother entered her oldest son as a pupil in the school of the radical community at New Harmony.

This establishment had been started as a westward outpost of the Pennsylvania Rappites. The Rapps, father and son, grown dictatorial, demanded celibacy of the inmates, who by fanatically forced labor broke in 30,000 acres of new land. Then the community was sold to Robert Owen, the Scottish philanthropist, for his socialist experiment. But even Owen's fortune could not support a thousand eaters with but few workers. In his turn he sold to William McClure, a wealthy Pennsylvanian, whose reform goal was educational. It was McClure who set up the famous school to demonstrate the (then) advanced principles of Pestalozzi.

Apparently Pestalozzi pleased Mrs. Trollope until she heard that the instructress in charge, Madame Fretagot, was McClure's mistress. In good Victorian fashion Frances Trollope then extracted young Anthony from the seminary. Later, in a special blasting, she accused New Harmony of starving its pupils.

This educational misadventure was the last straw for Frances Trollope. She terminated her three disastrous years in Ohio with a final verbal kick. "I am sure I should have liked Cincinnati much better if the people had not dealt so largely in hogs."

BACK TO CIVILIZATION

As she escaped from her valley of humiliation, bitterness dropped from the traveler's journal with every mile. Beyond Wheeling "the country wore an air of careful husbandry." The Allegheny mountain region was "a garden of rhododendrums, azaleas, sumacs, cedars and hemlocks such as I have never seen in Europe." The inns still offered only cold bedrooms and sheets which had been "previously used but for a few nights." When they week-ended at Hagerstown because coaches were not permitted to operate on the Sabbath, she called the town "a small neat place."

Baltimore was "one of the handsomest cities to approach in the Union," and the hotel there was excellent. On attending mass at the Catholic cathedral, she was "perfectly astonished at the beauty and splended appearance of the ladies who filled it." In the evening the Englishwoman visited an evangelical chapel where a woman fell from the gallery in a fit of ecstasy. At the hotel a colored maid explained that she "liked religion right well, but never took fits in it," because she didn't like to have "her best clothes broke up."

It was in Baltimore that the traveler found a fine "infant" school "for children from eighteen months to six years." Here little boys and girls were "elegantly neat" in dress, and their manners were well bred, "totally free from the rude indifference so markedly prevalent in the manners of American children."

Washington reminded Mrs. Trollope of a fashionable English watering-place, although female society was chiefly among the ladies of the foreign embassies. It also pleased her to find a ladies' gallery in the House of Representatives, at a date when they were rigorously excluded from the British House of Commons. At church she observed "a greater proportion of gentlemen than anywhere else . . . The general appearance of Washington on a Sunday is much less Puritanical than that of most other American towns. People walk about, and there are no chains in the streets as at Philadelphia, to prevent their riding or driving, if they like it."

But Philadelphia aroused the traveler's ire, because, at an exhibition of the Academy of Fine Arts, ladies and gentlemen were admitted separately to the gallery of antique statues. This separation of males and females to encounter the allurements of some fifty plaster casts she denounced as a "coarse minded custom" (Chapter Note 2). She also found "a prodigious majority of females" in the Philadelphia churches. In Baltimore, she wrote, church attire was characterized by gaudy splendor; in Philadelphia, by elegant simplicity.

Like all British visitors, Mrs. Trollope was amazed at the number of young married couples in cities who preferred living in boarding houses to "going to housekeeping." "I can hardly imagine a contrivance more effectual for ensuring the insignificance of a woman than marrying her at seventeen, and placing her in a boarding house," where she would clear-starch a little, iron a little and sit a great deal in rockingchairs. "The ordinary mode of living is abundant," she found, "but not delicate."

"Almost everyone drinks water at table; and . . . in a country where hard drinking is prevalent . . . there is less wine taken at dinner; ladies rarely exceed one glass and the great majority of females never take any. Mixed dinner parties of ladies and gentlemen are very rare." Even then it was the custom to seat the ladies at one end, the gentlemen at the other. "Unless several foreigners are present, but little conversation passes at table . . . Their large evening parties are supremely dull."

American ladies also powdered themselves "immoderately" with pulverized starch, and were "unhappily partial to false hair." Nor would they condescend to comfortable walking shoes. Even in midwinter they went "with their poor little toes pinched into a miniature slipper. I must say in their excuse, however, that they have almost universally, extremely pretty feet." The ladies of the Union were also "great workers." Perhaps, if they had their way, a little more relaxation would be permitted. But few ladies (and she gives this as a positive statement) "have any command of ready money entrusted to them."

Of all the cities, New York pleased her best. She praised the houses and their furnishings. Also, she went to the theatre and saw a good play—at least it was an English play. But when the curtain fell, to her horror, she saw a woman sitting "in the front row of a dress box" nursing her baby. On a Sunday she went by ferry to "a Pleasure Park at a place called Hoboken." There she found all the men who weren't in church, enjoying the park. For once the visiting lady was not scandalized. She even suggested that the health of American women would be improved by less constant church attendance, and more time spent outdoors.

So let us leave the Squire's lady once more among people she recognized as her own kind, who were willing to defer to a member of the British landed gentry. Her book, one notes, had not then been published.

MARK TWAIN VS. FRANCES TROLLOPE

These British observations will now be checked by two strictly American sources covering the same period. The first is the autobiography of Mark Twain, in which are his recollections of boyhood, jotted down in 1870. Admittedly this record of Samuel Clemens came through the haze of memory. Its importance, though, is that it is the frontier speaking for itself through a man who came from one of those little Mississippi towns that Mrs. Trollope found so dreary.

Around 1830, he relates, his father bought 75,000 acres of Tennessee land for about $400, becoming the most opulent citizen of Fentress County, for, besides his land, he had some $3,500. Most of that he lost in the financial crash of 1834. Thereupon the elder Clemens sold out and moved his family to Florida in Monroe County, Missouri.

"I suppose Florida had less than 300 inhabitants," its famous son recalled. "It had two streets, each a couple of hundred yards long; the rest of the avenues were mere lanes with rail fences and cornfields on either side." Both streets and lanes were paved with "tough black mud." Most of the houses were of logs, and there was a log church with a puncheon floor and slab benches. (Puncheon meant logs whose upper surfaces had been chipped flat with an adz.) The cracks between logs went unfilled. There was no carpet. The structure was perched upon short sections of logs, leaving a space of perhaps two feet between building and ground. "In this space, hogs slept. Whenever the local dogs got after them during services, the minister had to wait for the uproar to abate." The winter wind came up through the puncheon flooring and "in summer, there were fleas enough for all."

On weekdays the church served as schoolhouse. Twain remembered "a strapping girl of fifteen in sunbonnet and calico dress" who scorned him because, as a youngster of seven, he could not chew tobacco.

Florida also boasted two stores. When women or children made the smallest purchase, they were entitled to a handful of sugar from the barrel. A man customer was expected to "draw and swallow as big a drink of whiskey as he wanted." Everything was cheap, with apples, peaches, potatoes and corn at ten cents a bushel. Chickens were ten cents apiece and butter was six cents a pound.

MISSOURI PARADISE

Four miles out from Florida the boy's uncle had a farm which Samuel visited for two or three months every year. Uncle John had eight children and about twenty Negroes. "It was a heavenly place, that farm . . . The house was a double-log one with a spacious floor roofed in, connecting it with the kitchen. In the summer, the table was set in the middle of that shady and breezy floor, and the sumptuous meals . . ." Fried chicken, roast pig, wild and tame turkeys, ducks, geese, partridges, pheasant and venison were routine. From the kitchen came hot breads, fresh corn, succotash, and so on through vegetables and fruits. It ends with "apple pie, peach pie, pumpkin pie, peach cobbler—I can't remember the rest."

"I can see that farm yet," Mark Twain declared, "the family room . . . with a trundle bed in one corner and a spinning-wheel in another; the vast fireplace piled high on winter nights . . . the lazy cat spread out on the rough hearthstones; the drowsy dogs braced against the jambs; my aunt in one chimney corner, knitting; my uncle in the other, smoking his corncob pipe; the slick and carpetless floor . . . half a dozen children romping in the background . . . split-bottomed chairs here and there, some with rockers; a cradle, out of service but waiting with confidence." In the early morning a snuggle of children in shorts and chemises clung to the hearth, reluctant to go out into the "wind swept floor space between house and kitchen, where stood the general tin wash basin."

Certainly it is a far cry from Mark Twain's Missouri to the fever-ridden western settlers depicted by Dickens in *Martin Chuzzlewit*. But Twain was telling of his own experience. In his boyhood town of Hannibal everyone was poor, but didn't know it. "Everybody was comfortable and did know it . . . Everybody knew everybody, yet the class lines were clearly drawn." The social life of each class was restricted to that class. The local doctor took care of an entire family for 25 dollars a year, providing the medicines. How the patients were treated is perhaps another story. But there is the frontier town from the memory of a boy who came from it, and was to go far. What is lacking is the voice of the aunt who sat knitting, near the cradle, empty for the moment. How she lived, the reader can easily picture. But what she thought and felt while so living has gone down into silence. Many years afterwards Samuel Clemens visited the friends of his boyhood. The women, he noted truthfully, had aged much faster than the men.

THE REALLY WILD WEST

Twain's recollected Missouri of the '30's, though a newly settled region, was still within bounds of law and order. They had a church, a rudimentary school and a doctor. It was an organized community. But beyond Missouri was still newer country where the frontier farm was a clearing in the midst of what was still a hunter's paradise. In 1832 Washington Irving toured the region from the Missouri to the Arkansas, with a government commissioner charged with resettling Indian tribes west of the Mississippi. Protection was furnished by a troop from Fort Gibson, a post "surrounded by a village of Indian wigwams and Negro huts." The expedition's cook was Antoine, a "swarthy French creole" who had a small farm near St. Louis, with an Indian wife and "a brood of half-blood children." All the farms near the Fort were ravaged by fevers.

Toward the end of the expedition provisions had grown scarce. They were told that a white settler had a place nearby. Almost dropping with fatigue and hunger, they pushed on till they saw "a low tenement of logs overshadowed by great forest trees." There were a stable and barn, "granaries teeming with abundance." Soon the Captain was seated at a three-legged table, devouring a dish of boiled beef and turnips. "A fat, good humored Negress received me at the door," Irving recorded. "She was the mistress of the house, the spouse of the white man."

For still farther west there is the journal of Captain Bonneville, who left Fort Osage on the Missouri in 1832 for his exploration of the Rocky Mountain region "and beyond." The men of Bonneville's adventures were the free trappers or "mountain men." The women were Indians. Bonneville tells of a trapper who went to the Nez Percés for a wife. "Give me one from among your tribe. Not a young giddy-pated girl . . . but a sober, discreet hard-working squaw; one that will share my lot without flinching." To Captain Bonneville the duties of a squaw seemed "a little less onerous than a pack-horse." Then there was a Shoshone Indian whose wife was taken by a trapper, and he accepted two horses as compensation, saying "two horses were very good pay for one poor wife."

Bonneville (assisted by the pen of Washington Irving) also told the tale of a Blackfoot squaw. "I was the wife of a Blackfoot warrior and I served him faithfully . . . Whose lodge was so well provided and kept so clean? I brought wood in the morning and placed water always near at hand. I watched for his coming; he always found his meat cooked and ready . . . I searched the thought that was in his heart, to save him the trouble of speaking." When he returned from the hunt or the war-path, she met him at the door. "I took his gun . . . unloaded his horses . . . fetched him dry mocassins . . . dressed all the skins . . . and what was my reward? Who was it that scarred and bruised me?" At length she fled to the Nez Percés. When Bonneville met her, she had married a white trapper.

MR. HONE SEES THE LADIES

But the bulk of American women still lived in the older region between the Atlantic seaboard and the Alleghenies. In the 1830's they, too, had their chroniclers. Through American eyes we have the pages of Philip Hone, who ceased being Mayor of New York in 1827, and began to keep a journal. Fifty years later his diary was to make two fat printed volumes. Entries for 1830–40 present an unconscious sketch of the women of the decade, or at least of those sufficiently genteel to come within the ex-mayor's observation.

With New York as a base, politics carried Hone many times from Washington to Boston, with social side trips to Baltimore and Saratoga. Later he also made a "tour of the West" which took him as far as Chicago, then "a large town on a transcendently beautiful Mediterranean sea." Although Hone covered considerable territory, he always moved in the upper brackets. Page after page of his diary listed the names of guests at notable balls and parties and other social functions.

In Hone's notes women were always "the ladies." Thus, in 1832, the chapel of Columbia College was "filled with ladies and gentlemen, the fairest and best of our city," to hear an orator defend classical learning "against the hosts of utilitarians." Also a large number of ladies and gentlemen sampled the collation provided for the spring exhibition of the National Academy of Design. In 1835 came the wedding of an heiress whose "splendid estate" Hone was preparing to "transfer to her husband," a process in which he saw nothing amiss. That was the law, and also the custom (Chapter Note 3).

The most prized invitations were for balls, often costume parties—"My daughter went as Sweet Anne Page"—sometimes held at the City Hotel, but more often given in the capacious mansions of wealthy citizens. There was a dazzling party in 1836, where the premises were lighted with gas, then so much of an innovation that the lights gave out in the midst of a cotillion. "Gas . . . is a handsome light in a large room like Mr. Russell's, but illy calculated for the ordinary uses," the journal pronounced. Private or semi-public, the supper tables "were splendidly and most liberally furnished." Nevertheless, splendor was not always comfort. Hone noted his reluctance to attend evening parties in the winter, since that required his going upstairs into his unheated bedroom to change his clothes, at an hour which usually saw him headed for a warm bed. (Did that imply a warming pan?)

But, except for balls, the social life of the sexes was as clearly separate in Hone's pages as in Mrs. Trollope's. Hone, however, accepted this convention. For instance, when he attended the Concord Jubilee of 1835, "our party went from the dinner table to visit the ladies who had invited us to drink coffee with them at their banquet." He enjoyed talking to the "fine Yankee women and the blooming

Yankee girls," but didn't see anything odd in their being excluded from the main banquet.

Yet, in Boston, these same Yankee women were beginning to make themselves felt. When the Perkins Institution for the Blind was founded, its donor offered an endowment conditional on the city's raising 50,000 dollars for the purpose. Hone recorded that more than 11,000 dollars of this sum were proceeds of a "ladies fair." This, in 1834, seems to be the first mention of American women acting publicly as money-raisers.

But, in New York, the dining clubs, the reading clubs, were all strictly masculine, even when the dinners were given in the homes of gentlemen members. Did the mistress of the house, having organized the feast, then content herself with tea and toast sent upstairs on a tray? The diary does not tell, but we do learn that Hone's domestic staff included two maids, a houseman and a colored cook. The money lavished on eating and toasting in these club dinners was astounding. Later, during the Irish famine, two of Hone's club members forewent their dinner parties to contribute to a famine relief fund. The cost of those two dinners, converted to charity, was 360 dollars.

Already the distinction between northern and southern ladies was apparent. In July, 1836, Hone took his daughter Mary abroad, embarking on one of the new steamboats. "We have two ladies, passengers who exemplify the two extremes in American female character," the diarist wrote. "Mrs. May of Boston is a regular Yankee, quick of apprehension, intelligent, handy, self-confident, a person qualified to take care of herself in every situation . . . Mrs. Hammond is soft, languishing and inert, her listlessness . . . proclaiming her at once a South Carolinian . . . All day long she lounges on sofas in the cabin and on deck . . . and would starve, I verily believe, if she had nobody to help her to her food." But after that comment, Hone awarded the palm for "feminine loveliness" to the lady who languished.

It should be remembered that the year 1837 was one of severe financial upset. Starting in the big cities, carrying banks and insurance companies down to ruin, repercussions of the crash reached out to the farthest western settlements, where cash of any kind became increasingly scarce. Consequently, when the Quakers of Philadelphia began their anti-slavery agitation, Hone did not approve. It was very bad for business. To him and to others of his kind, financial recovery ranked first.

Hone deplored especially the part played by Quaker women. The rioting which led to the burning of Pennsylvania Hall in May, 1838, he attributed to "the outrage of public opinion in the exhibition in public streets of white men and women walking arm in arm with blacks." The names of either the sisters Grimké or of Lucretia Mott are never mentioned by Hone. He does report, however, the presence in the hall of many "females of whom several harangued the meeting and were foremost in arousing the excited populace." These radicals of Philadelphia, one notes, were classified strictly as females. They were not ladies.

As a wealthy and prominent citizen, Hone also served as host to visiting European notables, including even actors who brought sufficiently good introductions. Thus Fanny Kemble, the youthful leading lady of London, dined at the Hones'. There was also Harriet Martineau, whom he feared to find "a little too blue." But her book, he noted, "could not be neglected if one would be in the fashion . . . some say saucy and some say very good."

On her part, Fanny Kemble was somewhat critical of dining out in New York. Even at Hone's house, one of the city's show-places, "the food was plenteous and tolerably well dressed, but ill-served. There were not half servants enough to do the work."

The ladies at the table were "in a sort of French demitoilette, bare necks and long sleeves, heads frizzed out . . . thread net handkerchiefs and capes . . . The women here, like those of most warm climates, ripen very early and decay proportionately young. There was a fair young thing at dinner who did not look above seventeen and she is a wife. . . . These American women have pretty feet and ankles, but are brought up effeminately, take little exercise, sallow their complexions and destroy their constitutions." Having published this blast, Miss Kemble left the stage to marry Pierce Butler, a wealthy gentleman of Philadelphia and Georgia.

Still, even Hone's polite restricted world did move a little. In December, 1841, his diary sets forth a great social innovation. When the annual dinner of the New England Society was held at the Astor House "the tables were graced with the presence of ladies . . . a

81

Yankee invention." But those tables, he lamented, were "chilled by exclusion of all beverages but water." The speaking that evening, he argued, would have gotten off better with some good Madeira or a sparkling tumbler of champagne. Also after dinner broke up, "the barrooms in the neighborhood of the Astor House had an unusual run of custom."

A FAMOUS MURDER

There were darker happenings in New York which were entirely omitted from Hone's genteel jottings, for New York was also a seaport. At about the time when Hone was transferring his wine cellar of 2,180 quart bottles plus a hundred or more gallons of Madeira, from his old down-town house to a newer location uptown (Broadway and Great Jones Street), a very famous murder was committed within a half-mile of Hone's old address. This was the case of Ellen Jewett which has appeared and reappeared in legal legend and in fiction, because it was an unsolved murder involving families of standing and notable courtroom oratory.

In Thomas Street, up from the west side waterfront, Mrs. Roxina Townsend maintained "a house," well patronized by seafaring men. Ellen Jewett was said to be the handsomest of its inmates, and was often seen promenading near the Battery, always clad in green silk. Among her lovers, under a false name, was a young man of good family, employed in a well known mercantile firm, and engaged to marry "a young lady of the utmost respectability." Her name, incidentally, never appeared in the public prints. Apparently the young man was trying to break off with Ellen Jewett. Perhaps, as in the old melodramas, he was trying to regain letters that he had written to Ellen, for there were such letters.

One May evening, he called "as usual," and had champagne sent up to Ellen's room, which had its separate hall. In the early morning, a horrible screaming arose from Ellen's room. While "watchmen" were entering at the front door, the murderer escaped unseen at the rear, along the fences. Hours later, a hatchet was found in a nearby backyard, and roughly identified as "the murder weapon," but in the days before fingerprinting and laboratory tests, this was only circumstantial. The young man of standing was arrested, apparently asleep in his own boarding place. He protested his innocence, and the foremost criminal lawyers in the city were retained in his behalf.

In New York at this time there was also an ambitious young printer named Horace Greeley who, plagued by small capital and many debts, was trying to establish a weekly magazine. This struggling venture with only a few hundred subscribers was called "The New Yorker." From the start young Greeley seized on the Jewett murder. Contrary to all accepted rules of etiquette, he interviewed Ellen's fellow-inmates in Mrs. Townsend's establishment, and gained access to Ellen's letters. By the rules then prevailing, evidence from "unlawful characters" was limited in court. Still, Greeley printed his stories. The circulation of his little weekly leaped, though in the end the prisoner, whose employer was an Alderman, was acquitted. So the case of Ellen Jewett went down on the list of unsolved murders, with Greeley stoutly maintaining that Robinson's release had been a miscarriage of justice.

But public indignation over the slaying of Ellen Jewett was short lived. The night-life of New York was soon once more in full swing. Spectacular evidence of this was provided by the famous fire of 1841, of which a vivid account is given in the diary of George Templeton Strong. In the burning down-town district stood the Dutch Reformed Church, and its neighbor, the French Eglise du St. Esprit. Nearby was a flourishing "temple of Venus," a dwelling demolished by the falling walls of its more reputable neighbors. Mrs. Brown's young ladies rushed into the street *en deshabille*. One girl turned back into the house and was killed.

A few days afterwards this "Margaret Yagers" was identified by the *New York Firemen's Journal* as Ellen Roberts, with a "moral" case-history added. She was the daughter of a Philadelphia widow of good family who had forbidden the girl's marriage to an anonymous young man-about-town. Defying her mother, Ellen had followed her lover to New York for a few weeks of lavish spending. Then the lover, tiring of her, had placed her with Mrs. Brown. She had been in the "temple of Venus" only a few days when the fire occurred. The reporter gave a final touch of pathos to his story by having Margaret-Ellen rush back into the falling building to save a locket that contained a "likeness" of her mother. That, in the terms of the day, represented repentance. A dead girl could not speak for herself, but the dates on record speak for her. Born in May, 1824, she had just turned seventeen on that fatal 29th of May (Chapter Note 4).

CAPTAIN MARRYAT IN SELECT SOCIETY

There was no mention of such affairs in Mr. Hone's decorous pages, nor was murder accepted as table talk during the visit of Captain Marryat in 1837. The author of the famous slogan "duty before decency, Mr. Chuck," was informed that the word "leg" was never to be used before ladies. Exercising his wit, the Englishman told of seeing the statue of the Apollo Belvidere "hung with drapery" in the Boston house of Governor Everett. Also, in a young ladies' seminary, he encountered the square piano "with its four limbs in modest little trousers with frills at the bottom of them."

Having had his joke, the noted novelist penetrated as far as White Sulphur Springs, and liked it. Feminine society there he found well worth observation. Many of the buildings were little cottages and log houses, still "a decided spirit of aristocracy prevailed." No one was given accomodation who was not well known, and usually only "to those families who travel in their private carriages. It is here and here only in the States that you meet what may be fairly considered as select society." Several belles from several states were on view at White Sulphur "nor is there a scarcity of pretty and wealthy widows."

Today the amusements of the resort sound very tame. A walk down to the springs before breakfast, then rest till a midday dinner, after which guests "rode out" or paid visits. The day always ended in the ballroom. With rising enthusiasm, the Captain proclaimed that he was never at any watering-place in England "where the company was so good, and so select."

Captain Marryat was not the only Britisher to fall afoul of the niceties of speech prescribed in the upper brackets. The Scottish-born James Gordon Bennett (the elder) began in his *Herald* "the battle of the petticoat." In New York, between 1830 and 1840, Mr. Bennett complained, the most harmless words were excluded from newspaper columns. In public print, "trousers became 'unmentionables'; legs and arms were 'branches of the human body.' " Linen was the accepted synonym for shirts, while petticoats could not be mentioned at all. "Petticoats, petticoats, petticoats," was Mr. Bennett's battle-cry. "There, you fastidious fools, vent your mawkishness on that." Mr. Bennett thus became a scandal at a time when prize fighters fought with bare knuckles, and a rising fury of dueling was sweeping the South and Southwest.

LOWELL'S LADY PIONEERS

That Captain Marryat did not visit the young textile city of Lowell, one can understand. But that Philip Hone, concerned with steamboats, canals and the start of coal mining, should have omitted this early American enterprise is surprising. For Hone attended the Whig convention of 1840 in Boston. He described the Harrison parade out to Bunker Hill, past balconies and windows "filled with women, well dressed, with bright eyes and bounding bosoms, waving handkerchiefs." But Hone did not follow "Tippecanoe" out to Lowell, where the lady operatives, "all dressed out with parasols and silk stockings" gave their greeting to the old General.

To Hone, women earning their living in a mill could not be ladies. But within their own circle these first loom operatives were select specimens. Frances Cabot Lowell had planned this as a model industry, a place where the young misses were as carefully guarded as the machinery. Technical specialists were imported from England, but the girls who ran the power looms came straight from the neighboring countryside. They were housed in "corporation" establishments, where the fixed board fee was well within their weekly wage. In 1836, a widow named Larcom became one of these housemothers. She found her margin of profit so small that her daughter Lucy, at twelve, hired out as a bobbin girl, and lived to become the notable head-mistress at Wheaton.

It was Charles Dickens, coming a year after General Harrison, who first told the world about the ladies of Lowell. He visited the mills and read the *Lowell Offering,* that "respository of original articles written exclusively by females actively employed in the mills." He thought it a remarkable production to come from women "who worked a twelve-hour day, and pretty tight work, too." He admired the procession of young ladies, two by two, neatly bonneted and shawled, on their way between boarding house and mill, and learned that 978 of the young ladies had savings bank accounts amounting to a total of 100,000 dollars. The operatives, he noted, usually came from the farm, spent a few years in the mills, and then went back with their savings. In contrast with "those great haunts of desperate misery" that he had known in England, this was a model town.

AN ITEM FOR HISTORY

But there was an occurrence in early Lowell that escaped both Hone and Dickens. In 1836, the loom-ladies staged the first organized strike of women workers in this country's annals. It was called a turn-out, and was done to protest a pay cut—managerial retrenchment was part of the financial troubles of the '30's. That first turn-out was lost. The ladies went back to their looms at the lowered rates. But they did organize a strike more than two generations before the notable victory of New York's shirt-waist makers. So, the bonneted ladies of Lowell made history, although nobody noticed it at the time.

To Europeans, these women operators seemed to be amassing marriage *dots*. Even Dickens failed to visualize women dedicating their savings to further education. But many a Yankee "schoolmarm" of the next decade got her start at the Lowell mills. For the ambitious daughters of New England, Lowell's looms spelled opportunity.

AT THE CLOSE OF THE DECADE

The last travelers' tale will be that of Mrs. Steele who, in 1840, made *A Summer Journey to the West*. Little is known of the author, except that she had some connection with the old John Street Methodist Church in New York.

She started west from Albany, described as "a city of very moral and religious people." To Schenectady she proceeded by railroad "which renders the landscape blurred with speed." Utica, "now on the Erie Canal," had a population of 10,000 and sixteen churches. By canal she reached Auburn, pausing there to visit the penitentiary, and to applaud the rule of silence for the prisoners. "This life of La Trappe monks is said to be a most successful method of reforming the unhappy convicts . . . I cannot but think it a very efficient arrangement."

From Rochester the traveler went by stage to Lockport, the fare of $2.50 including the dinner. Then there was a railroad, fare 94¢, to Niagara, the engineer stopping to pick up an Indian woman who was walking along the tracks. From the Cataract House, she visited the Canadian side of the Falls, where she bought a Scots kilt as a souvenir. This garment she rated as "picturesque but cold," deploring the lack of "a pantaloon over the naked knee."

"Buffalo," pronounced the lady firmly, "is a frontier town." It was home to some 25,000 boatmen, "the lowest and most worthless class of men." German immigrants, heading west, looked "comical." There were also "sturdy, gaitered English farmers," and a Tonawanda squaw with a papoose on her back. From Buffalo she went by boat to Cleveland, "a lady with a foreign lady's maid" being also a passenger.

Among Cleveland's 7,000 inhabitants, Germans and Swiss were noticeable. Detroit, with only 2,200 people, disappointed her. The houses were "very plain," but she was assured that Michigan would soon fill up. A Sunday found Mrs. Steele embarked on Lake Superior. To atone for this breach of the Sabbath, she had brought with her "a package of well selected tracts," which she set out on the table in the "ladies saloon." To her delight, these were snatched up by all, including some rough looking crew members. But, honestly, she attributed the unexpected popularity of her tracts to "a great scarcity of books in all this new territory."

When Mrs. Steele reached Milwaukee, that place had only 1,000 inhabitants, though people assured her that "Wisconsin will soon be covered with a dense population." The soil, she noted, was very rich, and already Madison was a "pretty, thriving town." Chicago, in 1833, had only three frame houses; by 1840 it had six churches ready for Mrs. Steele's inspection. The lady also counted 100 shops, and rated the Lake House "a very good hotel."

From Chicago to Peoria, the trip was made by stagecoach, the driver losing the road—such as it was—during the night, and not being able to relocate himself till daylight. The passengers breakfasted at a log cabin farmhouse, where they were amply fed by the farmer's wife and daughter. But the coffee was definitely "not good." Nearing Joliet, the stagecoach overtook trains of covered wagons, filled with men, women, children, dogs and cats. The Joliet hotel's tablecloth was soiled, its knives and forks were iron. "While traveling in unsettled countries," the author warned her readers, "one must leave all one's niceties at home."

At Peoria, they rested at the Clinton House ($1.20 daily), waiting for a steamer to take them to St. Louis. Peoria, which had started out French, she found a pretty town with six churches, "academies," shops, mills and a brewery. Its cottages were neat, but the women and children living in them were thin and pale, from fever and ague. Everyone had come west to get rich.

But the river boat was a sad surprise to the Methodist devotee. Liquors were on the table. There was gambling in the gentlemen's cabin, and the Negress chambermaid was the captain's slave. Yet traveling safely alone to join a brother in St. Louis was a country girl of sixteen. She eagerly inspected Mrs. Steele's wardrobe to learn the eastern fashions, displaying her own one treasured possession, a topaz brooch. It had "lasted wonderfully, considering how much it had been borrowed." The ornament had been "to every dance, ten miles around."

Checking the artless notes made in 1840 by Mrs. Steele against the more literary observations of Frances Trollope in 1830, it seems that the Englishwoman was not far off on her facts. But while an American traveler instinctively made allowances for the newness of the country, the Britisher merely looked down her nose. Frances Trollope, in financial desperation wrote a book to sell to the British reading public. And it did. Today her artificial novels are completely dated, but *The Domestic Manners of the Americans* has survived.

The decade of the '30's offers few women of outstanding personality. Abigail Adams had long since gone to her reward. Dolly Madison, close to 70, was content with tributes to her past. Louisa Adams, widow of the controversial John Quincy, spent her last years in seclusion. The crudely valiant Anne Royall became a public figure only by way of the ducking stool.

By strange irony, in a period when ladies were held to the strictest propriety, the only two women who have come down to our own generation as personalities, made their mark by breaking the rules. They were Peggy Eaton of Washington, by this time safely removed to Spain, and Madame Jumel of New York. The career of Peggy Eaton, made familiar in print and film, needs no repetition here. (Her last appearance will be treated in a later chapter.) The case of Madame Jumel is less known and more remarkable.

THE AMAZING ELIZA

She entered the picture as Mademoiselle Eliza, supposedly a refugee from slave insurrections in the West Indies. She was young, handsome and spoke just enough English to describe her family, slain, their plantation destroyed. True, she had arrived at New York under the somewhat dubious protection of a French ship captain, but her story was one that had been honestly duplicated a hundred times in various Atlantic ports. The French captain brought his charge to the attention of Stephen Jumel, the wealthy French merchant, noted for his generosity to his stranded compatriots. Then one fine day, off sailed the French captain, leaving Mademoiselle Eliza to Jumel, then a man of middle age.

But Mademoiselle Eliza did not remain long in an extra-legal category. Soon she had become Madame Jumel, gossip accusing her of having tricked Jumel into a promise of marriage. Tricked or no, the infatuated merchant was soon spending lavishly to secure his wife's social acceptance. Their names began to appear as supporters of the city's charities. Still the best families remained stiff-necked. The next move was the purchase of that fine country place overlooking the Hudson, originally built by a Philipse son-in-law.

With the Bourbon restoration in France, Jumel learned that he might regain his family's confiscated estates. Necessary business arrangements were made for an extended absence, and the Jumels left for Paris. There his wealth and her beauty won speedy entrance into the new court circles, but this personal success was offset by the extremely slow progress of Jumel's petition. According to custom, it was also an expensive progress. By the time Jumel was once more in legal possession, he no longer had in hand the capital needed to restore the neglected lands. His presence being required in France, he dispatched his wife to New York with the power of attorney to convert assets there into cash.

Eliza apparently had no intention of ending her days in a French country house surrounded by her husband's relatives. From New York she reported delays, not surprising since much of Jumel's wealth was in real estate. After waiting two years for money that did not come, Jumel returned to New York. There he learned that Eliza had obtained possession of his property. The legal excuse was that with advancing years, Jumel was no longer competent. He soon became too old, too battered, to fight it out, and spent his last years as an aging pensioner living on his wife's bounty in his wife's mansion. It was Madame who drove into town in state behind four horses, leaving the old man pottering among his vegetables.

At this juncture, Madame made what, after her death, was to prove the one mistake of her life. While she was inspecting some property in the Greenwich section, Madame met on the sidewalk a woman who recognized her as her sister, and addressed her as Betsy Bowen. The consequences of this recognition were afterwards the core of a famous lawsuit brought to break the will of Eliza Jumel.

Apparently Madame paid several visits, incognito, to the home of this sister, a respectable matron whose husband had left Providence to establish himself as a baker in Manhattan. Later Eliza took the more dangerous step of inviting her sister's children to visit her. Soon there were quarrels and the visits ceased. But the harm had been done. Two plain hard-working women knew that their sister, now the wealthy Madame Jumel, had once been Betsy Bowen of Providence.

BETSY BOWEN'S BASTARD

In the past the Bowens had been part of the sailors' quarter of that prosperous and godly city. The father was a Yankee seaman with wife and children, a flock that increased annually whether the sailor was at home or off on some lengthy voyage to the South Pacific. Finally, returning to Providence, Bowen, drunk, fell into his own home harbor and was drowned.

His widow, already in the bad books of the local authorities, was banished outside the town limits, where she made an honest woman of herself by marrying a wandering cobbler. He, too, was a drunkard but also a man of some learning, for he taught the Bowen children to read. They had never been to school.

Once more authority intervened. The older girls, barely in their teens, were placed as household help in respectable families. With two of the sisters, these protective measures worked. Betsy Bowen, though, was soon back on the streets of sailor-town. Soon, also, she became mother of a baby boy, known locally as Betsy Bowen's bastard. She seemed proud of the child, and had him christened George Washington Bowen. Then one day Betsy disappeared. That happened rather often in such cases, yet here was to be a difference. Although Betsy was not yet seventeen, year after year sums of money reached the midwife for the support of the child.

That made a deep impression on Betsy's former neighbors. When the boy was old enough for school (and there was money to send him), someone told the boy that his father had been George Washington, and the child believed it. Meanwhile, Betsy was never seen again in the streets of Providence.

Of the four years intervening before Mademoiselle Eliza arrived in New York, nothing is known. Perhaps the French sea captain could have told if he wanted to. So Mademoiselle Eliza became Madame Jumel of New York and Paris. Apparently, she never gave herself away until that day when she was greeted on the street by her own sister.

Nothing came of this indiscretion for many years. Finally old Jumel died. In 1835, his widow met Aaron Burr, recently cleared of his treason charge. Madame Jumel put some small legal business in his way and then married him, causing ex-Mayor Hone to include an acid commentary on the romance in his July entry. Soon Eliza was suspecting Burr of designs on her property (Chapter Note 5). She promptly divorced him, and resumed her widowed name.

After this humiliation, Madame began to age. She was living alone in her fine mansion, no longer able to get about much. She had no real friends, and few people ever came to see her. But one day she had an unexpected caller, an Episcopal clergyman in search of support for local charities. Given some small aid at the time, he continued to call on her occasionally. Years later, when Eliza

Jumel was in her coffin, it was found that the bulk of her estate was left to those charities which the visiting clergyman had advocated.

Then it was that the two surviving Bowen sisters began their suit to break the will. It went through several courts with voluminous testimony from witnesses brought from Providence. Nothing in the history of Betsy Bowen was left untold. In the end, the sisters won some share of the estate. The rest went to the charities and to the lawyers who defended the will. Probably the greatest sufferer was the boy who had come up from sailor-town believing that George Washington was his father. So believing, he had fought his way up to a highly respected position in the city from which Betsy Bowen had fled.

Whether we like her or not, Eliza Jumel was a remarkable woman. In an era when most girls of her kind died unmourned in the poorhouse, she achieved success. Her monument is the mansion that Stephen Jumel bought for her, and which today remains an architectural treasure.

Finally, mention must be made of a woman who became briefly a national figure of the epoch. She was Maria Monk, figurehead of the anti-Catholic movement of the late '30's. Soon she became its victim. Maria herself was a Canadian, but her short tenure of fame centered on New York, also the place of her downfall.

This anti-Catholic surge had grown out of economic pressure. Earlier immigration had been absorbed by an expanding republic, but the arrival of some 80,000 French and Irish in 1837 made trouble in seaport cities struggling with financial collapse. Since most of the newcomers were of the Roman persuasion, opposition became anti-Catholic.

In Canada the Rev. W. K. Hoyt, leader of an association "to arrest the progress of popery" brought forward a girl of sixteen who told a lurid tale of infants smothered by the dozen in the cellar of Montreal's Hotel de Dieu. In New York, these charges took published form as "Maria Monk's *Awful Disclosure* . . . A Narrative of her Sufferings during a residence of Five Years . . . as a novice and a Black Nun." This production, published by no less a firm than Harpers, sold by the thousand.

A committee of responsible Protestants was appointed to investigate Maria Monk, who at length was pronounced mentally irresponsible. She was not a Catholic, had never been either a novice or a nun, but rather a charge of the Magdalene Asylum. Meanwhile the *Awful Disclosure* continued to sell, reaching a probable total of 300,000 copies. Maria herself had followed Hoyt to New York, where their child was born at Bellevue Hospital. Next, the Rev. J. L. Slocum, more enterprising than reverend, carried Maria off from Hoyt. Then he sued the publishers for 30,000 dollars, alleged to be her share of the royalties.

When the investigating committee's report was made public, the bubble burst. Maria was cast off by her promoters, to become a drunken wreck. In 1849, she was arrested for picking pockets in a Five Points dive. Still under thirty she died in prison. The one hopeful item in this sorry episode was the rescue of Maria's child by Canadian relatives. Surprisingly, the daughter of this pitiable creature grew up normal, and later married well, far from the scene of her mother's degradation.

Special thanks are due the New York Historical Society for use of their rare collection of Anne Royall's works. Some biographers have tried to account for her talents by identifying her father as the Newport who was an illegitimate offshoot of the Calvert family. Evidence to this effect is very incomplete.

1   After the closing of Nashoba in 1829, Frances Wright continued to function as the stormy petrel of early American liberalism. But she herself was an importation. Born in 1795 in the staid gray town of Dundee in Scotland, she had been left a wealthy orphan at nine years. She had been dispatched to France for education, where she quickly joined the radicals of that day. Her first trip to the United States was in 1818. She wrote a book about it, and returned as Lafayette's ward on his famous visit here in 1825. Next came Nashoba. The freeing of her colored pupils and resettling them in Hayti cost her dearly. Nothing daunted, the red-haired Miss Wright then joined Robert Dale Owen (son of Robert Owen of the New Harmony community) in the founding of a radical journal, *The New York Enquirer*. Young Owen saw to it that the magazine paid her a living. It was the only venture in her career in which she was not left to foot the bills.

After a series of "advanced" lectures for what is now called feminism, Miss Wright revisited France and there married Phiquepal d'Arusmont, a French radical who had previously been a teacher at New Harmony. They quarreled over money, Madame d'Arusmont once more returning to the United States and the lecture platform. Always in controversy, she died in 1852.

Today, tourists on Highway 70 outside of Memphis, Tenn., can read a marker placed by the Tennessee Historical Commission. "Here in 1827, a Scottish spinster heiress named Frances Wright set up a colony whose aims were the enforcement of cooperative living and other advanced sociological experiments. It failed in 1830."

The site of Miss Wright's disaster is now a colored rural school still called Nashoba by the Shelby County Board of Education. The only monument to Miss Wright's idealism seems to be the liberal laws for women incorporated in the Indiana constitution of 1850. These were sponsored by Robert Dale Owen, her former partner in radical journalism, who had settled down to be a leading citizen of Indiana.

2   Philadelphia was not alone in separating the sexes for the viewing of art. A decade later when Sophia Peabody—youngest of the three sisters from Salem—visited art exhibitions at the Boston Athenaeum, there were special hours reserved for ladies. On a more mundane plane, in December, 1859, John Templeton Strong made mention in his diary of the women's afternoon of the Bank for Savings in New York. No "he-depositors" were admitted on the women's afternoon.

3   An authentic picture of marriage etiquette in the upper strata is provided in an unpublished letter of a son to his parents, dated 1826. As a perfect period piece, this letter is given here, slightly shortened.

"Respected Parents:
      There is one subject that I did not intend to communicate to you at present but as I have already hinted at it in some of my former letters, I fear you will think I act too reservedly towards you unless I disclose the whole.
      I shall be short. I have selected among the female sex one that I have determined to make a partner for life. More than a year ago I disclosed my passion and made the proposals to her. They were accepted after modestly evading the subject for some time and we mutually engaged to have each other if it would meet the approbation of her Father. His conduct towards me has always been such as to secure my esteem and to insure success, and when I was in Milton last I took occasion to introduce the subject to him, and received as favorable an answer as I could wish. . . .
      The girl's name is Catherine, a daughter of Mr. Sand's. My partiality towards her forbids me from enumerating all her good qualities, but I never should have sought to enter into such a connexion with her unless I had weighed her merits. I had impartially considered her accomplished, virtuous, industrious and possessed of an aimable disposition, altogether such an one as would suit me as a companion and not disgrace you as a daughter.
      I have always determined never to get married without the consent of my parents and the object of this communication is to obtain it. Therefore if I have your consent and approbation please inform me of it by letter as soon as you receive this . . . it is Catherine's wish as well as mine that we should have your consent.

                              I would wish to remain your
                              Dutiful Son,
                              Jas."

      Unromantic as this sounds to modern ears, James and Catherine were married, and this letter has been passed down from generation to generation of their descendants.

4 Two other famous New York murders of this same decade have come down to us in literature. Most notable was that of Mary Rogers who sold tobacco in John Anderson's shop on lower Broadway. Edgar Allan Poe changed the setting of the crime to Paris, renamed the victim Marie Roget, and added his own solution. The body of Mary Rogers was found mutilated in the Hudson river, and the murder remained unsolved.

More sordid was the Mary Hodine case which J. F. Cooper used for his novel *Ways of the Hour,* by providing a greatly expurgated version. In the court records, Mary Hodine on circumstantial evidence, was accused of stealing her brother's property, murdering his wife and child, and then setting fire to his house to hide the crime. Mary Hodine's only defense was an unedifying alibi. Married but separated from her husband, she had been visiting an abortionist when the crime was committed. Because of local outcry, there were two changes of venue. At a third trial, Mrs. Hodine was acquitted.

5 Burr meanwhile had brought down destruction on another notable woman, Mary Blennerhassett, the young Irish bride whom the wealthy Harman Blennerhassett had brought to his Island near Marietta, Ohio. There Aaron Burr had been their guest. Apparently they were duped into supporting Burr's venture, and when, in 1806, President Jefferson ordered the arrest of "the offending parties," the Blennerhassetts fled. In their absence the island property was ravaged by drunken militiamen; in 1811, their mansion was destroyed by fire. Meanwhile the Blennerhassetts sped from a southern refuge in Louisiana to a northern one in Montreal, and finally overseas to Guernsey, losing money with each remove. In 1842 the widowed Mary returned to this country to push her claim for compensation for the destruction of the island estate. Henry Clay presented her petition, but she died before it was granted. Descendants of one of her five sons now reside in California.

CHAPTER FOUR

A Parade of Pathfinders

O_{UR} panorama of three decades of the new republic has supplied many glimpses of inarticulate women. But where were the articulate ones? Where were the women who might have been daughters of Mercy Warren or Abigail Adams or Catherine Greene or Rebecca Motte? Search of the record gives no answer. Except for the scholarly Hannah Adams and Anne Royall's self-taught journalism, the young republic had produced no woman approaching the stature of a dozen Revolutionary figures. The women succeeding them could spell better, but they had less to say.

For its females, the new regime had created only one thing— its concept of the lady. There had been ladies before of course, great ladies of wealth and position. But the lady of the republic was something different—a conscious effort of expanding prosperity to mold its daughters to a new ideal.

This lady also marked an achievement, for she embodied the surmounting of pioneer harshness. She was an early version of Thorstein Veblen's "conspicuous expenditure." Her many ruffles proclaimed the financial status of father or husband. Indeed, one contemporary writer defined a gentlewoman as the daughter of a rich man. This lady demanded that over-niceness of speech, which amused Europeans but which was a reaction from the rougher usage of trade and farm.

Rules for the young lady were strict. She must never "run, jump, scream, scramble or push." With young gentlemen, she must never join in any rude games, nor suffer her hand to be held without showing instant displeasure. She must not accept overmuch assistance in the putting on of cloaks or overshoes, nor be lifted out of a carriage or off a horse. She must not sit with a member of the opposite sex "in a space too narrow," nor read with him out of the same book. When asked out to dinner, she must enter the drawing-room with her parents, and make a formal curtsy to her hostess. After that, five topics of conversation were allotted: "a child, a picture, an animal, a worked ottoman or a bunch of flowers . . . These and many other little points of delicacy" must become fixed habits for the lady.

For the most part, the new republic's females aspired chiefly to attain this delicate ladyhood. But under its stultifying surface, something was stirring. As the Yankee love of learning had become the flowering of New England, the '30's were to mark the awakening of American women. This generation was to see the pioneer intelligentsia of their sex, women trying to do something. Out of three decades of genteel silence emerged pathfinders in many fields—educators, writers, reformers, doctors, and at last, artists.

Because they were the first, their professional techniques fall far below today's standards. But because they were pioneers, they were interesting human beings. The earliest, and to be presented here, are: Emma Willard, Sarah Josepha Hale, Lydia Huntley Sigourney, Lucretia Mott, Mary Lyon, Catharine Beecher, Dorothea Lynde Dix, Lydia Maria Child, Margaret Fuller and Dr. Harriot Hunt. They will be shown chronologically; it is difficult to sort them by vocation, since educators and reformers often wrote or lectured as well.

Here these pre-feminists will be rated as exceptional women of their times. Especially we want to know how and why they got that way, for they were a minority of discontent that wanted something beyond the charms of the lady. For these victorious adventurers, there must have been thousands of other women, like-minded, but less forceful. The few trailblazers testify to a much more general ferment of opinion that helped to carry them to the top.

The drives were twofold. There was a compulsion to pierce through prevailing restrictions—educational, economic, and then political. Also there was a release of intense moral fervor in reform, a zeal which took on organized life later in the abolition, temperance and women's rights movements.

All of the very first pioneers were New Englanders. The grinding discipline of the farm ("one hill of corn between two rocks") was part of their inheritance. Those traits that had turned this region into a forcing-bed of masculine culture now produced their petticoated counterparts, women warmed through with the fire of faith that belonged to old New England. They were the spiritual sisters of the young men who left the plough for the pulpit.

EMMA WILLARD, THE VERY FIRST

The initial restrictions to be assaulted were those that limited women to the three R's, with a few accomplishments on the side. The earliest champion of women's civic right to a modest portion of higher education was Emma Willard.

She was born Hart, in Connecticut, 1787, a sixteenth child. But Samuel Hart was no mere man with the hoe. He busied himself with his children's book learning, and often read to them. Milton was his favorite poet. Beyond this patriarchal home study, Emma had exactly two years at an academy. Then at seventeen she was ready to begin her own adventure in pedagogy. On her first day of schoolmarming, she threw away the literal rod, resolved to stand on her ability to interest her pupils. That, in the year of the birch, 1804, was progressive education.

From this village school, Miss Hart was called to go higher up, to Hartford and to Westfield, Massachusetts. In 1807, when she was only twenty years old, she became headmistress of the "Female Academy" at Middlebury, Vermont, an early college town. The big, open schoolroom there was heated by one fireplace, though Vermont winters were no milder then than now. When her young ladies got too chilly, the enterprising Miss Hart set them to doing country dances.

In 1809, the preceptress quit her post to marry Dr. John Willard, a well-to-do scholarly physician nearly thirty years her senior. Under his guidance she began studying such subjects as Dr. Willard had had in his training—geometry, natural philosophy, physiology. At the same time, she was gathering in the winter apples, potatoes and buckwheat, and overseeing the making of twenty-three barrels of household cider, says an old letter. Her son was born in 1810. But a local banking disaster wrecked the family finances, and in 1814 Mrs. Willard turned her handsome brick house into a ladies' seminary of the accepted pattern. Spurred on by higher learning for men at Middlebury College, Emma soon found her Cause. Girls also could profit by the same education as that given their brothers, and to provide such education was the duty of the state. That thesis, in 1818, was distinctly new. It was too new for Middlebury.

Her plan, worked over for the seventh time, was presented (1818) to Governor Clinton of New York, who awarded her some support from the state's somewhat nebulous "literature fund." The next year, at Waterford, Mrs. Willard opened her "Academy for Female Education," precursor of the real colleges for women that were not to come, most of them, for another half-century. Shortly afterward, citizens of Troy offered to furnish grounds and building if Mrs. Willard would remove her progressive establishment to Troy. The rest is history.

Among Emma Willard's innovations was her emphasis on physical culture. During her own long life, often working fourteen hours a day, teaching, writing, preparing necessary textbooks, she would stop every two hours, fling open the windows, and take a few exercises. That was genuine pioneering at a time when fashionable delicacy of females only too often led to an equally fashionable "decline."

Yet the reformer would not permit her students to speak on the school platform. "Public speaking," she announced firmly, "forms no part of female education."

Outside her own field, Emma Willard deflates into a provincial lady. When she made the grand European tour during the '30's, she paid her respects to Monsieur and Madame de Lafayette. She was profoundly impressed, but she couldn't understand their French. Also, there was that questionable statuary in the Tuileries Gardens. The traveler thanked Heaven, by pen, that her dear school girls were spared such a spectacle, which could only bring blushes to the cheeks of the young and pure. A souvenir of Emma's European venture was her poem, "Rocked in the Cradle of the Deep." It is the only bit of her voluminous writing to achieve survival though in their day her textbooks on geography and American history were the best in these fields.

Financially, also, Mrs. Willard won success. She made money and dressed handsomely. At the height of her career came her one mistake, a mistake that sheds a human light on the woman herself. When she passed 50, she turned over active management of her school to her son, retaining, however, financial control. Then, a widow of long standing, in 1836 she made a second marriage. The new husband was a Boston dentist named Yates, considerably her junior. He apparently expected, as her husband, to administer her income. (That first liberal "married woman's property law" did not come till 1848.) But Emma had been independent too long. She had earned that money.

So the second marriage went from quarrel to quarrel, including one with Mrs. Hale of *Godey's Lady's Book*. Mrs. Hale, also a good-looking widow, had accepted Dr. Yates's escort to a Harvard class day. After that, for many years, those two notable ladies were on non-speaking terms, though the editor continued to publish Mrs. Willard-Yates's very popular articles. At length, to avoid surrendering her fortune to her husband, Mrs. Yates quietly got a divorce, regaining the use of her more famous name. For the rest of her long career, she was Emma Willard. She died, still a success, at 83.

SARAH JOSEPHA HALE, EDITOR

Strictly by birthdate, next after Emma Willard comes this same Sarah Josepha Hale, born in 1788. But because she was 40 years old before she began her career, both her novel, *Northwood* (1827), and her first editorial efforts were antedated by Lydia Maria Child, who was fourteen years her junior. But from 1837 on, well past the Civil War, the lady of *Godey's Lady's Book* was the leading magazine personage of her sex.

There had been a touch of the colonial to Sarah's youth. Her people, named Buell, had emigrated from colonial Connecticut to open land in New Hampshire. On this ancestral farm her only schooling came from her mother and then from a brother, one of the early Dartmouth students. Thus prepared, she put in seven years teaching school, till in 1813 she married David Hale, a lawyer of Newport. He died nine years later, leaving her with five children and not too much property.

The widow's first effort was a volume of verse. It amounted to little, but three years later one of her poems won a prize offered by a Boston magazine. This award brought her the editorship of *The Ladies' Magazine,* a new Boston publishing venture. Ten years later, Louis Godey of Philadelphia bought out his Boston rival, and merged two journals into his famous *Lady's Book*. He also annexed his competitor's editor, then close to 50. But the sprightly Sarah had brought a strong constitution out of New Hampshire. She continued an active editor for 40 years, and finally died at 92.

Even in her own day, Mrs. Hale led the conservatives. When the embattled '40's produced "the woman question," *Godey's* was vigorously *anti*. In her columns Sarah laid down the law. Women were "God's appointed agents for morality . . . On the right influence depends the moral improvement of men . . . no ideal of masculine nature is so perfect in moral values as the feminine." But they should rest content with being an influence.

This lofty tone of the editor was balanced for her readers by the excellent colored fashion plates for which *Godey's* became famous. Liberals might denounce the editor as timeserving, but her public liked her as she was. At the peak of her popularity, just before the Civil War, Mrs. Hale turned out volume after volume. Her *Woman's Record* became a bone of contention between the radical and conservative factions of the "women's cause." Except as research items her writings are now forgotten. Even the prize poem which started the widow on her path to fame is lost. There remains, though, her classic of childhood, "Mary's Little Lamb," published in 1830.

If the lady-editor of *Godey's* cannot be ranked too highly for either vision or intellect, Sarah Josepha Hale marks a milestone. She proved that a woman, even untrained, could have a profession outside of schoolteaching, a very important innovation. This pioneer paid her way—early women writers were rarely self-supporting—and opened paid columns to women writers of articles and romances. Nor should those fashion plates be overlooked. The task of coloring gave full-time employment to seven art-minded ladies in a period when there was no place for women in the graphic field.

LYDIA HUNTLEY SIGOURNEY

Another success story is that of Lydia Huntley Sigourney, of Hartford, schoolmistress, wife, mother and stepmother, and the first American woman to become a best seller. Born in 1791, she produced 57 volumes of prose and verse between 1815 and 1866. She died in the midst of her honors at 75.

She came from Norwich, Connecticut, of prosperous New England stock, and was what was a rarity in those days, an only child. Spared the common task of rocking the cradle of the next, she was given an unusually good education. Little Lydia started school at four. After the three R's and needlework, she received a genteel grounding in "music, painting and embroidery," all before she was nine years old. Later a school on Norwich Green introduced her to the English classics and Latin. Then she was sent to Hartford for two years "in the higher ornamental branches," unfortunately not specified.

But Lydia Huntley loved her books, for after two years of ornamentation, she tackled the Scriptures in Hebrew. In her nineteenth year she opened "a select school for girls" in Norwich, and then a larger one in Hartford. In 1815, she published her first volume of verse. Four years later she married a wealthy Hartford widower, brought up his three children, had two of her own, and still published continuously. In 1841 a London edition of her work was issued, and by 1842 some 8,000 copies of her poems had been sold in her own country.

Thus Mrs. Sigourney made herself the leading poetess of her

period. No new magazine thought of bringing out an opening issue without a poem from her. In her own judgment, she "wrote too much for highest success," and she never questioned the taste of her time. Her book *The Square Table* was intended to correct "the harmful tendencies of Arthur's Round Table." A European critic called her "a kind little sentimentalist, but an excellent housekeeper." Today, only her name survives. Yet nearly 100 years before the word feminist was heard, she had home, children, and a career.

THE GREAT LUCRETIA MOTT

In quite a different key is the tale of Lucretia Mott, of the Friends, born in 1793, and later described by Elizabeth Cady Stanton as the first "liberal-minded woman" she ever encountered. All her long life Lucretia dealt with ideas, leaving no monument in school or institution. Among the causes she served were abolition of slavery, temperance, equal rights for women, religious freedom, peace, and the plight of the little man against what she called "monopolies." More than 100 years later her causes are still with us, most of them having grown to global dimensions.

Lucretia Coffin Mott came from a family of seagoing Nantucket Quakers. There is the breadth of ocean in her views, and that same ocean also provided a practical school of feminism. Nantucket women expected to manage while their husbands were making those memorable sailing voyages that carried the Stars and Stripes from the whaling waters of the Antarctic to far islands in the South Pacific. Should a sailor fail to return, his widow was ready to open a shop and support her family.

As a child, Lucretia saw this happen. Her own father, a rather scholarly sea captain, was wrecked off the Chile coast and given up for lost. When finally restored to his home three years afterwards, he had had enough of the sea. He launched himself in business, first in Boston, later in Philadelphia. The small Lucretia's first school was a private establishment. Then Thomas Coffin deliberately put his girls into the newly opened Boston public school because he wished his children to "mix with all classes of society."

For such higher learning as there was, Lucretia and her sisters were sent to a Friends' boarding school at Nine Partners, Dutchess County, New York. (That school has disappeared in the passage of a century, but Nine Partners Road today crosses the Taconic motor parkway.)

This boarding school was called coeducational, though boys and girls lived in separate houses and were taught and kept strictly separate. The schooling was good. Lucretia qualified to become a teacher, only to learn that her stipend would be half that accorded to young men assistants similarly trained. All her long life Lucretia's feet were to be planted solidly in practical realities.

Teachers of the separate schools at Nine Partners were permitted to join for special studies. So James Mott and Lucretia Coffin met in a French class. They loved, and were married, with the approval of their families, when Lucretia was not yet nineteen. The bridegroom of twenty-two was taken into Thomas Coffin's nail manufacturing plant, and Lucretia began to raise a family.

All went happily till the War of 1812 wrecked the nail business. The young couple first tried keeping store together. When that also failed, Lucretia opened a school for the Pine Street "meeting," and continued teaching there till just before the birth of another child. James, meanwhile, had been taking work wherever he could find it. Eventually the young Motts were on their feet again, but the knowledge of business that Lucretia had gained through these hard knocks gave her a respect for commerce that later distinguished her from more visionary reformers.

It was the death of their (then) only son that turned Lucretia into an unsalaried Quaker preacher. Encouraged by her "meeting" she began a thorough study of Quaker history and theology which gave substance to a natural gift of eloquence. (Sarah Josepha Hale, who disapproved of Lucretia, complained that her sermons "sounded better, heard, than when read in print.") On her long list of "firsts," Lucretia Mott was the first American woman to speak at a masculine gathering. Also, her woman's anti-slavery society in Philadelphia antedated Garrison's Boston *Liberator* by two years. These advanced ladies, though, were so unversed in parliamentary procedure that they had had to call on an educated colored man to organize their first meeting.

Lucretia became an abolitionist the hard way, accompanying some Quaker women going South to address gatherings of Friends within slave territory. They met strong opposition even within their own sect, and Lucretia learned what it was like to face a mob. In a later midwestern venture of hers, abolitionists were in such disfavor that a Quaker physician refused to attend Lucretia. There were also fiery verbal attacks on the Quaker women from orthodox pulpits. These gave her, Lucretia said wryly, an opportunity to practice the nonresistance that the Friends preached.

Within her own family there was a practical problem, since James Mott's income came from handling cotton. When he, too, became a convinced abolitionist, conscience obliged him to give up that business and start another. This was a real sacrifice for parents with five children to support. When the Motts were both selected as delegates to the World Antislavery Convention in London (1840), friends had to help with traveling costs, though later the staunch James once more attained prosperity. While most of the American delegates were making conventional rounds of museums and art galleries, Lucretia Mott was out in the manufacturing areas studying the living conditions of English workmen.

Her most famous adventure in liberalism stemmed from her English experience, for the London convention committee had refused to seat any delegate from a woman's society. This exclusion supplied the impulse for the calling of that first women's rights convention at Seneca Falls in 1848.

Gradually Lucretia Mott had become the most distinguished American woman of her day, and a notable speaker. Though her mind ranged far, she always clung to her plain Quaker habit, and loyally attended "the yearly meeting." (The Motts were identified with the liberal wing of the Friends.) Recognized both at home and abroad, Lucretia remained remarkably active till near the end of a long life. She made her last platform address in Boston when she was past 79, and died in 1880.

THREE NOTABLE SPINSTERS

So far, it must be granted, these pathfinders have been very normal women endowed with vision and energy far beyond the line of domestic duty, but otherwise belonging to their time and place. All four were happily married. They had their children first and their careers afterwards.

But with Mary Lyon, born 1797 in western Massachusetts, the pattern changed. She came from a mountain farm where religion was the only luxury. The father's death left children "dependent on their own exertions." Mary Lyon hired out to other farm households for spinning and weaving, then became an untaught country school-marm, paid 75¢ a week, and "boarded around." By desperate frugality, at twenty she was able to enter the academy at Ashfield. When her scanty funds gave out, they kept her on, noting her "unusual aptitude for learning," shown in the "verbal accuracy" of her recitations. Better equipped, she went back to teaching and saving until she had accumulated 50 dollars of her own.

Then came the decision of a lifetime. Should she "marry and settle down," or use that hard-earned fortune to enter the Reverend Joseph Emerson's famous school at Byfield? Unlike Emma, Sarah, Lydia, and Lucretia, Mary Lyon cast her deciding vote against matrimony, or against the particular "matrimonial offer" open to her. In 1822 she went from Byfield to assist at the founding of Adams Academy at Derry, New Hampshire. But this first so-scantily endowed school for girls couldn't keep a winter term. Back went Mary Lyon to her own hills to put in the frozen months teaching farm daughters like herself who had become teachers by main strength.

There she had her vision—a permanent seminary "designed exclusively for young ladies preparing to teach . . . in the cause of education and religion." She had no money and no influential friends, only faith and enthusiasm. To extract "free-will offerings from an enlightened Christian public" took six years of gruelling canvassing. Mt. Holyoke Female Seminary, the first to own its buildings and equipment, was opened in November, 1837, with 80 pupils. They were girls more or less like herself, willing to do housework to keep down the cost of their superior schooling.

Yet not too superior by present standards. Latin was not included in the curriculum for the first ten years. Instead, Mary Lyon proposed, "a lady should be so educated that she can go as a missionary at a fortnight's notice." And some of them did that literally (Chapter Note 1).

For a little more than ten years Mary Lyon had the joy of teaching young women "to live for God and do something." But she had driven herself too hard. She died in 1849 of so-called "brain fever."

This death of Mary Lyon at 52 deserves special attention, for she was the only one of the pioneer intellectuals to succumb to disease under 70. (Margaret Fuller's death was by shipwreck.) All the others proved hardy specimens of the human race. Some had serious illnesses midway in their careers but recovered to round out many busy years. Most of them ended as octogenarians, which was unusual in those days, suffering only from what one old lady called "chronic longevity."

This extraordinary vitality in an era of fashionable female delicacy raises another question. Was it a common denominator in their rebellion against restrictions? Or being rebellious spirits, did their vigor enable them to make headway against almost universal apathy? Either theory can be argued, but one thing is certain: physical resilience was an important characteristic of these exceptional women.

Consider the case of another notable spinster, Catharine Beecher, born in 1800—teacher, publicist, and protagonist of domestic science as a career for women. In her we encounter that remarkable Beecher family—Lyman, the father, and three of his eight children, Catharine, Harriet, and Henry Ward. Catharine was another leader of the conservative opposition. She was strongly for woman-in-the-home, and as strongly against anything that might lead beyond it. Teaching and education were to be rated chiefly as they prepared women for intramural activities.

When a cause has long since been won, it is too easy to see the losers as ridiculously short-sighted. But while the conflict was on, the *antis* claimed thousands of sincere believers. Such a one was Catharine Beecher, an unreconstructed female who spoke for the multitude of her less articulate sisters.

Her story began with her father, a vigorous, zealous, opinionated orthodox clergyman who started preaching at Easthampton, Long Island, on a yearly stipend of 400 dollars. When this could not provide for five children, he removed to Litchfield, Connecticut, lured by 800 dollars plus the household firewood, no small item in

New England. Another advantage at Litchfield was Miss Pierce's Academy, where the Beecher daughters were accepted without fee. By 1816 the parsonage housed eight children, but their mother had gone into a rapid "decline." Now part of the burden fell on Catharine, who, at sixteen, was making all the clothing for herself and her seven brothers and sisters.

Discipline was supplied by the father, who demanded "exact, prompt and cheerful obedience" at the risk of punishment "so severe that it was thoroughly remembered." Within a year after the death of Roxanna, his devoted first wife, the Reverend Lyman had found another superior woman to share his parsonage. But money pressure grew more stringent. Now Catharine, always handy around the house, but not too keen a student, put herself through a year of drawing, painting and piano, to qualify herself for the one profession open to females.

During her first year of teaching at New London, this oldest daughter met and fell in love with a promising young professor at Yale. He had been granted a year of study abroad by the college, and on his return the young couple were to be married. But in June, 1822, his ship went down with all hands, off the Irish coast.

Deeply in love, Catharine had welcomed domesticity as woman's divinely appointed province. Now in her bereavement she accepted teaching as a substitute for the home she would never have. Her grief was aggravated by theological torment, for the lost lover, though deeply Christian, had never been "converted" as demanded by Lyman Beecher's code of salvation. It was to take his favorite daughter fifteen years to think her way into a less dogmatic theology. She was never able to go beyond her inherited assumption of woman's limited sphere in society.

Her first career project was a school of her own, in Hartford, with a younger sister to help with the teaching. Beginning with seven pupils in one room over a harness shop, by 1826 she was presiding over 80 girls in the basement of a church. Mary Beecher had married, but a younger sister named Harriet was drafted to fill the vacancy. An appeal to the citizens of Hartford for 5,000 dollars gave the Hartford Female Seminary a house of its own, with separate rooms for each grade, blackboards, maps, and similar equipment, altogether a very progressive school. Like Emma Willard, Miss

Beecher advocated physical exercise, to which she gave an impressive name from the Greek—calisthenics.

But Catharine's real career was to develop outside the classroom. The Reverend Lyman had received a call to become president of Lane Seminary in Cincinnati. Young and struggling as this seminary was, Lyman Beecher saw an opportunity for wholesale evangelism in the western territories. Daughter Catharine went dutifully along with the family to start a new school. This time, though, she persuaded someone else to preside over the classrooms, while she devoted herself to organizing a Board of National Popular Education. It was to select and train young ladies to teach in the newly opened regions, but the first requirement on any candidate's credentials must be a detailed recommendation from her clergyman.

Miss Beecher organized everything. She also wrote an address to commend the project to the public. But like a perfect lady, she sat silent on the platform while a male Beecher—her brother Thomas—read her speech, all through an extended fund raising tour. As her own contribution, she offered a share of the sales of her recently published *Treatise on Domestic Economy*. This was a pioneer volume of its kind. Revised in 1869, by famous sister Harriet under the title "The American Woman's Home," it became a post-Civil War best seller.

Catharine Beecher reached intellectual maturity in her *Letters on the Difficulties of Religion* (1836). In these she rejected the Calvinist doctrine of total depravity, which would condemn the soul of her "unconverted" lost lover. The achievement of this position had cost her fifteen years of mental struggle. Another twenty years later sister Harriet was to use the doctrinal arguments of Catharine's essay as the theme of her popular novel, *The Minister's Wooing*. But while Catharine had cast off theological leading strings, she clung all the more strongly to social chains. In 1837 she took pen in hand to rebuke the early abolitionists. Women might band together for "piety, charity, maternal and domestic duty," but to attempt "coercive influences" was outside their sphere.

Though she would remain completely *anti*, Catharine Beecher was a pathfinder in domestic science. She advocated planning a house in sections, so that it could be expanded later for a family.

She devised built-in shelves and cupboards near the stove for cooking utensils, and a hinged cover to turn a sink into a worktable. Laundry tubs were to be fitted with spigots and plugs to save labor in filling and emptying. More important, she advised methods of ventilation that were afterward used successfully in Washington's Civil War hospitals. Though she defined cosmetics as "preparations which some people foolishly think will preserve and beautify the skin," she commended dancing as healthy exercise. Thus Catharine Beecher, a New England girl who was always handy around the house, made herself into this country's first domestic scientist.

She died in May, 1878, a fine, upright, opinionated old lady, still planning "an extended tour for the improvement of common school education among the working classes" (Chapter Note 2).

By right of birthdate, the place of pioneer social worker goes to Dorothea Lynde Dix, protagonist of jail and asylum reform. Though born in 1802, it was not till nearly 40 years later that Miss Dix found her lifework, the cause that sent her before Congress (1852) as the first woman lobbyist. The irony of this was that Miss Dix was a stiff antisuffragist, standing always on her prerogatives as a lady.

The life of Dorothea Dix might almost be a textbook for modern psychology. This child did not come from an exemplary home. Her father, usually deleted from early official sketches of the reformer, was the black sheep of a sternly upright New England family. When she was twelve Dorothea fled for refuge to her Boston grandmother. Madam Dix evidently had no wish to see the curse of shiftlessness bequeathed unto a third and fourth generation. The grandchild was given some schooling, and then turned out at fourteen to try her hand at teaching.

For twenty years, till 1836, Miss Dix was a walking New England conscience. Then she collapsed into five years of invalidism. Dimly in the background were the ashes of a lost love, and finally a substantial legacy from that Spartan grandmother who had set those rebellious young feet in the path of duty. As a semi-invalid, Miss Dix became a sermon copier for Dr. William Ellery Channing, the famous liberal preacher of Boston. In 1841, quite by accident, she found her cause. One day she was asked to substitute for a theological student who taught a class of prisoners in the East Cambridge jail. It was a winter day, but the East Cambridge jail had no stove. From that moment Miss Dix ceased to be an invalid.

She recovered to campaign for jail and asylum reform for 40 years in nearly every state in the Union and over most of Europe. In April, 1861, she followed the Sixth Massachusetts regiment into Washington, where she was at once appointed Superintendent of Women Nurses for the Civil War. Well past 60, she survived four hard-pressed years to pursue hospital reform for two decades of peace. She kept on working till a few years before her death in 1887. She was then 85. Clara Barton, popularly ranked as this country's nursing pioneer, was still teaching school during this earlier period. Not until she encountered the Franco-Prussian war in Europe did Miss Barton adopt the life work with which her name is associated today, the American Red Cross.

As a woman lobbyist, Miss Dix did not invade state legislatures from any sense of her own political rights, but from flaming zeal for other people's wrongs. Literally, she did not invade. From one state capitol to another, she made no addresses, appeared at no meetings. A special room or separate alcove would be set off for this very conservative lady with a mission. Thither the masculine advocates of hospital betterment would conduct reluctant legislators, to be won over by Miss Dix's vivid description of local abuses.

After successes in many states, Miss Dix sponsored a bill to give national support to the reform movement. At the Capitol, the same procedure was followed. The lady did not call on Congressmen or Senators. They were led to her secluded alcove. The national bill failed. Miss Dix later called politicians "the meanest and lowest party demagogues, the basest characters." This country's first woman lobbyist lived and died firmly convinced that women should hold themselves aloof from all political concerns.

LYDIA MARIA CHILD, AUTHOR-REFORMER

We turn once more to Massachusetts for Lydia Maria Child whose *Hobomok,* published anonymously in 1821, made her the first American woman novelist. Nine years later, this enterprising soul projected a *History of the Condition of Women in All Ages,* which was to embrace all races and religions. Left to Lydia, doubtless this monumental task would have been accomplished. But her publisher, a mere man, went bankrupt at the fifth volume.

The dauntless Lydia was born (1802) in Medford, Massachusetts. Her people—the family name was Francis—were shrewdly comfortable businessmen, known locally for love of learning. An older son, Convers Francis, later became an advanced thinker in that new advanced sect, the Unitarians. Lydia, the youngest of six children, started school with her brothers under the tutelage of "Ma'am Betty," an undistinguished spinster who solaced her sour lot by chewing tobacco. After Ma'am Betty's, Convers headed for Harvard, while Lydia was left to the district school, and finally "finished" with one year at Medford Academy.

She manifested a bent for letters early. At nineteen, she read in the new North American Review a suggestion that fiction could be written using early American history as a background. Young Lydia's brain took fire. It was a Sunday. Between morning and afternoon church services, she wrote the first chapter of this, the first novel to come from any American woman. *Hobomok* was an Indian romance laid in early Salem where her Indian hero was associated with the friendly Massasoit. Irving's American sketches and Cooper's early novels were then coming into vogue, so *Hobomok* for all its crudity had a speedy local success. A second romance, laid in pre-Revolutionary Boston, followed.

But fame came easier than fortune. Lydia was obliged to return to schoolteaching to make a living. On the side, she started *The Juvenile Miscellany,* a pioneer magazine for children that survived eight years. It was as a "juvenile" editor that Lydia Maria tossed off the children's classic that has outlived its author—"Over the river and through the woods, to grandmother's house we go." Her volumes of erudite theological argument have long since been forgotten; causes for which she suffered have been won and lost; but this delightful jingle of New England childhood lingers on. She was an interesting precursor of more notable women authors.

In 1823, Lydia Maria married David Child, a lawyer. A year later she was publishing a cookbook. Under the title *The Frugal Housewife,* this went through 50 editions. Her *Mother's Book,* two years later, had eight American editions, twelve English, and was then translated into German. It was after her *Girls' Own Book* that Mrs. Child started that over-ambitious history of women which ruined her publisher.

At this point the success story ceases. Both Mrs. Child and her husband became ardent abolitionists, she to be known as the first antislavery pamphleteer. That ruined her book market, since more than half of her readers had been ladies of the South. Two more books were published, but they failed to sell.

In 1841 husband and wife came to New York to edit an abolitionist weekly, living meanwhile at the home of Isaac Hopper, the Quaker philanthropist. As an extra, Lydia wrote two volumes of *Letters from New York,* besides Hopper's biography. Then in 1855 she published *The Progress of Religious Ideas Through the Ages.* She had worked on the book for six years, and Lucretia Mott praised it, but it brought no profit. A hotly controversial pamphlet on John Brown's raid made more trouble.

Then when complete disaster threatened, Lydia received a legacy from her father, author of the more remunerative Medford crackers. The crusader and her semi-invalid husband retired to the quiet of a New England village. But even in Wayland, Massachusetts, there could be no peace for Lydia. With the close of the Civil War she published a novel dealing with the social status of the quadroon, *A Romance of the Republic.* Such was the final blast from this literary reformer, whom Frederika Bremer, the visiting Swedish novelist, called "a beautiful soul, but too angular to be happy." She died in 1880 (Chapter Note 3).

MARGARET FULLER, OF BOSTON AND ROME

Like Mrs. Child, Margaret Fuller, later the Countess Ossoli, was born in 1802. But there resemblance ceases. Lydia was a zealot, Margaret Fuller a personage. She was not only the first American woman to become a literary critic, but she was also the first critic to apply European standards to American work. Even today her name strikes a chord of memory. People recall her vaguely as somehow connected with Brook Farm and Hawthorne. Oh, yes, she was his Zenobia in *Blithedale Romance.* But most of all, people remember the Emerson story. According to tradition, Emerson took Margaret Fuller to see Fanny Ellsler dance, saying, "Margaret, this is poetry!" Rolling her eyes to Heaven, Margaret corrected him, "No, Ralph, this is religion!"

This is more than an anecdote. It is a phase of a woman of extreme contradictions, a woman of brilliant intellectual attainments, yet one who could be a plain fool in human relations. The idealist, reaching for the stars only to fall flat on her face, can be either tragedy or comedy. Margaret Fuller was both.

There is no mystery as to what made her like that. Sarah Margaret Fuller (she soon dropped the Sarah) was born in Cambridgeport, Massachusetts, the eldest child in a substantial family that was to send three sons to Harvard. Harvard was also her father's college. Thus she was born into that group of writers and scholars who were soon to make Boston famous. Also, she was born with a mind that made her, said Thomas Wentworth Higginson, "the queen of Cambridge with a large majority of rather unwilling and insurrectionary subjects."

If most of our pathfinding women suffered from lack of education, Margaret Fuller was surfeited with it. Timothy Fuller, her father, had the unusual ambition of raising his oldest daughter to be man's intellectual equal. He succeeded only too well. Since a second girl had died when Margaret was only three, for several years Timothy concentrated all his adult love of learning on this small survivor. Margaret had no childhood. When other tots played with their dolls, she was mastering Latin declensions. Caesar, Ovid, Horace and Homer were her playmates.

When she was seven a merciful Providence sent Timothy Fuller to Congress. From Washington he wrote home demanding why she had delayed sending him Goldsmith's "Deserted Village" done into Latin. Back from Congress, Timothy was annoyed to see his ten-year-old prodigy squinting and short-sighted. So he bundled her off to a Boston school where she found herself much cleverer than the other girls. They retaliated by calling her fat. Timothy next tried the establishment of the Misses Prescott at Groton. There for another three years Margaret was in continual warfare with her schoolmates, one against the mob. In the end the mob reduced her to convulsions. Thus, at sixteen, a genius had to learn painfully the lessons that most children master before the alphabet.

She came home to rock the newest baby's cradle, and to study Greek, French, Italian and philosophy. There was something merely pedantic, however, in this flourish of languages, for in after years, although she had conducted classes for the study of Dante, Margaret lacked enough spoken Italian to get herself around Italy without a courier.

Meanwhile Timothy Fuller had prospered sufficiently to move himself to the Dana mansion in Cambridge, under the critical eye of Harvard. John Quincy Adams, then President of the United States, accepted Timothy's invitation to visit him. This occasion the father chose for Margaret's introduction to society. Mrs. Fuller, awaiting the birth of an eighth child, was in that state of retirement that had been hers almost continuously since her marriage. It was Margaret's father who countenanced the lacing of this large and learned debutante into a brilliant pink dress, cut so tightly that she could scarcely raise her arms. Margaret, "receiving" beside her father, met the great world, particularly the local great world of Harvard. The Harvard ladies admitted her brains, and later one of them sent her to a good dressmaker. Thereafter Margaret Fuller might be called queenly, but never fat.

At this time, too, the debutante tried to temper somewhat the brusqueness of her manner. She took for her model a young lady from New Orleans, then visiting one of the faculty wives. But she didn't get very far in remaking herself in the pattern of southern charm, since she was also busy reading Goethe, Schiller and Richter, and keeping an elaborate journal in which her own thoughts seemed to her very interesting and important.

The sudden death of Timothy Fuller changed the later current of his daughter's life. She was then 24. Her entire blue-stocking accomplishment was one unsigned article in the *North American Review*. Now, though, she found herself the head of the family. Her mother emerged from a penumbra of pregnancy (there were nine Fuller children), a gentle, much-effaced woman, always in need of a strong arm and a strong mind to cling to. Since her sons were mere lads, she turned to this brilliant oldest daughter. When the Fuller estate proved smaller than had been supposed, Margaret set herself to teaching Latin and French in Bronson Alcott's experimental school in Boston, supplementing its rather doubtful payroll with private evening classes in German and Italian. In spare moments she also made excellent German translations, and began outlining a life of Goethe.

Within two years she had gained such a reputation for learning that she was offered 1,000 dollars a year (then an enormous sum for a woman) to go to a school in Providence, Rhode Island. Boston, though, was home. By 1839 she was back there again, to institute her famous classes in conversation for women. This was really adult education in general culture, designed to round out the limited schooling of the average "lady" of the day. The classes were an enormous success, with Margaret doing most of the conversing. They also furnished another famous Fuller story. In the course of a lecture she announced grandly, "I accept the universe." This being related to Carlyle in one of his dyspeptic moments, drew from him the famous retort, "By God, she'd better."

At the peak of professional success Margaret suffered the first of those personal humiliations that were to mark her career. While queening it over the best minds in Boston, Miss Fuller had acquired an admirer, a lofty, transcendental sort of lover, tagged by the workaday name of Samuel. Samuel's letters began to grow cold. He failed to appear for walks around Walden Pond. Then Samuel faded out. Margaret heard that the young lady from New Orleans was again visiting in Cambridge, and that Samuel was about to marry her. Which he did. The young bride joined Margaret's classes to improve her mind.

The learned Miss Fuller was also very hard working. Outside her classes, she was editor of the *Dial* when that magazine achieved esthetic renown on a circulation of 500 copies, though it rarely paid either editor or contributors. Essays, criticisms and translations flowed from her pen, till in 1844 Horace Greeley invited her to become literary editor of his *Tribune* in New York. She grasped at this remarkable opportunity, pausing only for a characteristic farewell entry in her diary, under date of April 28, 1844. "It was the last day of my class. How noble has been my experience of such a relation now for six years, and with so many and so various minds! Life is worth living, is it not?"

Since a lady, even though a critic, had to be in someone's home, the intelligent but eccentric Mrs. Greeley took the Bostonian into her household. There, by the shores of Turtle Bay, Horace would come home to find his guest-author holding court for a dozen women, instead of writing her book review. To Horace this was very irritating. Still he admitted that her articles, when done, were adding both distinction and circulation to the *Tribune*.

Just when the famous Miss Fuller was becoming considerably engrossed with her own importance, came another personal jolt. In New York she met a young Jew, James Nathan by name. This was her first encounter with a cultured European outside of book covers. His romantic attitudes took her fancy. To Horace Greeley Nathan was just an obscure young foreigner, but to Margaret he seemed the embodiment of an older civilization. Since the Greeleys did not approve, she began meeting him by stealth for walks and talks, and fervent letters passed between them. But as the lady swept forward, the gentleman withdrew. Instead of receiving a proposal of marriage, Miss Fuller was asked to find a wealthy patron to finance an exploration of the Holy Land, which was Nathan's life ambition.

Never doubting, Margaret begged favors from influential friends, and James Nathan sailed for Germany, leaving Margaret to look after his dog. Margaret, still trusting, arranged to follow him abroad, though forced to borrow money for the trip. She reached Liverpool only to learn that Nathan had just married someone in Hamburg. The critic returned to her literary labors.

Later on Miss Fuller was able to compass an extensive European tour. With her instinct for drama, she reached Rome in time for the siege of 1848. From there she wrote back to Boston that "the hour of love" had come to her. According to Frederika Bremer, she also wrote enthusiastically of the joys of motherhood that awaited her, omitting any specific details of marriage. Her friends were to "learn all" later. Naturally, there was considerable talk in Boston, especially since there was no cable service to expedite queries. At length Boston was relieved to know that, at the age of 37, their queen of Cambridge had married. Her husband, much younger than herself, was Giovanni Angelo, Marquis Ossoli, who had renounced his noble family to throw in his lot with the short-lived Roman republic. Their son was born in September, 1848, in a comfortless peasant house, with the ministration of a village midwife.

At the fall of the republic the Ossolis had to flee. They sailed from Leghorn, in May, 1850, in the bark *Elizabeth,* which was wrecked in a sudden gale off Fire Island, within a hundred yards of shore. Sailors offered to save Margaret, as they had another woman, by binding her to a plank and having some strong swimmer in the crew tow her to shore. But Margaret refused to be parted from husband and child, a last romantic gesture. Its sincerity can scarcely be doubted, since she vouched for it with her life.

Thus, at 40, perished the woman who, whether one likes her or not, must be credited with having done most to win recognition of intellectual equality for the women who came after her.

ENTER DR. HUNT

It was also Boston which produced the first accredited woman physician, who had to acquire her training by apprenticeship, since no medical school would then accept women. This notable pathfinder, Harriot Kezia Hunt, opened an office of her own in 1835. In 1853 the Female Medical College of Philadelphia conferred an honorary degree on Harriot after she had been in successful practice for nearly eighteen years.

Born in 1805, Harriot came to her chosen profession from the accepted female treadmill of teaching (1827–1833). She was led to medicine by the severe illness of a younger sister who was under the care of a Mrs. Mott. Mrs. Mott's position is illuminating. She had no official standing whatsoever, but was the wife of an English doctor who turned his women patients over to her. For three years, Sarah Hunt was a patient of Mrs. Mott, who finally cured her. Thereupon Harriot gave up her school to become secretary-apprentice for Mrs. Mott, to train by office study and observation. Upon the death of Dr. Mott, his widow decided to return to England.

Recognizing an opportunity, both sisters, Harriot and Sarah, opened their own office. Their venture was successful. Their patients praised them. They made a specialty of hydrotherapy, then coming into vogue, and Harriot practiced a homemade psychotherapy of her own invention. She afterward wrote that she was always surprised when it worked, and a patient recovered from some psychosomatic illness. Incidentally, Boston seems to have had its share of neurotic women back in the good old days.

Sarah Hunt now married, but Dr. Harriot kept going. In spite of her success, Harvard Medical School, close at hand, looked askance. Her two applications for entrance, in 1847 and 1850, were refused. Finally Harriot achieved that belated honorary degree from Philadelphia. To Frederika Bremer from Stockholm, Dr. Hunt of Boston was "a zealous little creature . . . a very peculiar individual." Still Miss Bremer was "delighted" with her.

Dr. Hunt's zeal was rewarded with a lucrative practice which turned her into a city taxpayer. For the rest of her life (she died in 1875) she paid her rates under protest. Since she was voteless, she insisted, this was a flagrant case of "taxation without representation" (Chapter Note 4).

A search of old sources indicates that women's interest in medical enterprise antedates considerably Dr. Hunt's struggle to enter the profession. Data are fragmentary but a few facts stand out. For instance, in 1813, following an outbreak of yellow fever in South Carolina, the Ladies Benevolent Society of Charleston was founded. Later on the organization was maintaining sixteen hospital wards. These were nonsectarian, and until the Civil War, drew no color line. Far to the north, in 1828, the women of Portland, Maine, started their Female Samaritan Association. The earliest hospital for women in the United States was the New York Asylum for Lying-in Women, established in 1822. Its founders were said all to have been women, but so far research has failed to discover their names.

These instances support the theory that the few pioneer women who won public recognition represented the protests of many hundreds of their sisters who lived and died unknown.

For the ten women sketched here were most truly pioneers. They also blazed the trail for those who would soon follow, women whose names are more generally remembered in our own era. Whatever the limitations of our pathfinders, they were the ones who did the first hard spade work.

Different as these ten were in personality and outlook, they had one thing in common. They had all taught school, either starting from that to their individual goals, or returning to it when the going was tough. In their time teaching was the one breadwinning vocation open to literate women. Perhaps the entire forward movement of American women—as Sir Anthony Absolute maintained elsewhere—was the fatal consequence of teaching girls to read.

Where early career women are concerned, varying dates often appear in different sources. Dates in this chapter have been checked wherever possible, especially in assigning priority in any field. Thus the novels of Catherine Sedgwick of Stockbridge came closely after *Hobomok* and *Northfield,* but the most reliable records accord priority to Mrs. Child and Mrs. Hale.

There was the famous *Charlotte Temple* published in Boston in 1804, but its author, Susanna Rowson, was an Englishwoman. She came to this country with her husband on a theatrical venture, and stayed on to teach in Medford, Newton and Boston. *Charlotte Temple* was considered a moral novel because it depicted the horrible end of a young lady who disobeyed her parents.

It should also be noted that unpublished letters of Lucretia Mott and the papers of Clara Barton are now in the Smith College Library.

1 Mount Holyoke Seminary's pioneer missionary graduates should not be forgotten. Fidelia Fiske (born 1816) went to Persia, the first unmarried woman missionary. She returned in 1847 and was briefly President of Mt. Holyoke. But her health failed and she died at the age of 48. Anne Wilkens (born 1806) went out to Liberia in 1837, and survived for twenty years. Mrs. R. B. Lytle reached the Fiji Islands in 1836–37, saw real cannibals there, and survived till 1899.

Preceding the Mt. Holyoke women by a decade, seven untrained men missionaries went to Sierra Leone, taking with them five young wives—anonymous. In less than two years all of the women were dead and there were also three dead babies.

The first named missionary wife on record was Harriet Newell of Haverhill, Massachusetts. She married at nineteen and set out with her husband for Burma, along with the famous Adoniram Judson. Three weeks before reaching Burma Harriet's baby was born, to live only five days. The mother died shortly afterwards, just turned twenty.

The rollcall of Adoniram Judson's wives was hardly encouraging. The first wife worked in Burma, 1813–1821, and then returned to this country, ill. She went back in 1823, had a child in 1826, and died. The infant survived for six months. The second Mrs. Judson was the widow of a missionary in India. During six years there she had three children, two of whom died. In 1825 she became the second Mrs. Judson and bore

122

her fourth child. Ill herself, she died on the voyage home. The third Mrs. Judson had been a child laborer in a New York state textile mill, working to pay for schooling. Later a writer for the Baptist Sunday School publishing house, she met Judson in 1846 and married him. She had two children in Burma, one of whom lived. Then Judson himself died. His widow, still comparatively young, returned to this country to die at 37.

Then there were Elizabeth Baker Dwight who caught the plague at Constantinople and died (1837) in her 29th year; Sarah Lanman Smith reached Syria in 1833, started a girls' school, and died within three years. Eleanor Macomber and Sarah Davis Comstock went out to Burma, and died there in 1836 and 1843 respectively. The first American woman missionary to China was Harriet Shuck of Virginia who arrived in China with her husband in 1835. She learned Chinese, started a school there, and died in 1847, following the birth of a fifth child.

The ghastly roll of early women missionaries can be continued almost indefinitely.

2 In her later years, Catharine Beecher felt that no restrictions on women applied to her. When about seventy she called on the President of Cornell, announcing her intention of enrolling for a certain course. Dr. White explained that no Cornell courses were open to women. That was quite all right, Miss Beecher explained. She really preferred to take the course along with men. Also she proposed to live in a college dormitory. "As for those young men who are of appropriate ages to be my grandsons, they will not trouble me in the least." So, long before Cornell admitted women, Miss Beecher made herself a resident student there. This anecdote is told in Margaret Thorpe's *Female Persuasion*.

3 Lydia Maria Child appears in Lowell's "Fable for Critics" as Philothea, with the lines beginning:

> "Here comes Philothea, her face all aglow,
>   She has just been dividing some poor creature's woe"

The passage ends:

> "If her heart at high flood swamps her brain now and then
>   'Tis but richer for that when the tide ebbs again.
>   What a wealth it would bring to the narrow and sour
>   Could they be as a Child but for one little hour."

4 The cry against taxation without representation was a suffragist strategy of the post-Civil War decade. An amusing example was that of the Smith sisters of Glastonbury, Connecticut, who refused to pay outright. The local sheriff, not wishing to start suit against two spinster ladies of 76 and 81, merely removed their cows to the village pound. The Misses Smith then paid the sum to release the cows—but they did not pay taxes—and everyone was happy. There were originally five sisters, two of whom learned Greek and Hebrew from their clerical brother-in-law; becoming dissatisfied with the King James version of the Bible, they made their own, and paid for its printing. Long before their advocacy of equal suffrage, they had been ardent abolitionists; the claim is made that Mrs. Smith, their mother, joined them in drawing up the first antislavery petition to be submitted by John Quincy Adams to Congress. These sisters furnish an example of the mental ferment among women of the mid-19th century, although their activities were largely restricted to their own home town.

Another instance of local pioneering that had repercussions far beyond state boundaries was the school kept by Prudence Crandall in Canterbury, Connecticut. In 1832 Miss Crandall, a Quaker, admitted a Negro girl to her select private establishment. When the white misses were promptly withdrawn by indignant parents, Miss Crandall filled the vacancies with "young ladies of color." The resulting furore produced the state's "Black Law" (1833) which prohibited the teaching of Negroes except in public schools. Miss Crandall refused to yield, was mobbed and fled. In 1883 the same state of Connecticut awarded an annual pension of 400 dollars to the intrepid innovator who had been driven out 50 years earlier.

CHAPTER FIVE

The Parade Marches On

*T*HE years between 1805 and 1820 supply the birthdates of another group of notable pre-feminists, including some names still heard a hundred years later.

But significant changes have occurred since Emma Willard began talking about education for women as a duty of the state. The mental ferment had spread far beyond New England which first gave it nurture. As the territory widened, so did the scope of activity. The battle against restrictions swung from educational to economic and political fields. Movements were organized: for abolition, for temperance, for "women's rights"—causes all pursued with flaming missionary zeal.

In this second group of pre-feminists, only three came from New England. South Carolina provided two; New Jersey and western Pennsylvania, one apiece, while up-state New York can claim three well known names. Four out of the ten women were to be associated with areas west of the Ohio.

As the ferment spread, personal contact developed. Those first pathfinders were localized in place or purpose, each in her separate star. Except for that unfortunate encounter between Emma Willard and Sara Josepha Hale, there is no record of early fellowship. In the

'30's the canal boat represented rapid transit in bulk, but by the '40's steamboats had multiplied and trains were beginning to roll. Nearly everyone got around a little more. So did ideas, books and magazines. Individual crusaders learned to pool their efforts. Varied scope and terrain were to produce some striking personalities, although the women themselves were less strictly pioneers.

THE GRIMKÉ SISTERS

At the van of the second parade were those surprising aristocrats from South Carolina, Sarah Moore Grimké, (born 1792) and her sister Angelina Emily, born in 1805. They became the first women to speak for abolition at public meetings, open to both men and women. It was around the genteel heads of these two southern ladies that the stones flew.

For such daring, their background was extraordinary. Their father, John F. Grimké, was a distinguished Charleston judge, who had been educated abroad at Cambridge and in London. In all, there were fourteen Grimké offspring, brought up in the best of a strict tradition. Yet two daughters, Sarah, the oldest, and Angelina, thirteen years her junior, became imbued with a religious hatred of slavery.

The abolition idea had its germ for Sarah in the trip that she made to Philadelphia, accompanying her father who went there for medical treatment. The sojourn was extended, bringing Sarah into touch with the Friends. Following a return to Charleston and the death of Judge Grimké, both sisters came north. They made their home in Philadelphia with sufficient income for their needs. But if spared bread-and-butter urgency, that of conscience soon had them in its grip. Joining the Friends, they became the storm center of the early antislavery movement.

Angelina Emily, the younger and prettier of the two, was the more "forth putting." Sarah, reserved and more of a student, was the balance wheel. Angelina was just past 30 when she wrote *An Appeal to the Christian Women of the South* (1836). This pamphlet was to be circulated by the Anti-Slavery Society of Philadelphia. Anticipating a favorable reception for it in the author's own state, many copies were shipped there. This proved a gross miscalculation. The pamphlets were burned, not by the Christian women, but by post-masters throughout South Carolina. Later when Angelina attempted to visit her mother, she was forbidden to land from the steamer under threat of mobbing. Not wishing to involve her family, she yielded. But after this forced return north, both sisters volunteered as lectur-ers and speakers for the antislavery cause.

Women, in 1836, were not given platform hearing at public gatherings. So the sisters began with private meetings for ladies only. But some Congregational clergymen of Massachusetts commenced denouncing them as women preachers. Even the gentle Whittier wished they would confine themselves to the written word. Soon abolition had become enmeshed with the issue of free speech for women, and the fat was in the fire.

For nearly four years, the devoted sisters persevered. Some-times, usually in churches, they would address enthusiastic gather-ings. Again, a minister would close his church against them, and less protected quarters had to be found. Billboard notices were torn down, and even in the North the women speakers were attacked by mobs with stones and rotten eggs. On one occasion, Angelina Emily faced a mob boldly, continuing her address while windows were shattered all around her. That was her last public effort. First one sister and then the other lost the use of her voice, a circumstance that modern psychology would quickly label a defense mechanism. They were never able to speak from a platform again.

Sarah and Angelina withdrew to private life. In retirement, however, they made a practical demonstration for the cause. They persuaded their mother to allot to them, as their share of the family estate, as many as possible of the Grimké Negroes. These slaves were shipped to Philadelphia and there freed by their new owners. (1838)

The sisters' further gesture caused a stir even in advanced cir-cles. They had brought to the North a young mulatto, admittedly the son of a brother. This youth they welcomed as a member of the family, and had him educated in the best schools available. Such an extreme protest against racial discrimination at that early date was too much for most Philadelphians, including some in the antislavery movement.

In 1838, Angelina married Theodore Weld, a teacher of social-istic leanings, later identified with "The Phalanstery," an early cooperative venture in New Jersey. Following his marriage and with the two sisters to help in the teaching, Weld opened a "liberal" school in Belleville, New Jersey. There Angelina had one child who lived to grow up. In the '50's Frederika Bremer visited the noted ex-reformers. She found the two sisters more concerned with a new diet for little Charles than with public affairs. Miss Bremer thought the boy looked fragile and wanted to recommend some good hearty Swedish food for him, but tactfully confined her advice to her journal.

When the sisters died in the '70's—Sarah in 1873, Angelina six years later—they were almost forgotten. But 40 years earlier these quiet women had faced mobs.

FANNY FERN, JOURNALIST

Shifting from the Grimkés to Fanny Fern exchanges the fires of moral conviction for the genial warmth of a September noon. Fanny Fern was that rare thing, a really blithe spirit. This is the more striking since her inheritance was on the stern side. But that native gaiety was to prove her salvation and make her our first thoroughgoing woman journalist.

"Fanny Fern" was the pen name of Sara Willis Eldredge Parton, born in 1811. She was a sister of N. P. Willis, leading author, editor and founder of *Town and Country* magazine. Their father, Nathaniel Willis, had edited a Boston religious journal, and "N. P.'s" first literary effort had been the rendering of Old Testament stories in verse. At sixteen Sara was dispatched to the Hartford seminary of the highminded Catharine Beecher. There Sara distinguished herself chiefly by tearing the pages of her geometry book into curl-papers. Her instructor was Harriet Beecher, exactly Sara's age, but decidedly serious. Since both pupil and teacher were to become literary figures, the curl-paper incident is worth recalling. On leaving Miss Beecher's, Sara Willis promptly married. Nothing but necessity, twenty years later, forced her to take pen in hand.

Sara's husband, a bank cashier named Eldredge, died suddenly, leaving his widow and two little girls without income. Dependence on her father-in-law proved unpleasant, so Mrs. Eldredge married again, evidently unwisely. Soon she had separated from her new husband, who departed for Chicago. From that safe distance he began divorce proceedings. Our Sara now found herself in a serious predicament. Etiquette demanded that she should seek reconciliation with her husband, or return to the father of her first husband. Otherwise she must expect social ostracism. Instead, this untrained, double-widow of 40 struck out for independence.

Under the name "Fanny Fern" she penned her first sketch. After many rebuffs she sold it to a Boston editor for exactly fifty cents. But the despised little piece pleased its readers, and more were ordered at slightly better rates. Then an enterprising publisher bound together the first *Fern Leaves,* which sold to the astonishing number of 70,000. A juvenile version followed, and a "second series," with a total sales of nearly 200,000. Next came two novels, now forgotten, but popular enough in their day to be translated into French and German.

Fanny Fern, best-seller, married for the third time in 1856. This husband, James Parton, was ten years her junior, and the country's most popular biographer. The two Partons then became staff writers for Bonner's famous *Ledger* in New York. But Boston had its parting shot. When "Fanny" quit her magazine there someone in that office published a good-sized volume attacking her, anonymously. Aspersions were cast on everything connected with her, from morals to punctuation. The nameless gentleman-author also complained that some of the lady's humor was not strictly ladylike.

But New York accepted the Partons promptly as "writers whose province borders on Bohemia." "Can any good come out of Fifth Avenue?" Fanny demanded in one of her columns. This attitude was far more suspect in 1850 than it would be today. It was in especial contrast to the aristocratic tone of Fanny's brother, "N. P."

Fanny Fern made herself the first salaried columnist of American journalism. For fourteen long years she produced her weekly piece for the *Ledger,* never missing an issue. For that record let Sara Willis be acclaimed as no mean practitioner of her craft.

She died in 1872. The next year, James Parton published a memorial volume in her honor. Then, in 1876, the widower married Ethel Eldredge, Fanny's daughter by her first marriage. Again there were upraised eyebrows in the best Boston circles. After all, those Partons had never really belonged!

THE WOMAN WHO WROTE UNCLE TOM

In the year 1823, a twelve-year-old girl of Litchfield, Connecticut, composed an essay—"Can the Immortality of the Soul be Proved by the Light of Reason?"—and offered her creation in a competition at the academy there. It took the prize and also impressed the author's father. That was no small feat, since the girl named Harriet was one of the numerous children in the Beecher parsonage. This was the first literary venture of the person who three decades later produced what Lord Macauley called "the most valuable addition that America has made to English literature." He gave that rating to *Uncle Tom's Cabin,* although he didn't like the book, which he found powerful and disagreeable, "too dark and Spagnoletto for my taste" (Chapter Note 1).

The literary merits of Harriet Beecher Stowe will not be considered here. But Harriet herself, girl and woman, is a marvelous example of genius in adversity.

Adversity began with the death of Harriet's mother of "galloping consumption," following the birth of a ninth child. Harriet had been the seventh. Undeterred by this misfortune, or income limitations, the Reverend Lyman Beecher was soon married to another fervent and saintly woman, and recording further additions to the family flock.

The highlight of Harriet's youth was the finding of a copy of *The Arabian Nights* at the bottom of a barrel of sermons. At twelve she was struggling with the immortality of the soul. At fourteen she was duly "converted" according to the rites of Calvinism with a violence that nearly threw her off-balance mentally. Three years later she was an assistant teacher in Catharine's school, "carrying two young ladies through Virgil." That phrase of Harriet's was to prove symbolic, for until middle age this Harriet was always carrying somebody or something—husband, children, household finances.

Next came the call for the Reverend Lyman to head the Lane Theological Seminary in Cincinnati, a splendid visionary establishment that was always short of funds. Harriet was soon suffering the inconvenience of Cincinnati housing and the prevalence of hogs. The youngest Beechers made pets of those running the roads. Depressed and harassed, Harriet wrote a short story for the *Western Monthly,* which won a prize of fifty dollars. That suggested to her a way out of the poverty that was to dog her steps for twenty more years to come.

At the age of 25, Harriet married Professor Calvin Stowe, one of the minutely paid intellectuals of the theological school. Stowe, a widower, was many years older than she, and was already oppressed by mental difficulties akin to hallucinations. Certainly no one could ever picture him as a good provider.

Why, then did Harriet marry him? Was he, for her, a lost cause, a man who needed taking care of, an emotional outlet for a highly emotional woman? Or, at 25, did she prefer to be almost any man's wife, rather than face a prolonged spinsterhood of teaching? No ready answer can be given, but story-book romance played little part. A half hour before the wedding Harriet was writing a letter to her best friend, back in Connecticut, that said, "I feel nothing at all." Three months later the bride described herself and husband to the same friend as sitting opposite each other at table "like domestic tame fowls."

The first consequence of this "marriage into poverty, without a dowry" was the birth of twins. They were girls. Professor Stowe named one after his departed spouse, and the other for his present one. When another child was born in 1838 Harriet was gladly writing at two dollars a page whenever she had a chance. "I am but a mere drudge," the exile told Connecticut. By 1840 there were four children, admittedly "delicate, nervous and excitable." The arrival of a fifth child in 1843 brought protracted illness to the mother, and more than usual financial stringency, for Lane Seminary was cutting the already scanty salaries of its faculty.

"I am sick of the smell of sour milk, sour meat, sour everything," the mother confided to her absent schoolmate. Alarmed by the situation, old friends in the East raised the money to send her to the "water-cure" at Brattleboro, Vermont, and to keep her there for nine months recuperating.

Harriet's sixth child, Charles, was born in 1848. It is sober fact —much meaner than fiction—that following the arrival of the sixth little Stowe, the Professor broke down and was forced to retire to Brattleboro to recover. Harriet remained in Cincinnati with the six children, taking boarders, writing, doing anything she could to keep the wolf from the door. This was the cholera year—1849. To top all other anxieties, baby Charles died of it.

At this dark moment Professor Stowe was called to his own college, Bowdoin, in Maine. The salary was only 1,000 dollars. But, unlike Cincinnati, it would be paid, and house rent in Brunswick would be less than 100 dollars a year. Professor Stowe with the older children remained to close out in Cincinnati, while Harriet with the younger ones, made the long journey to Maine. She rested one week in Brooklyn, visiting her famous preacher-brother, Henry, and another week in Hartford, with old friends. Then on to Brunswick, where she revarnished furniture and painted rooms till interrupted by the birth of her seventh child. "I was glad of an excuse to lie in bed," she confessed to her former schoolmate, "for I was full tired."

The year 1851 was the best the Stowe family had ever known. Their total income was 1,700 dollars, of which Harriet had earned nearly half. But, oh marvel, their expenditures were only 1,300 dollars, leaving a margin of 400 dollars, something the household had never known before. Now the wife, mother and authoress, deeply stirred over the recent Fugitive Slave Law, permitted herself a labor of love, the writing of a serial for a poor abolition journal. It is part of the New Brunswick story that Harriet saw the death of Uncle Tom in a vision, while sitting in a pew of the old First Congregational Church. Vision or no, Harriet's serial was the world-shattering *Uncle Tom's Cabin,* for which she was paid 300 dollars. Quickly republished in book form, it brought fame and fortune almost overnight. Harriet's share of royalties for the first three months was 10,000 dollars. In her later prosperity Mrs. Stowe seems to have washed her early struggles right out of her mind.

From solid novels like *The Minister's Wooing* which popularized the use of a realistic background in American fiction, she dropped to fictionalized essays for the *Christian Union.* In these, she proclaimed the ideal of protected womanhood in a social order in which women—frail, gentle creatures—were shielded from the rough things of life. She who had once been sick of the smell of sour milk and sour everything, now extolled the bliss of love in a cottage and the blessings of poverty.

132

One more significant fact remains. Throughout all Harriet's long struggle she was never without some kind of hired assistance in her home. No matter how pinched for money she was, there were always women glad to work in the Stowe household. What these women were paid, or how paid, we do not know, but from old letters and journals, we can find the names of those domestic lifesavers. Harriet may have been obliged to write and sell a story to purchase her first featherbed (that is a matter of record), but on the arrival of the twins there were Mina and "the nurse" ready to help. Another document shows the mother of three sitting in her kitchen, alternately penning the next installment of a love-and-moonlight romance, and training a new cook to make baked beans and brown bread, still typical New England fare.

Later, in even greater poverty and sickness, she had a governess. While Professor Stowe was at the water cure, a helper named Anna Smith took the children off Harriet's hands, so that she might go on with that necessary potboiling. There was also a colored cook named Eliza Buck, and a faithful old laundress called Aunt Frankie. "If you want to see a black face look handsome," said one of Harriet's letters, "picture me with four children sick in the nursery, and no one downstairs to do a turn of housework, and then behold Aunt Frankie waddle into the yard." Though the Stowes were poor, there were always women worse off than Harriet. Exceptional talent could thrust aside restrictions, but dependant females were glad to work for a pittance—and a home.

Of course Harriet kept on writing. Royalties paid for two extensive trips to Europe and a house in Andover, Massachusetts, where the professor taught at the theological seminary. Besides a house in Hartford for Professor Stowe's retirement, there was a winter home, Mandarin, on the St. John's River in Florida. There, according to local report, visiting tourists were offered—for a fee— the spectacle of the famous authoress driving her pen quite unconscious of spectators.

It was this period of affluence that produced the two sensational episodes of the novelist's later years. In September, 1869, she published in the *Atlantic Monthly* an article "vindicating" Lady Byron's separation from her famous poet-husband in 1818. Now Mrs. Stowe flatly stated that the cause of Lady Byron's return to her father's roof was the poet's incest with an anonymous, "very near blood relation," easily identifiable as Byron's half-sister.

Mrs. Stowe revealed that on her second trip to England in 1856, Lady Byron had entrusted her with suppressed facts, she and Lady Byron having become friends in the antislavery cause. Lady Byron had died in 1860; the half-sister also was dead, and the poet had been in his grave nearly 50 years when the American author decided to tell all. Her exercise of the crusading spirit created a tremendous furore in foreign literary circles. Byron's admirers loosed pens in his defense; Harriet came back with her longer and stronger *Lady Byron Vindicated* (1870). To this day, the truth of these accusations has never been fully established.

Repercussions of the Byron affair were chiefly transatlantic. A few years later, however, an American audience, large and vocal, learned that the two notable Beecher sisters were policing the doors of Plymouth Church on Brooklyn Heights. This time Harriet was for the defense. Victoria Woodhull, famous militant suffragist of the post-Civil War decade, was making charges of personal misconduct against Henry Ward Beecher. Rumor had it that she would invade Plymouth Church to confront the preacher in his pulpit.

So Sunday after Sunday Catharine and Harriet stood watchfully by. Miss Woodhull never appeared though her continued charges resulted in the notorious Beecher Church trial. This, in the Centennial year 1876, and the jailing of Victoria Woodhull, were post-Civil War spectacles, well beyond the time limit of these pages.

Professor Stowe died in 1886. Harriet's sturdy frame went on functioning for another ten years, but her mind became much clouded. God, she used to tell visitors, had written *Uncle Tom's Cabin.*

AND NOW A WOMAN SURGEON

The first American woman surgeon was Clemence Harned Lozier of New York (1813–1888). Born during the War of 1812, it took her 40 years to achieve her medical degree, in 1853. Perhaps this long postponement was what made a surgeon of her, for after 1850 New York hospitals were using chloroform and ether. It is difficult to visualize a woman operating in the ghastly years before the introduction of anesthetics. (That began in Boston, 1848.)

Clemence Lozier was no hedgerow practitioner, but a competent professional, undertaking major operations "that would appal the lay mind," says an old memoir. She became Professor of Gynecology, Dean and founder of the New York Medical College and Hospital for Women (1863). She was able to keep the infant institution going for its first seven years out of the proceeds of her own practice. For 1864 her professional income was 25,000 dollars, a sum worth noting today, and breath taking for a woman of the hoop-skirt epoch.

Dr. Lozier's first surgical venture was on the family dog which had been run over and its legs broken. Usually a dog in such plight would be shot. But it was her children's pet, so she set to work with home-made skill and home-made splints. The operation was successful and the patient was soon running around again. This, in her pre-diploma period, served to set her mind all the more firmly on the goal of becoming a licensed surgeon herself. Incidentally, though a gentle, friendly woman all her life long, the one thing that could move her to instant wrath was cruelty to animals.

Her story stems from the early American scene, when outside of seacoast cities, scarcity of trained physicians was an accepted state of affairs. If a household was to survive, someone had to be a fairly skilled first-aid practitioner. Thus many women were actually engaged in healing long before any schools were open to them. Clemence Lozier's Quaker mother was such. She had come up in those western counties of Virginia that eventually became Kentucky, accepted peacefully as a medicine woman by hostile Indians. Later the family moved North, and this last daughter was born in Plainfield, New Jersey, the youngest of thirteen children.

Her name was always spelled Clemence, but in the family it was pronounced Clemency, just as girls were named Charity or Patience. The mother's medical bent reappeared in two older brothers, who were soon studying to be doctors. To them, the mother wrote that their little sister was a child of unusual mind, worthy of the best education. But the mother died when her youngest was only eleven, and the oldest doctor-brother was down in New Orleans working in a yellow fever outbreak. Clemence was placed in Plainfield Academy, but took matters in her own hands by marrying at sixteen.

Her husband, Abraham W. Lozier, was much older than herself, and their home was at 22 West Tenth Street, New York City. In obituary accounts of this notable woman surgeon her long-dead husband is carefully designated as an architect, though the old city directories of the '30's list him as a carpenter. Still, at that time, a carpenter might be called upon to build anything from a fence to the county courthouse. Obviously this Lozier built select houses for select people.

There, in Tenth Street, the young wife had at least five children, though only one son lived to grow up. He, too, became a well known physician. Of those lost children, two died in accidents, unspecified, and two died, so the mother believed, from the drastic drugging that then prevailed in "old school" medicine.

By 1837 Clemency was a young widow with children to bring up, and some property in city real estate. She had always wanted to be a doctor like her mother and brothers. But since no medical school at that date would take a woman, she turned her house into a "select" school. Old city directories list her as a teacher from 1833 on, evidence that her school was functioning during her husband's prolonged illness. It was later that she startled conservatives by introducing physiology, anatomy and hygiene as suitable subjects for young ladies.

Not till she was past 35 could Clemency find a medical school that would accept her. In 1849 she was permitted to attend lectures at the Rochester Eclectic Medical School. Four years later she had won a degree from the Syracuse Medical College. Then she returned to Tenth Street to hang out her shingle and become the republic's first woman surgeon.

The doctor was a handsome woman, with large dark eyes, a straight, finely cut nose and dark hair that curled thickly. Though small, she was described later by another doctor as "the most ceaseless, tireless, sleepless worker I have ever seen." She was trained in the "new school of homeopathy," but she held no exclusive brief for it. She took ideas and methods where she found them. Soon her practice was lucrative as well as busy.

Elements both general and personal explain Dr. Lozier's swift rise to local eminence without the gruelling struggle faced by other women doctors. The period of her venture saw the introduction of anesthetics and surgery in obstetrical work, Queen Victoria having given chloroform the royal sanction for the birth of her seventh child in 1853. In New York many of Clemence's former young lady pupils were now married and in need of her medical techniques. Beyond question the professional blessing of her older brothers also worked strongly in her favor.

No controversy whatsoever centered around Dr. Lozier till the Civil War years, when she was founding her hospital-school with its medical staff of "four gentlemen and four ladies." Legally, the lady students had a right to attend the Bellevue hospital clinics. But their presence there was assailed so raucously by both professors and men students, that finally police protection had to be invoked for the young ladies. It hardly needs adding that by that time Dr. Lozier had become an ardent suffragist.

With the end of the war Dr. Lozier resigned her professorship, and left her thriving practice to study in Europe. She came back to refurbish the equipment and curriculum of the women's hospital school, and to continue in active practice till within a few years of her death of a heart attack, June 1888. A few days before, she had delivered the chief address at the 25th commencement of the Medical College for Women (Chapter Note 2).

A curious postscript to this successfully adventurous professional career is the fact that, somewhere along the years, Dr. Lozier made an unsuccessful second marriage that was terminated by a divorce. The whole affair was treated with such strict Victorian reticence that 100 years later names, dates and details are unobtainable. There is written evidence of Elizabeth Cady Stanton's, describing Mrs. Lozier's consulting with her on the law and ethics of divorcing this second husband. The date of the meeting is not given.

If this episode belonged to Dr. Lozier's later career, the presence of a second husband in the house would hardly have passed unnoticed. But in premedical years there is a possible time gap. The latest date found for Mrs. Lozier's "select school" was 1844. Five years after that she was studying first at Rochester, then at Syracuse, locations not far removed from Mrs. Stanton's home in Seneca Falls.

A remarriage then, ending in a divorce and the reclaiming of her own name, would have sent Clemence Lozier back to Manhattan with no public mention of her personal misfortune. That is hypothetical. But somewhere, behind a curtain of silence, a second husband was sunk without trace. This also puts Clemence Lozier on the list of early divorcées, along with Emma Willard and Fanny Fern.

HORACE GREELEY'S "SISTER JANE"

A salute in passing now goes to Jane Swisshelm who was, very briefly, a Washington correspondent of the famous *Tribune,* making her the first American woman to attain a reporter's desk at the Capitol.

Jane Swisshelm also embodies the western trend of reform. She was completely apart from the intellectual circles of New England, having been born in Pittsburgh, Pennsylvania, when that new community could claim only 6,000 inhabitants. Of middle-class Scotch-Irish stock, the family name was Cannon. When Jane's father died (she was only seven), her mother took over the breadwinning, keeping shop, plaiting innumerable fine straw bonnets. A year later the small girl with clever fingers was being paid to give lessons in lace making to grownup women. She was teaching school at fourteen, a tiny bit of a creature who never passed five feet.

Chance played its part in shaping her career. At twenty-one, she married herself into a sectarian feud, for the Swisshelms were frontier Methodists, while the Cannons had always been strict Calvinists. Both mothers-in-law held firmly to their tenets. To escape embroilment the young couple departed for Louisville, Kentucky, where the bridegroom could enter a relative's lumber business. Jane's deft fingers added to the income, for she became a corsetmaker, one of the early "cottage trades" open to women.

The failure of the lumber business and the illness of Mrs. Cannon brought Jane and her handsome husband back north to a renewal of family dissensions, with neither side yielding a doctrinal inch. Soon the young Swisshelms had only one interest in common. Their sojourn in Louisville had made blazing abolitionists of them both. Jane, who had been turning an honest penny by providing stories for the Philadelphia newspapers, now felt a call to write for a small antislavery magazine published in Pittsburgh. In 1847, with a legacy from her mother as capital, she started her own abolitionist journal. She called it *The Saturday Visiter* (spelled with an "e"), and took for its motto the command to Moses at the Red Sea, "Speak unto the children of Israel that they go forward."

To go forward in print 100 years ago could be a shoestring venture. A Pittsburgh newspaper did the *Visiter's* weekly printing, and supplied its editor with a spot of office space. Libel suits held no terror for a reformer whose enterprise owned nothing against which a legal judgment could be executed. The more common threat of horse-whipping an offending editor was scarcely applicable to a lady. So Jane's editorial zeal was guided chiefly by conscience. Soon *The Saturday Visiter's* vigorous propaganda caught the eye of Horace Greeley, who began calling her Sister Jane, and quoting her sharp paragraphs in his *Tribune*. Not long afterwards, he offered to pay her 5 dollars a column for signed correspondence from Washington.

Jane's first despatch from the Capitol was dated April 12, 1850. Then came beginner's luck. In the course of a heated debate on the Fugitive Slave Law Senator Foote drew a gun on the notable Thomas Hart Benton of Missouri, and Mr. Greeley's lady reporter was right there with her pencil. On the days following, the visitors' gallery of the Senate became overcrowded. Unable to push her way in, Sister Jane applied to President Fillmore for a desk on the Senate floor along with the gentlemen of the press. Fillmore (husband of the up-and-coming Abigail who put books and plumbing into the White House) granted this radical request. It should also be recorded that the gentlemen of the press behaved like gentlemen, receiving Jane politely as belonging to the trade. Someone even surrendered his desk for her use.

But her triumph was brief. Shortly afterwards she sent along a snappy story, totally unverified, accusing the great Daniel Webster of rearing a family of eight mulattoes. Horace Greeley and Sister Jane quickly parted company. "A serious illness," so the *Tribune* announced, required the return of the lady reporter to her own home.

There, unfortunately, the *Saturday Visiter* was heading for the rocks. So also was the Swisshelm ménage. Since her husband refused to accept a legal separation, Jane resolved to go West, taking their one child with her, to join a married sister. In a later chapter, the reader will meet Jane Swisshelm there, a pioneer editor in pioneer Minnesota.

"TEMPERANCE" AND THE BLOOMER

Contrary to popular opinion, total abstinence and not dress reform was the primary activity of Amelia Jenks Bloomer. Thanks to the garment trade and a recent costume comedy, her name is much better known today than that of more original women of her era. She invented neither the temperance movement, nor the garb which so plentifully recalls her name.

But she was a keen advocate of total abstinence, and as editor of *The Lily* she gave first journalistic recognition to the reform garment. Actually, she had never even seen the costume when, in 1851, she began commending it in her columns. But it was her picture, clad in modest near-Turkish trousers, which a little later caught the public eye. It was her name, with its undeniably humorous sound, that became the word-of-the-hour.

The Bloomer was the furore of the '50's. Even the very first issue of *The New York Times,* September 18, 1851, gave front page mention to it. "A Bloomer Costume" had appeared in Sixth Avenue, where "a crowd of 'conservatives' manifested their hostility to this progressive movement by derision." The day before "two Bloomers" had appeared on Broadway, and two in Washington Square.

Years before all this outcry Amelia had taken over *The Lily,* started as a mouthpiece for the Seneca Falls Ladies Temperance Society. She was then 30 years old, and had already served an apprenticeship helping her husband, Dexter Bloomer, part owner of a newspaper in Seneca County, New York. If Amelia cannot be praised for inventing the bloomer, she should not be blamed for the name of her magazine. That had already been affixed. Amelia merely assumed responsibility, dedicating *The Lily* to "The Emancipation of Woman from Intemperance, Injustice, Prejudice and Bigotry."

To see the editor as she was, with her virtues and her limitations, one must also see that early temperance movement as part of a world now a hundred years gone. The plain fact was that the new republic was a hard-drinking concern. Rum from the West Indies was cheap and plentiful, and usually handled by country storekeepers over the counter, just like cheese or sugar. Whiskey was still cheaper, often homemade, with a daily dram part of the worker's wages. What the laboring man, and sometimes his wife, consumed was hard raw stuff. Wine, imported, was the luxury of the wealthy. Commercial beer making had yet to be brought to this country.

The abuses of the bottle were flagrant, and its hazards were aggravated by prevailing laws under which a sober workman could not obtain damages for injury resulting from an alcoholic fellow employee. Nor could a married woman, working, legally withhold her wages from a drinking husband. To the early crusading reformers there was no middle-of-the-road. For them, "temperance" must mean total abstinence.

Such a zealot was Amelia Bloomer, born Jenks, in a small Cortland County, New York, town (1818) into a home background of strict Presbyterianism and hard work. She had a few terms in her local district school, and at seventeen began as a country schoolmarm. Later, a small slight body with blue eyes and red hair, she went as a governess to Waterloo in Seneca County. There she met a young Quaker law student who worked for the (Whig) Seneca County *Courier*. In their day, these two were an advanced couple, for whom the clergyman omitted the word "obey" from the wedding ceremony—April, 1840.

Already the bride was a convinced teetotaller. She refused even a glass of wine at the wedding reception which her husband's publishing partner gave for them at Seneca Falls. Soon Amelia was helping write the newspaper, which was campaigning hotly for Harrison in the famous log-cabin election. Just how she reconciled herself to the hard cider that went along with the log cabin, history does not explain. Soon also, Mrs. Bloomer was a vice-president of the Seneca Falls Ladies Temperance Society, and editor of its *Lily*.

Suddenly Seneca Falls, till then just a thriving milltown, put itself on the map as the reform capital of the United States by that startling summons to the first Woman's Rights Convention of 1848. Amelia Bloomer attended that gathering but did not sign her name to the famous Declaration of Women's Rights. It was several years before Amelia was willing to align herself with the advance guard.

The Lily meanwhile divided its pages between very moral literature and "temperance." The lady-editor's news instinct listed in
her columns all the horrible deaths attributable to alcohol, culled
from other columns—suicides, murders, bloody accidents. She also
lashed out against local hostesses who "deliberately fill the intoxi-
cating cup" for New Year's callers. Later she included in her de-
nunciations ladies "who stood greatly in the way of temperance reform" by using alcoholic "poison" to flavor mince pies. For a reform
journal, this made lively reading, though it drew the only criticism
of Mrs. Bloomer that ever came from her admiring husband. She
had a tendency, he agreed, to notice "the mistakes and failings of
others, perhaps, too freely."

But *The Lily* prospered, and so did the Bloomer family. The
newspaper-husband was rewarded for his political services with the
postmastership of Seneca Falls. Since the Bloomers had no children,
he appointed Amelia as his deputy. She, in turn, arranged her room
off the post office as an informal club-room for the ladies of Seneca
Falls, something certainly new in the annals of western New York.

To this receptive audience, then, came the bloomer. In spite of
its speedy notoriety, no one really knows who invented the garment.
It seems first to have been used in 1848, as a work uniform by the
very advanced women of the famous Oneida community. (See Chapter VI) It was probably designed by the early philosopher, William
Gerrit Smith, or by his married daughter, Elizabeth Smith Miller,
who brought the trousers with her on a visit to the Stantons at Seneca
Falls. She was (this much is known) the first woman to wear the
"Turkish costume" in public. "She walked our street" said *The Lily*
"in a skirt that came a little below the knee, and trousers of the same
material—black satin."

The editor saw and was conquered. She "donned the new costume" and announced that fact to her readers. Within a year Amelia
was "the Bloomer." The publicity spread even to Europe. The Duke
of Wellington in his 82nd year wrote to Lady Salisbury (1850), "I
am vastly amused by the Bloomer discussion . . . it is impossible
that the Costume should be adopted."

Meanwhile the modest subscription list of *The Lily* climbed into the thousands. Amelia became a personage. Clad in the near-trousers, she had her daguerreotype taken along with Elizabeth Cady Stanton, and printed the engraving in her magazine. Then, in 1851, Mrs. Bloomer "came out for suffrage." The year following saw her a platform speaker for "temperance," advocating a woman's right to divorce a drunken husband.

But by 1853 the hoots and howlings of the mob had driven the radicals back to their petticoats, while Mr. and Mrs. Bloomer were leaving for the uncontaminated West. Pausing briefly in Ohio where Amelia sold her journal, the enterprising pair crossed the Mississippi, to settle in Council Bluffs, Iowa, where we shall rejoin them (Chapter VI). The transplanted family prospered mightily, but except for house cleaning, Amelia discarded her famous costume. It was, she explained with dubious logic, unsuitable for the high winds of Iowa. Besides, hoop-skirts had now become fashionable.

ELIZABETH CADY STANTON, 1816–1902

The story of Elizabeth Cady Stanton, who along with Lucretia Mott first called for "women's rights" at Seneca Falls, is laid among "the aristocracy." Margaret Fuller exemplified a Massachusetts variety, the Grimké's, that of South Carolina. Elizabeth Cady (born in 1816, and later Mrs. Stanton) belonged to a leading family of central New York. Her father was a lawyer and, in her youth, a judge. The pressures that made her a thoroughgoing feminist were personal, never economic.

The household had five daughters and one son, a happy family, devoted to an affectionate father. Then the blow fell, in the death of that only son, a brilliant student at Union College. Little Elizabeth, ten years old, torn by her father's grief, set herself to be a son to him, in her dead brother's place. A son, she knew, must ride horses and study Greek. The first step was easy for the Judge's stables were full of horses. For Greek she applied to their aging clergyman, a Presbyterian who had been schooled at a Scots university. He found his young pupil an apt student and a deep affection grew between them. On his death the old minister willed his Greek library to Elizabeth. No matter how radical her course in later years, she always maintained a membership in the church of her childhood. "But I was never happy," she afterwards confessed, "in that gloomy faith which dooms to eternal misery the greater part of the human family."

Alas, though, for young Elizabeth's plan of sonship. When the clergyman praised her Greek, Judge Cady merely responded, "She should have been a boy." When she won the Greek prize at Johnstown Academy, he said it again. It was added bitterness that though she kept ahead of the boys at the Academy, she could not go, like them, to Union College. She must be relegated to Mrs. Willard's Female Seminary. It was not a happy compromise. Years later she declared, "If there is one thing on earth from which I pray God to save my daughters, it is a girl's seminary."

The two years at Mrs. Willard's must have been an endurance test for both pupil and faculty, for Elizabeth deliberately set about breaking the rules. She did, however, reach graduation. Her journal records that, for this ceremony, she had a new muslin gown, a plaid of purple, white, blue and brown, with white linen undersleeves and collarette, and blue prunella gaiters. Her hair, done in four braids, was wound around a big shell comb. All of which sounds properly young ladylike.

The final urge to feminism was again administered by Elizabeth's father. Although he would never admit her to any equality with the son he had lost, when she returned home he could not bear to see her busied genteely at water-coloring or embroidery. He would stop her, present her with a heavy tome of law, and bid her read it, so as to have "something sensible to say" to the various legal luminaries who dined with Judge Cady. Thus Elizabeth began a home-study law course which was to stand her in good stead during her long years as an agitator.

She was 24 when she married Henry Stanton, already marked as an antislavery orator. The young couple started off on a true reformers' honeymoon. Their destination was the World's Anti-Slavery Convention of 1840, which was to be held in London. Thither also went Lucretia Mott, accredited delegate from the Female Antislavery Society of Philadelphia, and five other women representing their own organizations.

The lady delegates were received with all polite attention by their British hosts, and tactfully given the chief seats, but they were not permitted to vote. Smarting under this injustice, young Elizabeth Stanton and the older Lucretia Mott walked the British Museum together. They resolved to call a woman's convention as soon as they returned to the United States, a purpose, however, which could not be carried out for eight years longer. Returned home, when someone asked the bride what she had seen abroad that impressed her most, she answered "Lucretia Mott."

In the Stanton home the eight years after London represented the birth of three children. When, in 1848, the women's call was issued from Seneca Falls, its platform followed the form of the American Declaration of Independence. Elizabeth Stanton had the full backing of her husband, and James Mott, Lucretia's husband, presided at that first "women's rights" convention in the Wesleyan chapel. Their declaration was printed, reprinted, and widely circulated, for by 1848 railroads were facilitating a brisk exchange of newspapers. To editors of the period the women's charter was good comedy. Throughout the country, the general reaction was gigantic laughter, such as is apt to greet those who see too far ahead.

The laughter, though, had little effect on Elizabeth and Lucretia. They both survived it, to continue campaigning actively for more than three decades. Each passing year had its women's rights convention called in different cities, east and west. Even Judge Cady lived to be proud of the daughter whose feet he had unwittingly set on the path of protest. But he never really approved of her.

In 1856 Mrs. Stanton came upon the manuscript of her first public address, written for that first Convention, eighteen years previous. She put it aside for her own daughters, with this inscription:

"Dear Maggie and Hattie, this is my first speech. It was delivered several times after the first Woman's Rights Convention. It contains all I knew at that time. I did not speak again for several years. As I recall my younger days, I weep over the apathy and indifference of women concerning their own degradation. I give this manuscript to my precious daughters, in the hope that they will finish the work which I have begun."

The Hattie of this note became the Harriet Stanton Blatch of the early 20th Century. As a handsome, dark-eyed, white-haired woman, she lived to see "votes for women" become a fact.

SUSAN B. ANTHONY, WHO VOTED

The chosen companion of Mrs Stanton's militant career was Susan B. Anthony, born in 1820. Unlike most of the early suffragist leaders, she was a spinster, apparently by choice. Old records present her as an attractive young woman, with several beaux in the offing. Her slant to feminism was on strictly economic grounds. Educated in the Friends School of Philadelphia, the best of its day, she was paid eight dollars a month as a schoolteacher, while men in the same work received from 24 to 30 dollars a month. After fifteen years of thrift and hard labor she had been able to save exactly 300 dollars. That converted her to "women's rights" although she was not active in the cause till several years later.

This experience of Miss Anthony's did not derive from poverty but from a family of advanced social ideas. Her father, Daniel Anthony, ran a small "model" factory near Rochester, New York. There his workers had cottages with gardens, chicken yards, cow and pig pens, all designed to stabilize by husbandry their fluctuating pay as factory hands. The workers' wives were provided with spinning wheels and quilting frames. In their spare time, after making their men's clothing, they were also supposed to can vegetables and fruit, cure meat and dip candles.

Daniel gave his daughter Susan the best schooling available, and then as a matter of principle put her to earning her own living. It was a legacy from him that later enabled the daughter to make a profession of her cause.

Susan's entrance into public life was as a delegate to the (New York) Men's State Temperance Convention in the summer of 1849. There the gentlemen reformers were of the same mind as their anti-slavery brethren overseas. Women were not accepted as delegates. Elizabeth Stanton had met Lucretia Mott in London. So now Susan Anthony met Mrs. Stanton at Syracuse. The result was a life-long partnership in suffrage. Before political conventions, before state legislatures, before any gathering affecting the legal status of women, these two leaders of a forlorn hope appeared persistently with their resolutions. Usually they won only more laughter.

After the Civil War, Miss Anthony turned militant. In 1872,

she gathered together fourteen women to vote under Amendments XV and XVI, recently added to the Constitution. Such a clamor was raised by the Rochester newspapers that only one election official would receive the ballots. Miss Anthony voted, and was arrested for it, her attorney standing by with bail ready. At the trial the judge ordered a verdict of guilty on the evidence. She had voted and was proud of it. But the jury refused to convict, thus exercising that same jury right which had saved the skin of William Penn two hundred years before. However, any further attempt at voting by women was abandoned for that generation.

But, until 1890, each year Susan Anthony brought her suffrage amendment to the New York state legislature. Each year all the respectable legislators refused to present it, leaving the unwelcome task to Timothy Sullivan from the Bowery. A young reporter from the *Brooklyn Eagle* asked him why he thus offered himself up to annual ridicule. The Tammany leader answered simply, "Why, I respected those ladies." The same reporter recalled Miss Anthony at Albany, always handsomely dressed, dispensing home-baked gingerbread to her friends of the press. She was, however, he lamented, "entirely lacking in any sense of humor." Thirty years of uphill campaigning might do that to a woman.

NOW COMES LUCY STONE

Lucy Stone, who was Mrs. Henry Blackwell, but preferred to use her own name, was the last of these early feminists. That name-of-her-own has kept her memory fresh to the present, when thousands of women follow her example and think nothing of it.

Lucy was born in 1825, on that harsh farm in West Brookfield, Massachusetts, where her mother milked the cows the night before Lucy's arrival and regretted giving birth to another daughter, because a woman's lot was so hard. But poverty or no, this daughter worked her way to college and through it, the first of these early careerists to win that coveted college degree.

To do it Lucy had to go west to the Female Department of Oberlin, opened in 1837, for "the elevation of female character," and for the benefit of "a misguided and neglected sex." In that first year four piously daring young ladies had answered the challenge, consenting to live chiefly on bread and soup while preparing themselves to be the wives of clergymen (Chapter Note 3).

It was at this primitive fanatical Oberlin of the '40's that Lucy Stone discovered her great gift. She could speak in public, extemporaneously and movingly. With her hard-won diploma she returned to New England to become a paid lecturer for the Anti-slavery Society. She toured all the larger towns of the West, and even ventured into southern territory. Undoubtedly she was a better speaker than those first abolitionist women who had faced mobs. Besides, for more than a decade the public had become accustomed to women on a platform.

Even the newspapers had praise for young Lucy Stone, in spite of her short-cut hair and her bloomer-costume. The Cleveland *Plain Dealer* of October 1853 called her "a lady of no common abilities . . . She is as independent in mind as in dress . . . Without endorsing the elimination of petticoats, we cannot but admire Miss Stone's total independence of the god Fashion. Her dress is first a black velvet coat with collar, fastened in front with buttons, next a skirt of silk, reaching to the knees, then 'she wears the breeches' of black silk with neat fitting gaiters. Her hair is cut short and combed straight back. Her face is not beautiful, but there is mind in it; it is earnest, pleasant, prepossessing."

In 1855 Lucy Stone was married by a special ceremony in which the bridegroom renounced all the rights of authority and ownership which were his by law. The bride was to retain her own name. The pastor conducting this unconventional service was Thomas Wentworth Higginson of Boston, the noted Unitarian. Lucy's chosen mate, Henry Blackwell, was a feminist sympathizer, and a brother of Dr. Emily Blackwell, (the early English-born physician). After this fanfare of advanced thought, Lucy Stone retired to a happy private life, contenting herself with presiding over later "women's rights" conventions. After 1870 she became editor of *The Woman's Journal*, Boston mouthpiece of the suffrage cause.

Such then were the twenty pioneers who by the test of history were the forerunners of American women as we know them today. That, however, does not mean that their importance was widely recognized in their own time. On the contrary. For the most part their efforts were splendidly ignored in the day's best circles. They were actively opposed by many of the clergy. The noted novelist, J. Fenimore Cooper, liberally educated and an honorable gentleman, believed that the entire institution of marriage was undermined when his state (a little prior to 1850) passed a married women's property act.

This nonrecognition of the prophetess is also revealed by an *American Dictionary of Biography* dated 1857, and published in Boston. By measure, 29 finely printed columns are devoted in this to notable men, and less than one column to the lives of American women. Brief reference is made to Martha Washington, Abigail Adams and Dorothea Madison. Only one woman poet is mentioned, Maria Brooks, who lived and published in England. "The refinement of her taste has been questioned," is the curt summing up of her talents. Of all the trail blazers sketched in these pages, only one is included in this biographical dictionary of 1857. That one is Margaret Fuller. Listed as "Margaret Ossoli" she is rewarded with one and a-half inches of type.

With these two strictly literary exceptions, the women whose names are preserved in this summary were selected for outstanding piety. We have Mary Lake who went out with her husband to Marietta, Ohio, in 1789, and taught the catechism there under the Rev. Daniel Storey. "Her children were all pious." Then there was Beulah Gould, a milliner of Sharon, Connecticut, who over the course of ten years earned 350 dollars, and gave it all to missions. For this "unwearied industry and eminent piety" Mrs. Gould was given a listing denied to Lucretia Mott, Lydia Maria Child and Harriet Beecher Stowe (Chapter Note 4).

That was the point of view of a contemporary annalist. Making an allowance for masculine bias, it still seems probable that these standards of value reflected majority opinion. It is also more than likely that average feminine choice, with its deep reservoir of conservatism, would have followed the line laid down by this biographical editor.

It is against this framework of antagonism and indifference that the achievements of the republic's pre-feminists must be judged. Only from the safe hindsight of a century can we see clearly how right they were.

1   A severe critic of *Uncle Tom's Cabin* was Louisa Cheves McCord of South Carolina. An account of her model plantation and her writing will be found in Chapter VI.

2   Of Dr. Lozier's successful career, only one published work over her pen remains. That is a pamphlet, *Childbirth Made Easy,* written in 1870 as part of a project in what we now call adult education. Using non-technical language, Dr. Lozier urged the importance of fruits and vegetables in the diet of the expectant mother, stressing oranges, lemons and fresh salads. Two hours of mild exercise daily in the open air were also prescribed, together with a curious warning against nondistilled drinking water. This was not based on possible contamination of water sources, but on the chemical content of nondistilled water.

The booklet makes no mention of the use of anesthetics in delivery. Perhaps that was not thought sufficiently "lay" for the pamphlet. But public opinion had come a long way since Dr. Blackwell, an English-woman, had been forbidden to practice either pediatrics or gynecology in New York City in the early '50's.

3   The Female wing of Oberlin was opened in 1837, intended as a separate Ladies' Department. It became coeducational because of a faculty shortage. The students were taught together but were not allowed to associate outside the classrooms, and the "young ladies" were enjoined to keep silence in public. In classes, papers written by women students were read aloud by the men. That was early Oberlin,—Abolitionist, vegetarian, poor and pious. Yet in spite of its limitations, it was at Oberlin that Lucy Stone prepared her career of public speaking.

Other early higher schools for women include: The Wesleyan Female College of Macon, Georgia, chartered in 1836, opened in 1839; the Wesleyan at Cincinnati, Ohio, started in 1843; Antioch, 1853; Elmira (N.Y.) Female College, 1855; the Mary Sharp College for Women, of Winchester, Tennessee, which in 1855 issued diplomas in Latin to three women, and the University of Iowa, 1856.

In those pioneering days, the term college did not imply a curriculum of present college standards. When Horace Mann opened the famous "liberal" Antioch in 1853, he noted that many of the women applicants could not read intelligibly. "The profundity of their ignorance . . . was shocking." Yet three women were graduated in that first class of 1857, and there was one "professoress" on the teaching staff, Mann's niece, Rebecca Pennell.

Antioch's rules stated that "young gentlemen and ladies are not allowed to take walks or rides together unless accompanied by one of the teachers." The nearby Glen could be visited by the young gentlemen on odd days, and by the young ladies on even days of the month. Sixteen trustworthy youths were selected to bring in firewood for the numerous stoves that provided heating for the "female dormitory," called North Hall. Apparently the young ladies tended their own fires. As the college had no water-system, annexed to North Hall was a large brick privy-building.

4 It is not surprising that this *Dictionary of Biography* of 1857 made no mention of Emily Dickinson, later ranked as a really great woman poet. Although by birthdate she belonged to this period, her fame rests on poems not published until several years after her death in 1886. From 1856 on Miss Dickinson had made a recluse of herself within the family home in Amherst, Massachusetts. One surmises that even had her manuscript poems been available, editors of 1857 would not have saluted her very individual work as poetry.

Readers are also reminded that the notable Julia Ward Howe belongs largely to the post-Civil War picture. The daughter of a New York banker, in 1843 she married the famous New England philanthropist, Dr. Samuel Gridley Howe, who came of a wealthy shipping family. The Howes' honeymoon was a year in Europe where Dr. Howe was studying institutions for the blind. Their first daughter was born in Rome. Back in Boston, during the '50's, Mrs. Howe was her husband's assistant in editing his magazine, *Commonwealth*. Her poetry and plays of this period were mostly anonymous and sometimes unpublished. Her lectures were given in her own drawing room. It was "The Battle Hymn of the Republic," published (1862) in the Atlantic Monthly that carried her name beyond select Boston circles. After that she was a celebrity for nearly three decades of writing and public speaking.

CHAPTER SIX

In the 'Fifties, Befo' de War

*T*HE decade of the '50's in the slightly less new republic
was made up of extraordinary contrasts. A great burst of commercial
expansion, fostered by nearly 30,000 miles of railroad and some
2,000 river boats fetching cargoes up and down the Mississippi and
the Ohio, was balanced by the rise of communal groups like New
Harmony and Brook Farm, bent on getting away from the profit
motive. The California gold rush was offset by the financial crash
of 1857.

The '50's could choose between Queens of Society and heroines
of the Underground Railway, the elegancies of Saratoga, and harsh
Mormon wagons seeking refuge in the Rockies. There was the rare-
fied aspiration of the Transcendentalists, and the savagery of Osawatomie. While thousands paid out frantic sums to hear Jenny Lind,
coolie labor was pouring into California. The public that heard
Emerson lecture also saw the passage of the Fugitive Slave law.
The chill iron wealth of northern Michigan called its thousands.
Herds of cattle from the hot plains of Texas reached Chicago on the
hoof. Over all these contradictions hung the threat of a war that no
one wanted, except perhaps small groups of fanatics on both sides.

Through such diversity of place and purpose runs the trail of

American women. Now it is more plainly marked as they emerge from decades of official silence. We shall trace them north, east and south, and, in later chapters, west to the Golden Gate and to Oregon.

The chief foreign observer of the ways of women at this point was Frederika Bremer, the Swedish author, who came with a royal commission to report on the farming ventures of her fellow country-men settling the new raw lands in Michigan, Wisconsin and Minnesota. Miss Bremer, however, reached her objective by way of a leisurely circuit from Boston to New Orleans, with eyes sharpened to observe, and pencil poised to record. Enormously interested in people, especially in women, her previous experience with all classes of European society gave a sociological slant to her notes.

Her first stop was at the old Astor House in lower Broadway, "the great high street . . . of New York where people and carriages pour in one incessant stream." Even in 1850 a visitor must concentrate "on getting across the street alive." Inside the hotel were magnificent drawing rooms with velvet furniture and gilded mirrors, all brilliant from gas-lighted chandeliers. The famed chivalry of American men was quickly visible. Scarcely could a lady rise than immediately a gentleman was at hand to offer his arm.

Society had already overflowed the city to entrench itself in great estates along the Hudson Highlands. There Miss Bremer was a guest in the household of Downing, the early American landscape architect who resided outside of Newburgh, not too far from his wealthy clients. There were frequent breakfast parties, feasts graced with fresh meats, omelets and buckwheat cakes. One of Downing's neighbors gave such a breakfast in Miss Bremer's honor for 70 guests. The festivity, "magnificent" as to menu, was closed by a dance. To Swedish eyes the lively young girls were delicate in figure and lacking in strength. The older ladies, well dressed and with small hands and feet, reminded her of the French, though their faces seemed to lack expression. "Mrs. Downing is a thorough musician," the journal added, "a rare thing in this country."

Homes of the wealthy, whether up the Hudson or across the harbor on Staten Island, had one terror for the visitor—their un-heated bedrooms. "It is here as in England, not as in our good Sweden," moaned the exile. "I can hardly accustom myself to those cold bedchambers." In Brooklyn, in November, she again confided to her diary that she was nearly frozen. She had crossed the river to inspect the "Female Academy where five hundred young women study and graduate as young men do." Shortly after Miss Bremer's visit this academy was burned down, to be rebuilt afterwards as the Packer Collegiate Institute still functioning today.

But Frederika Bremer did not confine her sight-seeing to the opulent. Up the Hudson she likewise called at the house "of the man who drives carts of stones for the making of roads." She was amazed to find it "a beautiful little house," far superior to what such a man would have in Sweden. The tables of his farming neighbors were abundantly supplied with meats, vegetables and fruits, also "cakes of Indian meal and the most beautiful white bread." But in spite of all this good living, the country women were "too spare of figure."

One limitation of Frederika Bremer as an interpreter of American women is the fact that she had no contact with farm women in the East. When she later mingled with women of the Swedish settlements in the new West, she related their hardships entirely to immigrant pioneering.

Yet in the East was Mary Anne Day Brown, shortly to be the widow of John Brown of Osawatomie. At sixteen Mary Ann had married the widower, prepared to care for the five children of his first wife. She had thirteen children of her own, born while she followed John Brown from Pennsylvania, to Ohio, to Massachusetts. She either had a child or buried one in every town in which they lived. When John Brown was ready to go to Kansas, he drove her in an oxcart to a gaunt farmhouse at North Elba in the Adirondacks. Her children picked berries to pay for the postage stamps that carried her letters to Kansas. After John Brown had been made a martyr, his widow was taken to Boston to aid the abolitionist cause. Boston ladies noted that Mrs. Brown drank her tea from the saucer (Chapter Note 1).

Also one notes that Miss Bremer did not mingle with the Literati of New York, early art patrons who added elegance to the cult of letters. One wealthy man, planning to have his wife's poems published, paid Edgar Allen Poe 100 dollars to edit them. The Literati graced the salon of Ann Lynch in Waverly Place where Poe read his Raven, and joined the quiet circle of Alice and Phoebe Cary in their little house on Twentieth Street. But Frederika Bremer was not among those present at such literary gatherings, nor did she busy herself with the "rappings" of the young Fox sisters, then on display (Chapter Notes 2 and 3).

Instead, the Swedish traveler made the rounds of New York's charities, beginning with the Emigrant Asylum where incoming settlers for the West were sheltered and fed till their cross-country trains were ready. At Bloomingdale she found occupational therapy and music used for mental ailments. She was loud in her praise of a Miss Foster who had charge of the women in the old Tombs prison, but the men's side was "deplorable." Escorted by a "Quaker lady" (the daughter of Isaac Hopper) Miss Bremer inspected a home for fallen women and went through the notorious "Five Points." "There miserable women keep so-called 'fancy men' and the offscouring of society flows thither." But even among New York's lowest she found nothing worse than she had already known in London or Paris, or even in Stockholm.

SWEDEN SEES NEW ENGLAND

From Manhattan, the visitor turned towards New England. There she was to make what was to her a surprising discovery—the home without servants. The West had already drained the older farms of their hired help. Now factories and teaching were calling the young women. To find educated people living without servants was astounding to a European. Even the highest thought of Boston blossomed against a background of plain living. Miss Bremer found herself assisting at a sewing bee given by the wife of the president of Harvard to help a faculty household recently burned out. She called on Emerson's aunt, the learned Mrs. Ripley, "who examined me in Euclid while she shelled peas, and with one foot rocked the cradle of her grandson."

References to the New England feminists were far from flattering. She noted going out "to view the emancipated ladies delivering public lectures," something not done in her good Sweden. Lucy Stone "talked a full hour [on slavery] with perfect self-possession, but she merely repeated what the men had already said, and said better." As for Margaret Fuller, she was "devoid of beauty . . .

Among her faults was arrogance and a contemptuous manner towards others less gifted." Nevertheless, Miss Bremer credited her with "an actual genius for conversation."

The journal also described unnamed "ladies with splendid intelligent foreheads and beautiful forms" sitting spellbound while Bronson Alcott expounded his odd views on a fruit and vegetable diet. "I wonder that they could listen in silence!" The father of *Little Women* also told Miss Bremer that he wished to raise the status of marriage but "excused himself from treating such a subject in public conversation."

As for the Transcendentalists, the Swedish traveler wished that they would be "a little more rational." Still, something was to be said for a city where schoolteaching was honored and where Beethoven's symphonies were "well played." Not all Bostonians, however, aspired to the heights. There were ladies who prided themselves on having their clothes from Paris, and whose young people went sleigh riding on the Neck. She was taken in a "giant sledge" that held 50 people, and was drawn by four horses. "More beautiful carriages and driving I have never seen," she noted. A bit irrelevantly she concluded, "Nevertheless, how seldom one sees fat people or plump forms here."

The Swedish investigator did not fail to visit the model factories at Lowell, still in their uplift stage. "I saw the young ladies at work, saw their boarding houses, sleeping rooms, etc. All was comfortable and nice . . . The procession of the operators, two by two, in shawls, bonnets and green veils . . . produced a fine and imposing effect," even if some of the young ladies were nearing 50. Food, too, was sufficient and good, with meat, potatoes and "fruit tarts," undoubtedly New England's own apple pie. "Much stress is laid upon the good character of the young females—one or two elopements I heard spoken of, but the life of labor here is more powerful than the life of romance." To this pronouncement she added that, with the industrious able to earn nearly eight dollars a week, most of the young ladies were "laying something by."

For New England Miss Bremer was prepared to summarize: "The women have, in general, all the rule there that they wish to have." Educational opportunities for them were far superior to those of Europe. "Young girls of fortune devote themselves to teaching. The daughters of poor farmers go to work in the manufactures a sufficient time to put themselves to school . . . The young daughters of New England are universally commended for their character and ability. They learn . . . the classics, mathematics, physics and algebra with great ease. . . . Not long since, a young lady of Nantucket discovered a new planet . . . and received a medal from the King of Prussia." This anonymous young lady was Maria Mitchell. Unknown, cut off on her island, she was her Quaker father's assistant in teaching and making nautical calculations. Using homemade apparatus, she had detected the appearance of the new comet. Even after the regal medal had been bestowed, and she had been made a member of the American Academy of Arts and Sciences, she still clung to Nantucket. Not till the Civil War did she become a public figure, called in 1865 to the newly opened Vassar College. There this distinguished but difficult member of the faculty used to hold a watch, conspicuously timing the oratory of chapel preachers.

THE MINORITY OF PROTEST

After sampling New England Miss Bremer started on the more adventurous part of her tour in the course of which she would cover more American territory than any other woman journalist.

A nearby stop was at The Phalanstery, a Christian-Socialist enterprise near Red Bank, New Jersey. There some seventy members raised peaches, melons, tomatoes and hominy, which last they ground in their own mills. For the first time, the Swedish novelist beheld the bloomer costume. "Even the lady of the president of the Phalanstery wore a short dress and pantaloons." Worse, many of the young ladies danced in the evenings thus clad. "This costume . . . which might do for everyday occupations . . . was not at all becoming in the waltz." Miss Bremer's eye-witness report can be contrasted with Alexander Woolcott's sketches of the last days of the Phalanstery, memories from his own childhood.

The Phalanstery was only one of many experiments all the way from Brook Farm outside of Boston, to New Harmony in Indiana, and even farther west to a vegetarian community in Kansas. All of these spoke for some minority of protest. Earlier communal undertakings usually represented some religious sect transplanted in a group from Europe. Thus they preserved doctrinal tenets and lessened the financial hazards of resettling in a new world.

But the communities of the '40's and '50's were quite different, generally based on the socialism of Fourier translated into American terms. Members only too rarely were farmers and mechanics, and only too often idealists seeking escape from commercial drudgery. Where Rappites had expected to be governed by counsels of elders, these new communes attracted literate young people. Women in such groups were not docile peasant burden bearers but young ladies in search of something beyond the prescribed feminine routine.

Most famous was Brook Farm where New England's literary aspirants, Hawthorne among them, milked cows from necessity but preferred sitting around listening to visiting speakers. Margaret Fuller complained of "a good deal of sans-culotte tendency in their manner"—she was accustomed to a more deferential reception. Brook Farm youths and maidens sat on the floor, yawned and even left the room when they felt like it.

More industrial was the Cooperative at Florence, Massachusetts, just beyond Northampton. There a group of skilled workmen started a community based on silk weaving. By 1850, some 200 residents filled five frame houses, ranged around a ribbon mill. Everyone worked at wages a bit higher than the prevailing commercial scale. Women over seventeen received 6 cents an hour, men 10 cents. Older boys and girls were paid 4½ cents. Because this was a reform group, the working day was shortened from twelve to eleven hours, and everyone received an additional cash allotment for food. There was also a communal laundry, bath and kitchen, with free medical service provided by a physician member. So that labor and education might go hand in hand, the plant had its own school. Less literary than Brook Farm, this social project survived till 1866.

Plain as was the life, it attracted well bred women. A visitor who encountered brown bread, wooden chairs, and "apartments cold and comfortless," was surprised to find "ladies who had left good homes and the luxuries of refined life." There they were, surrounded by "half-abandoned children," trying to learn the trade of a factory operative.

The most notable woman of the group was the strange black

ex-slave, Sojourner Truth, heroine of many abolition gatherings. Between feats of oratory in behalf of her race the dark sibyl earned her keep as a member of the Florence community. (Sojourner Truth had been a northern, not a southern slave. The sufferings to which she gave eloquent tongue had been endured in "free" territory.)

THE ONEIDA LADIES

Most radical of all the protest communities was that of the Oneida Perfectionists in New York state. Not content with freeing themselves from the profit motive, Perfectionists also loosed themselves from the bonds of marriage. The leader of this controversial enterprise was the son of a country banker in Pultney, Vermont, who began gathering converts there. Fleeing Vermont's moral indignation, the Perfectionists found refuge in an abandoned settlement of the Oneida Indians. In the '50's the Perfectionists were keeping body and soul together by the heaviest toil. They ran a sawmill, cultivated and sold garden seed and were starting to manufacture a superior type of trap. It was the wide sale of this contrivance that raised the community from privation to comparative affluence.

Early membership included doctors, lawyers, farmers and mechanics. The women Perfectionists soon adopted the bloomer costume for their manual labors, for in this advanced group girls and men exchanged trades. Lady Perfectionists were not limited eternally to housework. Some even were trained to be mechanics and were considered "especially valuable for finer and more delicate lathe work." (A hundred years later modern shop managers made the same discovery in airplane production.)

Such were the women who, to the scandal of conventional morals, dedicated themselves to a very high-minded form of free love. Their first goal was a sinless life. They must achieve holiness of heart before they could win liberty in love, or as it was called, "complex marriage." Within the limits of the community any man or woman might freely cohabit, but no love making was permitted. Attachment between any couple, and the impulse to remain true to a chosen mate were rebuked as "selfish love." "Some suffering among their young people on that account" was recorded.

Arrangements for a "complex marriage" must be made through a third person, and not by courtship, and no man might force his attention on a woman. Propagation of children was on scientific principles. Some 24 men and 20 women were selected for this very early experiment in eugenics, which was called stirpiculture. Infants remained in the care of their mothers till weaned, and were then placed in a communal nursery which had both men and women caretakers. A visitor described the children as "plump and sound, but a little subdued and desolate looking."

Sundays at Oneida were a protest against the Sabbatarianism then prevailing in the outer world. There were no public prayers or sermons. After having sent off all the week's soiled clothing to the communal laundry, the Perfectionists gathered for their sessions of criticism in which the ladies were certainly vocal. An outsider at this ceremony heard a young man charged with having used slang in conversation, and also with having called some "sisters" pet names. It was a woman who brought that up. Another man was upbraided for having made "unnecessary remarks about food at table." A lady member was rated for "indolence and vanity," another for dislike of cold air, which was diagnosed as a form of fear.

Getting down to more serious misconduct, one Charles, who had been selected for stirpiculture, was accused of courting the mate chosen for him. This breach of code called for discipline. Charles, under community rebuke, agreed to isolate himself from his attractive mate, and to let another take his place with her. In community terms, Charles had "taken up his cross" and was "in a fair way to become a better man."

Curiously enough, the leading protest among Oneida ladies was not against the tenets of stirpiculture, but on the matter of dress. This important department was allotted to "a woman of good judgment and great patience." Originally materials had been selected from lists made up by the women members. But in the time elapsed between ordering and receiving, lady Perfectionists began to change their minds and were not content to abide within a meagre appropriation. As the colony prospered a clothing allowance was substituted. Living must still have been plain, for the official amount was 33 dollars per annum for each lady member. This sum was pronounced sufficient for all needs, minus the superfluities of fashion. Community workrooms produced two or three dresses for summer and winter, broadcloth coats, shawls, hoods and sunbonnets, also "the best underlinen."

In spite of its assault on conventional morals the Perfectionists flourished sufficiently to open a textile and silver-plating branch at Wallingford, Connecticut, and to maintain their own publishing plant at 43 Willow Place in Brooklyn. They rarely "lost their young people." It should be noted that the ingenuity of community workshops and forges produced one great luxury. Out in the wilds Perfectionists had steam heat while genteel society was still struggling with stoves and fireplaces. When the group finally disbanded long after the Civil War, its silver-plating department at Buffalo survived as a commercial enterprise, known today as Community Plate.

MISS BREMER IN THE SOUTH

Traveling South, the Swedish observer paused in Washington long enough to meet the first American woman lobbyist. In the library of the Capitol, she talked with Dorothea Dix, campaigning to have Congress allot 10,000,000 dollars of western land for asylum and poor-house reform. The great Henry Clay, so Miss Bremer noted, was "everywhere surrounded by female worshipers, and he himself seems to be a great worshiper of women."

Idyllic as Washington of the '50's seemed to a European visitor, it had its own system of spying and counterspying, and its own Mata Hari, in the person of Rose Oneal Greenhow. This accusation against Mrs. Greenhow as a spy was made directly by Jessie Benton Frémont to Josiah Royce (later of Harvard, but then in California) and her letter containing the charge is now in the Huntington Library (Chapter Note 4). Mrs. Greenhow was said to be secretly in British pay while her scholarly husband Robert served as translator for the state department during the Mexican War period.

After his death his widow remained in Washington, entertaining elegantly, receiving especially important members of the Senate and House. With the outbreak of the Civil War Rose Greenhow became an open Secessionist accused of having passed on the plans for the battle of Bull Run. She was arrested and held in the old Capitol prison along with her little girl, but was later released for deportation within the Confederate lines.

When last heard of she was a passenger on the S.S. *Condor* from London, which ran the blockade off the North Carolina coast. Two Confederate agents and Mrs. Greenhow were sent ashore in a small boat. It capsized in the surf. Mrs. Greenhow was drowned, carried under by weight of gold coins concealed under her dress. This was in 1864. Whether or not the gold was "British" has never been proved.

CHARLOTTESVILLE AND SOUTHERN ANTI-SLAVERY

Now Miss Bremer prepared to report on the southern scene. The idea of slavery was distasteful to her, but she tried to observe fairly. At the University of Virginia she was surprised to hear open anti-slavery arguments. There was, for example, a student oration condemning slavery because of its effect on the poorer whites. The system, so the speaker argued, was wrecking not the blacks, but the whites. "You in slavery territory do not labour for the lower classes of your countrymen" was the Swedish visitor's rendering of the student's thesis. She added: "It was really an uncommon speech."

Miss Bremer had never heard of the anti-slavery movement within the South that had centered around the American Colonization Society. Of Southern origin, this organization labored to ship freed Negroes to Liberia in Africa.

Faded records, now over 100 years old, show that Southern as well as Northern women were active in the cause. Miss Mary Brand of Richmond was treasurer of the Virginia branch of the American Colonization Society. Mary Blackford of Fredericksburg was trying to find "suitable teachers" for the voyagers. Jane T. English was treasurer of a Female Colonization Society in Georgetown. Hannah Whittebreit was sending "a liberated servant" to the colony. Miss Lucy Berkeley of Hanover had freed ten slaves and would send them to Africa. Miss Mary Moon of Wilmington, North Carolina, would liberate nine slaves if the Society would transport them to Liberia. "This is all the property Miss M. has, and no income . . . It is a matter of conscience with her."

Best known of these Southern reformers was Margaret Mercer whose memorial stands in an old churchyard in Belmont, Loudon County, Virginia. Miss Mercer's father had been a liberal minded governor of Maryland. On his death she freed her "inherited servants." Then she sold her property to buy and free other slaves for resettlement in Liberia. Now forced to support herself, she founded a girls' school in Loudon County.

Her sacrifices seem to have been in vain. A Negro whom she had trained as a doctor died within three years of his reaching Liberia. Her other protégées wrote back unhappily from free Africa: "We can't get no meat . . . The monkeys get so wild . . . the leopards howl . . . The savages caught us, but praise the Lord, they set us free." Resettlement in Liberia proved no solution for house-servants used to the amenities of Maryland and Virginia.

CHARLESTON AND POINTS SOUTH

Charleston, South Carolina, seemed to Miss Bremer a continental city. On the streets were fat Negro and mulatto women with bright handkerchiefs wound around their heads, "a thousand times preferable to the bonnets and caps which they wear in the Free States." But the hotel was not of the best, with its "throng of Negro lads about the dinner tables pretending to be waiters."

At a Charleston wedding Miss Bremer saw the family nurse "sitting near the altar. These black nurses," she recorded, "are cared for with great tenderness as long as they live . . . and, generally speaking, they deserve it . . . The house slaves here seem to be very well treated with quarters and comforts much better than those provided for the free servants of our country." Many Negroes, she wrote, were taught to read by their owners. But on the subject of slavery, "the women grieve me by being so short-sighted, and still more irritable and violent than the men."

As a guest of well known Charleston people, Miss Bremer found life very pleasant. There were oranges and bananas to eat, a new experience to the Swedish lady, also picnics on Sullivan Island. The world picnic was strange, and she defined it as an excursion into the country "where they go to eat and enjoy themselves in a merry company. . . . During mealtimes, one of the black boys or girls stands with a besom of peacocks' feathers to drive away the flies." Southern breakfasts were really too plentiful, but evenings were made pleasant with plays and dances.

But the visitor did not surrender entirely to surface charm. She recounts the story of "Mrs. Doctor Susan" as an instance of the intolerance meted out to white women who transgressed the conventions. Mrs. Doctor Susan was a physician and helper of the poor. She belonged to one of the good families, "but having made a false step in her youth, she became an outcast from society." As a physician for the poor she always made her rounds at night, lest by day she should encounter a friend of her youth. When some physicians fled Charleston during fever epidemics, Mrs. Doctor Susan stood by. Miss Bremer learned the story because she herself had encountered the woman doctor, then middle-aged, going her nocturnal rounds.

When Miss Bremer was taken to visit a plantation outside of Charleston she tasted the rations made up for the slaves, "and found the food better than what poor people in Sweden had . . . Certain it is that under a good master, they [the slaves] are far from unhappy and are much better provided for than the working people in many parts of Europe."

Unfortunately for the historian, Miss Bremer does not give the name of this plantation nor of its owners. One may suspect that the place described was that of Louisa Cheves McCord, one of the notable women of anti-bellum South Carolina, who, within the strict pattern of gentility, managed a model plantation.

LOUISA McCORD OF "LANG SYNE"

By the rule of contraries, an upbringing rather like that of the sisters Grimké produced also this protagonist of Negro slavery as a divine dispensation. In 1840, Louisa McCord believed this doctrine sincerely, accepting its corollary of white moral responsibility for the blacks committed to their charge.

Like Judge Grimké, Louisa McCord's father was a noted lawyer. She was an older daughter in a large family, apparently the fourth child among fourteen. As Sarah Grimké had accompanied her father north, so the two oldest Cheves girls went first to Washington when their father was in Congress, and then to Philadelphia when he served there as President of the Bank of the United States. Living in an atmosphere of political activity, Louisa received the best schooling obtainable in both cities.

Then the door closed. The Cheves family returned to Charleston where the two daughters were expected to refit themselves to the demands of southern charm. But Louisa was her father's own daughter, large, powerful, energetic. Though at forty she was an imposing matron, at twenty she was no southern belle. For her, release came through the inheritance of a plantation. Into its life and management she threw herself with all her father's vigor. After a few years her "Lang Syne" (the Cheves were of Scots descent) had been made a model establishment. There was a hospital with trained attendants for the 200 cotton hands, a day nursery where women field workers could leave their youngsters, and their own Baptist preacher for the slaves. It was this plantation to which northern visitors were often taken to demonstrate how different was the real South to that pictured by abolitionists. Certainly Louisa's "servants" had everything except their freedom.

Meanwhile, at the age of 30, (the year was 1840) the mistress of Lang Syne married, becoming the second wife of David McCord, lawyer-politician, and the editor of a "nullification" newspaper. To a household of step-children were added three children of her own. A literary career was still to come, but it was to be strictly on the southern pattern. Mrs. McCord took pen in hand only at the request of her husband. The occasion was the translation of a recently published French work on the errors of a protective tariff policy. Editor McCord believed that this would make good ammunition for the southern tariff case at Washington. So Louisa set to work. Her translation was published in 1848. It was followed by reviews for the *Southern Quarterly* over the initials L.S.M., which protected the identity of the author. "L.S.M." was the critic chosen by the *Southern Quarterly* in 1853 to review *Uncle Tom's Cabin* (Chapter Note 5).

There is a marked contrast between Frederika Bremer's reports and Fanny Kemble's *Journal of a Georgia Plantation*. This was written down ten years before Miss Bremer's travels, but not made public till 1863. Fanny Kemble, young and fresh from her theatrical triumphs, knowing the world only through the best artistic circles, found herself set down on her husband's sea island estate. There had been nothing in her experience to prepare her for what she encountered.

On the Butler plantations slaveholding was complicated with the evils of absentee landlordism. For nineteen years the Sapello Island acres with their 700 slaves had been left to the mercies of an overseer, with no questions asked as long as income was forthcoming. If Frederika Bremer saw the best in South Carolina, Pierce Butler's English bride encountered the opposite. She had expected the American equivalent of a well kept English country house. She found crude living and neglect with "house servants perfectly filthy in their persons and clothes."

Negro cabins, she noted, were revolting, the plantation infirmary horribly rundown. Women field hands were sent back to work three weeks after childbirth, their babies put in charge of "little nursemaids of ten or twelve, all very dirty." Infant mortality at the plantation was appalling. It was this part of her journal that was quoted in England twenty years later as an antislavery document (Chapter Note 6).

ACROSS THE ALLEGHENIES

Although Frederika Bremer covered more American territory than any other woman writer of her day, there were large sections of the republic where she never set foot. Undoubtedly she surveyed the shores of Mississippi and Tennessee on her river voyage north, but she never stopped there. For the women of this region other sources must be tapped.

By the '50's older towns of Kentucky and Tennessee had "select academies" for young ladies, usually conducted by an Episcopal clergyman. At Columbia, Tennessee, for instance, the Institute, "a noble edifice," sheltered some three hundred young ladies. In spite of its size, a New England traveler conceded that its "rector" maintained "perfect order and system."

Nashville, the capital, could then display mansions "richly furnished," and its ladies were said to be given over to the fashions. Their riding-habits, a Yankee governess wrote home, were especially "recherché." At the select Female Academy, the young ladies could bring their own maids.

But Tennessee was not Virginia. A much stricter Sabbatarian regime was in evidence. Earlier, when Mrs. Felix Grundy had tried to start a Sunday school, it was denounced, oddly enough, as a desecration of the Sabbath. The social acceptance of dancing was delayed for 25 years. When in 1844, the principal of the Academy, the Rev. C. D. Elliott, introduced instruction in dancing, there was an outcry in the local press. The Nashville *Christian Advocate* assailed the move as "vain, foolish and profitless." The journal was "against any institution . . . where such injurious practice is tolerated."

It was at this time that Sarah Polk, First Lady from Tennessee, stopped dancing at the White House in Washington. In Nashville, though, the Rev. Mr. Elliott stuck to his fiddles, and a few years later fancy dress balls were popular in the best circles.

This stricter atmosphere of western Tennessee is reflected in early records of old St. Agnes school in Memphis, founded in 1851 by six Dominican sisters from Springfield, Kentucky. "With a view to prevent extravagance" says a prospectus, "uniforms are enjoined." In winter the girls were limited to slate-colored merino dresses "and cape of same," with a black silk apron for Sunday and a white sunbonnet. In summer heat the blue gingham uniform had long sleeves, "to fit close to the neck, with a small white collar, a black silk apron and a white sunbonnet."

The old document gives no information as to studies, but "discipline and order require attendance at divine services on Sunday." St. Agnes graduated its first class in 1855. Commencement exercises, says an old letter, "lasted three days . . . Everything was very elegant . . . the rostrum of the large hall covered with fine velvet carpet and a square piano on each side . . . As we were called, we mounted the rostrum and made a courtsey . . . lovely Southern girls dressed in pure white, so graceful and innocent."

GOVERNESS DE LUXE

For prosperous plantations in Kentucky and Tennessee a family governess was the accepted agent for female education. Usually she

167

herself had been schooled in the north, and very often she was a New England Yankee. Sometimes, too, the governess would add to her income by writing accounts of her experiences "in the West" for some northern magazine.

One such imported teacher was greatly impressed with the easy luxury of her employer's household. She was the orphaned daughter of a naval officer and had learned French from a West Point brother during vacations. Her mother had taught her to draw. At fifteen the girl had "assisted" in the grade school at Portsmouth, New Hampshire. After that she had earned her way through a Massachusetts normal school.

Now, in Tennessee, Miss Anonymous was called at six each morning by her own maid, who had at first brought in something called a wine mint julep. But when it was learned that the governess was strictly "temperance," morning black coffee was substituted. Then the maid arranged the governess's hair. At seven there was family breakfast, over which "the colonel" asked a daily blessing. The meal would include "four or five warm breads, ham, succotash and hominey" and was served by two men and two women waitresses. At nine the governess and her young charges "take to our books and our needles," study however, being usually broken off for a morning drive.

Dinner was at two, "every dish elegantly served." After wine and dessert the ladies retired "to sleep till the cool of the day." Towards evening all was animation on the piazza or in the drawing room, where once more "attentive servants" brought refreshments such as tea, coffee and cakes. "Even Yankee girls would get helpless, too," the governess speculated.

The plantation hierarchy was evident. At the top were the house servants, pastry cooks, laundresses and seamstresses, who looked down on everybody else. Next in rank were stable and garden hands, and the chief dairywoman. At the bottom were some two hundred "agriculturalists." The visitor agreed that the colonel's slaves were better off and happier than free Negroes she had seen in the North. Yet when they "returned from work at sundown, their hoes across their shoulders," she noted that faces were unsmiling. One woman was carrying a huge basket on her head. In it were four naked colored babies who had been taken to the fields. There a young girl had looked after them while the mothers worked.

The governess also visited the colored chapel, where the daughter of the house played the organ, and a neighboring tutor read a printed sermon. "The slaves are more religiously disposed than middle-class whites . . . and colored women sing well," said the schoolteacher. Then she noted as an afterthought that her own personal maid, sixteen years old, could not read. Also in the South, she finished, "few females write." She had heard only one woman author mentioned, a poetess, "Amelia of Kentucky."

SONG BIRDS OF THE SOUTH

Such is the background against which to measure a literary phenomenon of the '50's, the rise of a group of Southern women poets. Both by date and content they were a regional counterpart of New York's literati. But there was one important difference. In the North, lady lyricists published proudly over their own names; in the South, genteel anonymity prevailed. Newspaper editors of Louisville and Memphis opened their columns to the new lady-poets, but it has taken research by modern Southern colleges to establish the identities behind the *noms de plume*.

Earliest and best known was "Amelia . . . the sweet poetess . . . embellishing the columns of the *Louisville Journal*." Born in Maryland, Amelia had removed to Kentucky with her family when she was fifteen. Admittedly she had been given no formal education, but three years after the migration to Kentucky, her poems began to appear in print. At this time also, she married. In 1844 a volume of her lyrics was published in Boston. Poe compared her to Mrs. Hemans . . . "songs of simple measure . . . from a gushing poetic nature." Amelia's book went through fifteen editions. It was still selling when she died young in 1852, leaving one son. "Amelia" was Mrs. G. B. Welby.

Next came "Miss L' Connue" called Tennessee's peerless queen of song. In 1852 she was producing a poem a week for *The Eagle* and *The Enquirer* in Memphis. In person L'Connue was Miss L. Virginia Smith, a northern-trained teacher from the eastern shore of Virginia, who had "accepted a tutorial position in the West." Then love at first sight turned "Miss L'Connue" into Mrs. J. H. French. From her new home in the Cumberland mountains she published, still anonymously, her volume *Wind Whispers*. A portrait of her shows hair parted in the long curls of the '50's. Her round-necked silk gown is fashionably cut. But the eyes looking out above this conventional elegance are bright and alert.

There was also "Annie," otherwise Mrs. Chambers Bradford of Kentucky, whose lyrics appeared in Memphis newspapers. A widow, she had come to Tennessee to teach for her living. Soon though, she remarried and ceased to publish.

"Estelle" wrote from Mississippi, where, in Holly Springs, she was Miss Martha Frazier. By 1850 she was Mrs. R. B. Brown.

"Mary P.," a third Memphis schoolteacher, expressed "the sweet murmuring of her muse . . . in doleful elegies." She has been identified as Mrs. Mary E. Pope, probably a widow.

Meanwhile, in the world of politics, relations between North and South grew increasingly strained. Southern readers took offense at northern magazines, and southern editors began founding their own. Soon, too, the ladies followed suit with "The Southern Parlor Magazine edited by a Southern Lady." She was Wilhelmine McCord, whose ambition carried her from Georgia to Tennessee. Spurred on by this example, "Annie" (now identified as Mrs. Ketcham) began publishing *The Lotus*. Then "Miss L'Connue" left the happy retirement of McMinnsville to edit *The Crusader* and *The Southern Ladies Book*.

As literature all this belonged to the period of wax flowers and painting on velvet. The magazines were short-lived, gone with the wind of the rising conflict. But the lady songbirds proved that they could both write and edit.

CLAY vs. CALHOUN

The political arena provides the wives of the great rivals, Henry Clay and James Calhoun. Neither man reached the presidency, but both were memorable figures. Their wives conformed to the pattern of anonymous aristocracy, scarcely emerging from the shadows cast by their notable husbands. Mrs. Clay belonged to Kentucky, Mrs. Calhoun to South Carolina. Even with husbands whose careers are voluminously documented, it is difficult to penetrate the silence that surrounded the women themselves.

THE RETIRING MRS. CLAY

Lucretia Hart, later Mrs. Henry Clay, was born in Hagerstown, Maryland, at the close of the Revolution. During her childhood, the family removed to Kentucky, resettling at Lexington. Twenty years of trading and land speculation had brought prosperity to this new and stormy political center. Since 1787 Lexington had had a grammar school and, in a decade, its Seminary became Transylvania University, dedicated to law, medicine and the arts. Such opportunities, however, were strictly masculine. The only educational recognition of the town's young ladies was a dancing academy.

Though Thomas Hart was a prominent citizen of Lexington, there is no school mentioned for his daughter Lucretia. Home tutoring seems probable. Long afterwards one of Clay's northern admirers dismissed his wife as "not a brilliant but an estimable woman." The first recorded fact of her life in Kentucky is her marriage at eighteen. That was in 1799, the year that the town's Seminary proclaimed itself a University, and horse-racing in the streets was forbidden.

Young Henry Clay who married Lucretia Hart had been born in Virginia, one of the seven children of a poor Baptist preacher. The father had died in 1781, and his widow did her best for her children by remarrying. It was Clay's step-father who secured him his chance as an apprentice-copyist of legal documents in Richmond. In true Horatio Alger style the youth had won his legal license by his twenty-first birthday. Then he chose Kentucky for a swift upward climb in his profession. Within a year he had become an acceptable son-in-law and was soon purchasing "Ashlands." He was still under thirty when he was appointed to fill out a term in the United States Senate.

That date was 1806. From then on Henry Clay was one of the great men of Washington—Senator, Speaker of the House, Secretary of State, leader of his party and somewhat perennial presidential

171

candidate. Today he is still remembered as protagonist of the Missouri Compromise and of the shorter-lived Compromise of 1850. Personally he was always popular, "fond of amusements, a great favorite with the ladies, in all parties of pleasure, out almost every evening," a colleague wrote of him.

Rarely though in all those decades of prominence was Mrs. Clay seen in the Capital, and never after 1825. In that year, when Clay was Secretary of State, Mrs. Clay started for Washington with two young-lady daughters. One girl died on the way, the other shortly afterwards. The mother then "retired altogether from society," and remained so until her death 49 years later.

Yet, in the background, she was an important part of her husband's fame. It was she who kept "Ashlands, that beautiful residence," going. Much of its 600 acres was under her management. It was she who kept the 50 slaves fed, clothed and healthy. When Clay's Washington expenditures mounted, she made the Ashland's blooded dairy herd pay. It is on record that she supplied the Phoenix hotel in Lexington with 30 gallons of milk daily. "Mrs. Clay was the first up in the morning, and the last to bed at night," states the same source. Like Letitia Tyler in Virginia and Rachel Jackson in Tennessee, this other lady of the plantation backed her husband's career by staying at home.

Another gap in the story of Lucretia Clay concerns her children. In all, there were eleven, five sons and six daughters. None of the girls survived their mother. Besides Eliza, and Lucretia who died on the way to Washington, two others succumbed as young children. Susan grew up and married, only to fall victim to yellow fever in New Orleans. Ann, the longest-lived, died suddenly in 1835 when she was only twenty-eight.

The record of the sons is equally tragic. Theodore, the oldest, was thrown from a horse at sixteen, fracturing his skull. His injury resulted in insanity and many years in an asylum. Henry Clay, junior, a West Point graduate, was killed at the battle of Buena Vista, 1847. Two other sons died in 1862 and 1864. Lucretia herself lived to be 83, with only the youngest, (John) of all her eleven children surviving her.

In the face of these successive blows (states an old chronicle) "the mother's manner grew cold and reserved." Yet through it all "she was sustained by the beautiful and childlike faith that had characterized her whole life."

FLORIDE CALHOUN FROM CAROLINA

In marked contrast was Floride Calhoun whose upright, fanatic husband became the spokesman for the South's slaveholding interests. Floride, although her husband's cousin, was half-French. One branch of the family, the less prosperous, had migrated upland into South Carolina's Piedmont region. Another had married into a wealthy Huguenot family of the coastal section. That was Floride's heritage.

She enters history when her mother, a wealthy Widow Calhoun, took her daughter on a summer tour north to Newport, a journey made in the widow's private traveling carriage. At New Haven she paused long enough to meet young John Calhoun, then finishing at Yale and soon to enter New England's first law school at Litchfield, Connecticut. Floride, born in 1792, was thirteen at the time. What this darkly beautiful young girl thought of her cousin will never be known. The mother, though, was much impressed. When Calhoun later entered a law office in Charleston, he was made welcome at Bonneau's Ferry, and was permitted to write to his cousin. In that strict household the favored cousin could only enclose a note for the girl (she was seventeen) within a letter to her mother.

Poor though the upstate Calhouns might be, Floride's French mother urged on the match. When family lawyers proposed a usual marriage settlement to protect the bride's inheritance, the cousin-suitor objected. Floride's mother then overruled the estate attorneys, and had the girl's dowry go directly into the hands of her husband. The wedding date set was January, 1811, when Floride was nearing nineteen. The groom was ten years older. So rigidly had the bride been kept at home that when her new husband took her to the theater in Charleston she was shocked.

With Calhoun's marked ability and his wife's money, success both in law and politics came speedily. He had been elected to Congress before his marriage. By 1823 he was in Monroe's cabinet as Secretary of War. After that he was Vice-President under John Quincy Adams and also for Andrew Jackson's first term. He resigned in 1832 to lead the nullification forces, becoming a senator almost in perpetuity. Under Tyler he was Secretary of State. Again a senator, he died in 1850, a power in the North-South controversy.

THE CALHOUNS IN PRIVATE LIFE

What now of his wife? The outer framework of her marriage is well documented. At first she accompanied him to Washington in spite of children born or on the way to be born, her first son coming within a year of her wedding. She had nine children, seven of whom (five sons and two daughters) lived to grow up, although the youngest daughter was accounted an invalid. Probably also she was a cripple, although this was never admitted in writing (Chapter Note 7).

Washington society reported favorably on young Mrs. Calhoun, who was mentioned as a musician and as a lady chess player. While Calhoun was in Monroe's cabinet the family lived on a fine estate in Georgetown which has come down in history as Dunbarton Oaks. But it was the wealthy widow who provided this handsome setting, apparently content to bask in the honors conferred on her brilliant son-in-law. At "Oakley," young Mrs. Calhoun presided in a gown of "elegant white velvet . . . trimmed with lace over white satin." Floride's turbans came from Washington's best milliners, and she drove about in her mother's coach with four horses.

Then the tune changed. In 1826 Calhoun invested his wife's dowry in the Fort Hill Plantation near Pendleton in the hilly western region of South Carolina. Though not as magnificent as the mansions of the rice planters near Charleston, it was a fine house with tall white pillars across the front. The 1,100 acres were worked by some 80 slaves for whose welfare Calhoun, by his own doctrine, must be responsible.

Now Floride went seldom to Washington, or even to Charleston, though her husband dispensed hospitality at Fort Hill to his many political visitors. It was open house, with one limit. If any guest failed to attend family prayers there was a standing order to "saddle his horse and let him go." The master's personal life was exemplary. He tolerated neither gambling nor heavy drinking. Definitely the lavish living of Washington was no more. Either there was less income, or it was being ploughed into an agricultural future.

There is a eulogistic description of the Fort Hill household from the pen of their New England governess. It was, Miss Bates maintained, a cheerful and happy home although never once did she hear the master utter a jest. His manner was always one of grave dignity. Should there be a visiting lady, Calhoun "paid his compliments by recognizing her soul, not by flattery." The plantation was producing fine crops as well as choice fruit. Daily the master rode the rounds of the estate while "the ladies did needle work." Now Calhoun was taking his oldest daughter to Washington, her mother "being often detained by family cares at Fort Hill . . . preferring the voice of friendship to the acclamations of the multitude." Quite the period piece for a southern lady of the '50's.

But beneath this smooth surface neighbors noted episodes in a different vein. For instance, one day, in anger, Mrs. Calhoun had thrown a silver pitcher. Apparently not surprised, the Great Nullifier had merely said "Tut, tut, Floride." There was also a story of the master's having ordered a flower bed planted thus-and-so. Whereupon the lady of the mansion ordered it dug up and replanted to her liking. If thwarted, so said the neighbors, "she would take to her bed and threaten to die."

All letters that passed between Calhoun and his wife were destroyed, and only three of his to his favorite daughter (Mrs. Clemson) are extant. In one of these Calhoun complains that Floride has not answered his letter. In another Calhoun reminds Anna that her mother's "nerves" were "the only cross in my life." But the harassed husband could always escape to his career in Washington. Altogether, historians have reckoned, he spent nearly half of their 35 years of marriage apart from his wife. It was also noted that Floride's "nerves" improved markedly in his absence.

To the hard working farmers of Marengo County Floride was spoiled. Yet there she was, year after year, compelled by law and custom to make her home among people alien to her. The neighborhood was peopled mostly by Ulster Irish to whom this half-French woman was a foreigner. In plain English, they didn't like her. Meanwhile Floride would find compensation for her resentments in ordering more rooms built onto Fort Hill. After Calhoun's death in 1850 (at Washington, not at home) his widow ceased her building operations. Calhoun left no will. Fort Hill was Floride's, bought with her money. Nearing 60, she stayed there sharing its seclusion with her invalid daughter. There, after the close of the Civil War, Floride Calhoun died at the age of 74.

ANOTHER EATON SCANDAL

One cannot dismiss Floride Calhoun without a parting mention of Peggy Eaton who in 1859, when she was well past 60, made her third marriage and suffered her last scandal.

The story of the first Eaton affair that disrupted Andrew Jackson's cabinet has been told only too often. The Calhouns were usually credited with heading the party which refused to accept Secretary Eaton's young and beautiful second wife. He had married her on New Year's day of 1829. As is well known, Andrew Jackson, believing that she was maligned, exerted presidential prestige in her behalf. Gossips rated Mrs. Calhoun as Peggy's chief enemy, though the well informed John Quincy Adams put the finger on John C. Calhoun, who had just opened a serious political feud with Jackson.

The new Mrs. Eaton was also rejected by the still stricter circles of Tennessee, where Eaton had taken his wife on a political mission. There opposition centered around Emily Donelson, Andrew Jackson's niece, whom Peggy had met in the White House and had called "a poor silly thing."

Finally, unable to force Mrs. Eaton's social acceptance, Jackson substituted the resignations of all his cabinet members, both pro- and anti-Eaton. The Calhouns returned to South Carolina. Eaton with his controversial wife was sent to govern Florida, then, later, to be Minister to Spain, where Peggy flourished and Eaton took to drink. On his death in 1856, the widow inherited a considerable fortune. Then Peggy Eaton committed her one disastrous folly. She married a handsome, very young Italian, Antoine Buchignani, who had been the dancing master for Eaton's grand-daughter by his first wife. The Eaton fortune passed into the hands of the new husband, who thereupon eloped with the grand-daughter.

Stripped of her wealth, Mrs. Buchignani sued for divorce and the resumption of her previous name. Once more Peggy Eaton, she spent her remaining years in obscure poverty. This she tried to remedy by writing her autobiography, which began: "I have had three husbands . . . I may have been vain and wayward, but with little longer to live . . . I have been spotlessly faithful to each of my three husbands."

The final exhibit in the case is Peggy Eaton's last portrait, painted before that third marriage terminated so ruinously. It shows Peggy, still handsome, seated, with her young husband standing behind her. Sometime in her aging poverty she either sold or gave away this canvas, with a request that the offending male be removed from the work of art. This, however, was not done. Peggy and the irreparable error of her career remain framed together and hanging in the Gloucester County Courthouse in Virginia (Chapter Note 8).

MISS BREMER SUMMARIZES

Meanwhile Frederika Bremer, embarked on one of the famous Mississippi steamboats, jotted down a few generalizations about the South and its women. She had met, she wrote, "many lovely, pious people," but their prayers were too long. Southern girls sang better than most ladies in America. As for the mistresses of families, she admired them greatly, but she thought that the young ladies should be "more helpful to their mothers . . . I saw many lovely young daughters of the South, but no great beauty; on the contrary, many were very pale." To the Swedish diarist beauty was synonymous with a right rosy complexion.

"THE PRAIRIES!"

Now Miss Bremer was ready for real adventure. Under date of September 13, 1850 comes the exclamation, "Prairies! A sight I shall never forget!" Chicago, though, let her down. It was one of the most miserable and ugly cities she had seen in America. It was then twenty years old, and had a population of 25,000. Beyond the city Miss Bremer came upon a log house, already a year old, but still partly open to the weather. "It was clean and orderly within, but the good woman was tired of the prairies." Life there was too monotonous.

Soon Miss Bremer reached the official object of her journey, the Swedish colonies of Michigan and Wisconsin. Ann Arbor was "a pretty little rural city," and she approved the liberal tone of Michigan law. But when, in Detroit, she found young ladies teaching French and the guitar to a young man imprisoned for attempted murder, she felt that sympathy was being carried too far. Michigan farmers, she noted, "work hard, live frugally, and bring up strong able families." But the children seldom seemed content to follow their father's occupation.

All was not rosy in the Swedish colonies. At Pine Lake a poor harvest had been followed by a winter so severe that a baby had been frozen to death in its bed. Again there was the difficulty of obtaining farm labor, male or female. "Colonists must pay for labor at high rates or do without." Mostly they did without. Miss Bremer met a farm wife of 50, bent double with rheumatism, "with eight children and no conveniences." She had had to work even while suckling her babies. "She must still wash, worn out, finished before her time. None who are not accustomed to hard agricultural work ought to become farmers in this country."

Miss Bremer reached Madison, Wisconsin, over roads "which were no roads at all . . . but a succession of hills, holes and water pools." At Madison the minister "preached a sermon strongly condemnatory of the gentlemen of the West," placing "all his hopes on the ladies." After that she learned that she must not go out on the lake on a Sunday. "On Sunday, people must not amuse themselves," she penned angrily, "not even in God's beautiful scenery. But sleep in church—that they may do."

Now she was coming close to frontier living. At Blue Mound a log farmhouse was both post-house and inn. Its only guest accommodation, a large garret in which six laboring men usually lodged, was cleared for the distinguished lady. But there was no lock on the door, only a piece of wood to fasten the latch. At meals she sat at table along with the men and maid servants of the family "just as they come in from work and not over-clean."

LOCAL ADDENDA

Other travelers supply items to supplement Miss Bremer's observations. But any mention of women is meager. Again and again one is told that John Doe "and wife" from Maine, Massachusetts or Vermont, here laid out a first farm or built a mill. When Moses Meeker led out a party to open the lead deposits he had discovered at Galena, Illinois, the pioneers were listed as "forty-two people, including women and children."

An early tradition, however, maintains that Ann Arbor was named for the wives of two founding fathers. The women were: Mary Ann Rumsey, wife of Walter, who came in February 1824 from New York state, and Ann Allen, wife of John, migrating from Virginia. "The arbor or tent which formed the first shelter for this little party . . . was made of their sleigh-box with a rag carpet spread over boughs of trees . . . They brought with them a few barrels of provisions and Indians agreed to supply them with corn and venison."

There is also mention of a woman innkeeper of early Kalamazoo. The inn was a log cabin with a sign "Entertainment for Man & Beast." Then the traveler added, "the landlady said it was pretty hard times when they had to live under their wagon," while the logs were being felled.

A local historian of the '50's contributes, without names, the story of a German farmer in Michigan, and his three wives. The first lasted just one year. The second survived for four years, then died leaving one child. Next a third spouse was summoned from Germany. She came bringing household furnishings as her marriage portion. But no one tells what urge brought that third wife, dowry included, to cross the Atlantic, to endure three days and nights on the wooden benches of an emigrant train, finally to reach Michigan, all for a husband who had already buried two wives.

Further North Mackinac had an early woman hotelkeeper, and an early schoolmarm, unfortunately anonymous. But the teacher "married a highly educated half-breed," the official Indian interpreter of Mackinac. Better known was Laura Haviland, a Quaker wife who reached northern Michigan in 1837. Having brought up her own children, she then started a school, the Raisen Institute. Quaker fashion, it was coeducational, and open to all races and colors.

The first white woman reported at Madison, Wisconsin, was Mrs. Rosaline Peck who in 1837 rode into the settlement on an Indian pony. She stayed to open an inn, eleven years before Wisconsin had a state capital. Mrs. Peck had been deserted by her husband, a Vermonter, who went on to Texas where he annexed a second wife and acquired five children.

Throughout the entire republic one keeps encountering the wide-ranging New England schoolteacher. Thus, when Catharine Beecher broke up her Hartford Seminary to start anew in Ohio, her assistant, Frances Strong, struck out for the deep South. In 1831, she founded the Huntsville Female Seminary in Alabama. Later Frederika Bremer noted that all the young ladies she had met teaching in southern seminaries had come from New England.

It must have been with women like those in mind that Miss Bremer wrote a final summary addressed to the Dowager Queen of Denmark. "Youthful daughters of America," she informed her royal correspondent, "are not kept in ignorance and inactivity as are still the great number of young girls in Europe. They are early taught that they must rely on God and themselves."

1   Another farm woman who long afterward became famous was Mary Ann Morse Baker, later known as Mother Eddy. For many years this remarkable woman was a farm reject, too frail to meet its physical demands. Born in 1821 at Bow, New Hampshire, she was the sixth child of a mother who had worked herself out. Her last fragile girl was not considered worth educating, although three older brothers were well schooled. There was nothing for this girl but marriage. Left a young widow with a posthumous child and no money, for 35 bitter years, she was an unwanted woman in a farm economy. Yet in 1870 she became the founder of Christian Science.

2   Records of the New York Historical Society give the Cary house address as 52 East 20th Street. The dwelling was twenty feet square, two storeys high, and located on the north side of the street just west of Fourth Avenue. Early in the 1900's the entire corner site was covered by a large loft building.

3   Although the Fox sisters played a leading role in the wave of spiritualism that swept through the United States during the '50's, they themselves (like Maria Monk of an earlier generation) were Canadians. Their father had moved to Wayne County, N.Y., in 1847 when Margaret was twelve years old. Together with her younger sister, Kate, she worked up a "rapping" performance as a prank to take in their very superstitious mother.

However, when the girls visited their married sister, Mrs. Leah Fish, at Rochester, this enterprising woman saw money making possibilities. Their technique was improved, and in 1850 Mrs. Fish took Margaret and Kate to New York where they were speedily being paid 100 dollars for an evening of "Rochester rappings." These the credulous interpreted as messages from the spirit world. This New York venture was followed by a still more prosperous road tour.

At Philadelphia Margaret encountered Dr. Elisha Kent Kane, noted scientist and explorer who was preparing his second Grinnell expedition in search of Dr. Franklin. Dr. Kane offered to provide schooling for Margaret, then about sixteen, if she would break away from the exhibitions. Unstable, she quit her schooling while Dr. Kane was off in the Arctic, and rejoined the family troupe. After Kane's death in Havana in 1857, Margaret claimed a secret marriage, and when Kane's executors refused her an annuity, she published (1866) his letters to her, some of which Kane's friends considered fraudulent.

Meanwhile the managing Mrs. Leah had taken the sisters to London where their advocates included Harriet Martineau and Elizabeth Barrett Browning. Once more Margaret broke away, confessing that the "rappings" had been produced by flexible toe joints, but a little later she recanted her confession. Spiritualist circles charged that the confession had been extorted from her under the influence of alcohol. Later Margaret took more and more to drink. Before her death in 1893, she was largely discredited.

4 These letters to Josiah Royce then preparing his history of early California, are now in the Huntington Library. According to Mrs. Frémont, Secretary of State Buchanan suspected Mrs. Greenhow of spying, and so sent all confidential Spanish papers to Senator Benton, to be translated by Benton's daughters. Buchanan "thought it best to cut off opportunity, but not to betray his knowledge," Jessie Benton Frémont recounted in 1885.

During the Civil War, Mrs. Greenhow was arrested after the battle of Bull Run. Her house was searched. Incriminating papers (Mrs. Frémont wrote to Josiah Royce) had been found, also "overly affectionate letters" from General Scott, commander of the Northern forces. On these letters, Mrs. Greenhow based "a large money demand." Royce's replies imply a distrust of Mrs. Frémont's recollections; Scott was 75 at the time. Letters alleged to be from Henry Wilson of the House Military Committee were exploited, but Wilson denounced them as forgeries.

5 Mrs. McCord criticized Mrs. Stowe for having her deep-South Negroes speak in border-state dialect, which was the only dialect that the famous author knew. Mrs. McCord also complained that educated Southerners were made to use New England colloquialisms.

6 Fanny Kemble's marriage to Pierce Butler broke up shortly after her plantation experience. More than twenty years afterwards, Miss Kemble sent her old journal to the London *Times*. It made a sensation in 1863.

7 Miss Mary Bates, the Yankee governess at Fort Hill for many years, never spoke of her pupil as crippled. In Miss Bates's monograph, Martha Calhoun merely "suffered from poor health." At present writing proof is lacking. Following her services in the Calhoun household Miss Bates opened a "female seminary" five miles from Fort Hill.

The Calhoun children were: Andrew, b. 1811; Floride, b. 1814, d. 1815; Anna Maria (Mrs. Clemson) b. 1817. In 1818, Mrs. Calhoun suffered a miscarriage. Then came Elizabeth, b. 1819, d. 1820; Patrick,

b. 1821, d. 1858; John C., born 1823, became a doctor; Martha Cornelia, the invalid who was born in 1824 and died in 1857. James, b. 1826, emigrated to California and died there, unmarried. The last child was William L., born 1829.

8   The dates of Peggy O'Neal's marriages were: Timberlake, 1816–1828; Eaton, 1829–1856; Buchignani, 1859. She died November 9, 1879, aged 80. Her body lies in an unmarked grave in Oak Hill Cemetery, Washington, D.C.

CHAPTER SEVEN

A Few Early Blooming Artists

(And the Soil from which they grew.)

*N*OTHING gives a clearer sense of this country's newness than the slow beginnings of American fine arts. Granted that
the colonists soon called on the skills of carpenter and joiner, pres-
ently employing woodcarvers and silversmiths for the fine houses
of the few pre-Revolutionary wealthy. But art for art's sake, whether
in music, painting or acting, had a late and lean start. First things,
like farms and ships and roads, had to come first. If this was true for
men, it was much more so for women. No notable female artist of
any kind appeared on the scene before Charlotte Cushman. Her
birthdate was 1816.

To explain Charlotte Cushman, one must recall the republic's
beginning in both music and the theater, for she had been trained
as a professional singer, and turned to the stage only when her voice
failed.

There had been occasional theater in the old colonies, the first
Shakespearian productions being attributed to early Williamsburg
and Annapolis. There was the Dock Street Theater in Charleston,
opened in 1736, probably the first building in America designed
solely for theatrical purposes. Previously planters met in deserted
tobacco warehouses to applaud tragedy and farce. From that time
on, dramatic art burgeoned spasmodically along the seacoast. The

performers were British, following their trade in the new world, in peril by land and by water.

Soon after the Revolution, American tours by English actors became profitable. By that time the largest cities provided theaters, sometimes camouflaged as a "museum" with "an edifying exhibit of stuffed animals, bones, mummies, minerals, wax figures and other curios." In Boston the Museum might not keep open on Saturday evening, lest godless entertainment encroach too closely on the approaching Sabbath. It is recorded as evidence of deep Christian charity that the ladies of Philadelphia actually ministered to the sick wife of an English manager there.

As for music, it too was imported, but mostly from the Continent. In England there had been a violent swing from the music-loving Elizabethans to the Puritans for whom song was a lure of the evil one. (John Bunyan, long before he wrote *Pilgrim's Progress,* reproved himself for enjoying the melodious ringing of church bells in his town of Bedford.) Approved music in colonial New England was restricted to Sabbath renderings from the Bay Psalm Book. In aristocratic Virginia music was merely an accomplishment for heiresses who played or sang at the spinet. Martha Washington was one of those; Thomas Jefferson's wife played accompaniments for his violin.

The scant instances of group musical performance stem from Europe, and were supplied by French Huguenots in South Carolina and Catholics in Louisiana. Further north credit goes to the Moravians for choral singing and for the first church organ brought here from the other side, to be installed later in Gloria Dei church in Philadelphia. When, in 1777, patriotic Philadelphians wished to celebrate the first anniversary of the Declaration of Independence, they had to commandeer the regimental band of the Hessians, captured at Trenton the previous Christmas.

The works of European composers followed in the wake of imported instruments and players. Haydn, for instance, (spelled both Heyden and Aiden) had reached New York by 1782, Philadelphia by 1786, and Boston by 1792. In that year, an "Aiden" symphony was performed at "Mons. Jacobus Pick's benefit at Concert Hall." The strings were played by "gentlemen amateurs of Boston," while two ladies, also strictly anonymous, furnished a song and "A

Sonata on the Piano Forte." The program was concluded with "several pieces on the Harmonica by Mons. Pick," who came from Brussels, and taught "vocal music by note" as well as "nearly all orchestral instruments."

By 1800 music, and especially church music, was expanding, though organs remained under suspicion as "popish." Scotch-Irish immigrants, coming to North Carolina with their ballads and homemade zithers, soon reached the Southern Appalachians, and followed the western surge out into Ohio. Hymn singing, as practiced by the Lutherans and Moravians, spread to New England, fostered by the singing schools planted by the Rev. Jonathan Tufts. Little by little choir singing became a slightly paid calling for well brought up young ladies, though the era of highly priced church soloists was still several decades in the future. So also was such a group as the Singing Hutchinsons, the famous family chorus which served both God and Mammon in the '50's by concertizing for Temperance, Abolition and similar approved causes (Chapter Note 1).

Meanwhile professional music and its performers were still imported. New York in the '30's patronized an English light opera company, and even a season of Italian grand opera. In 1833 the "new" Academy of Music was ready for the visiting grand opera. Boxes for subscribing proprietors were fitted out with armchairs and sofas, to help the wealthy auditors sustain listening to four hours of song in an unknown tongue. In his diary Philip Hone protested that it was much too long, but seemed proud that his box, shared with two other notable families, had cost 8,000 dollars.

Opera divas now presented a social problem. Did they or did they not rank as foreign *ladies,* and as suitable guests for the best houses? One daring hostess took a chance, inviting Signora Pedrotti to a large reception. To Mr. Hone's indignation, the Signora remained unimpressed by the honor, and refused to sing for nothing.

Such then was the meager background of music and drama against which the career of Charlotte Cushman must be measured.

ENTER MISS CUSHMAN

She was born in Boston in 1816, and lived to be called "the only actress native to our soil to whom the adjective great can be fitly applied." (That was written in 1870.) This genius was bone of the bone and flesh of the flesh of old New England. She was the eighth generation in direct descent from Robert Cushman who came over in the *Mayflower*. (He is mentioned in Bradford's diaries as "manager of business" for the infant settlement at Plymouth.) It should be noted that the *Mayflower* Pilgrims were somewhat less given to restrictions than were some later migrants to Massachusetts Bay.

Seafaring ran through the Cushman annals. Charlotte's father was a West India merchant who allowed his children to perform their own dramatization of "Bluebeard" in the family attic. A seagoing uncle was sufficiently liberal and sufficiently prosperous to be one of the stockholders in the first Tremont Theater. It was this uncle who took his niece to the theater as a reward for minding her books.

Charlotte, however, was never intended for the stage, though she had been noticed early as possessing a remarkable voice. It was the sudden death of Charlotte's father, leaving five children with but scanty support, that called for her removal from school at the age of thirteen. She was to be trained in singing as an aid to the family. Nothing more worldly than church music was in view, a modestly lucrative but still genteel calling for a young lady. Soon she was appearing with the Woodward sisters, the best church singers of their day. Then she was called upon for duets with the English professional, Mrs. Mary Anne Wood, who gave concerts at the old Boston Museum on the Saturday nights when theatrical performances were barred. (One hates to suggest Boston as the originator of the "sacred concerts" of later vaudeville utility, but such seems to be the case.)

It was this Mrs. Wood, whose English opera enlivened early New York, who urged Charlotte to train her voice for the stage. That in 1830 was not romantic. It was a genuine sacrifice of caste made on the altar of home. So, at less than twenty, Charlotte joined an early opera troupe, which after a few weeks in Boston, sailed for their main season in New Orleans among the music-loving French.

Six or seven performances a week proved too great a strain for so young a singer. To her horror Charlotte discovered that she was losing her voice. Desperate, she called on the manager of the English theater there for advice. To help this girl, stranded so far from friends, the tragedian of the company offered to let her play Lady Macbeth at his approaching benefit performance. Since Charlotte had no costumes nor money to buy them, the leading lady of the local French theater offered hers. Unfortunately the French tragedienne was four feet ten and fat; Charlotte was five feet six and thin. Necessity, though, was a stern driver. Charlotte went on, her length covered by two of the French woman's robes.

Proceeds from this extraordinary debut brought Charlotte to New York via sailing ship, an opera singer without a voice, an actress by virtue of one performance only. Nevertheless, she was taken on at the Bowery Theater as a "heavy woman." The salary was 25 dollars a week, with five dollars deducted to pay for costumes. On the strength of that remaining twenty dollars, Charlotte sent to Boston for the four younger children to come and live on her. One week after their arrival the theater burned. With it went Charlotte's costumes and her bread and butter. Only an unexpected five weeks' engagement at Albany, where the theater opened when the legislature met, saved the family from complete disaster (Chapter Note 2). Next Charlotte became a "walking lady" for the Park Theater in New York at 20 dollars a week. Then, after serving a three-year apprenticeship, this astounding young woman of 24 took over the management of the Walnut Street Theater in Philadelphia.

From this time on (1840), Charlotte Cushman's career was assured. But, although she was the republic's leading actress, much of her professional life was spent overseas in English theaters. The few large cities in this country could not support steadily even one highgrade company. Charlotte was forced to invade London which also proclaimed her genius. Moreover, her enunciation was pronounced perfect, score one for the schools of Boston!

Artistically, her best work was in Shakespeare, but her most popular role was Meg Merrilies, the gypsy, in the stage version of *Guy Mannering,* Scott's novels being at the zenith of their fame. Also, three generations before Sarah Bernhardt essayed male parts, Charlotte Cushman played Romeo and Cardinal Wolsey, as well as Hamlet. Whatever the part, all critics agreed that Miss Cushman conveyed a fierce intensity of emotion, a quality not usually attributed to New England women.

All through her life there ran a contradiction. In her art Charlotte Cushman was thoroughly international. Outside of that she was Boston transplanted to whatever part of the globe her profession might call her. Her European holidays were spent in Rome where she maintained a studio presided over by a strict New England spinster. When friends came in, she would sing for them the period's popular ballad, "Oh, Mary Go and Call the Cattle Home." For her portrait she sat to Emma Stebbins, an American woman sculptor (Chapter Note 7). During the Civil War Miss Cushman returned to her own country to give benefit performances for the Sanitary Commission, precursor of the Red Cross. Later, a victim of cancer, she no longer had strength for acting. Then she turned reader and continued that almost to the end. The glory of an art cursed by the Puritans, Charlotte Cushman lived and died a strict professor of their code, and the greatest actress of the republic's first hundred years.

AND NOW A PLAYWRIGHT

Another pioneer of the theater was Anna Cora Mowatt. Not as notable an actress as Charlotte Cushman, she was the first American woman to go in for practical play writing. Her famous comedy was *Fashion*. It is still revived by theater groups as a period piece more than a hundred years after its original production.

The first woman dramatist was no offspring of a vagabond theatrical troupe, but a lady who began and ended her days under the most correct auspices. She was born into a well known New York family in 1819. The very American ups and downs of her life began in Anna Cora's childhood. Her distinguished father, Samuel Ogden, had involved himself so deeply in a South American revolution that a long sojourn abroad was indicated. Anna Cora was born and educated in France. Exile terminated when she was fourteen, and her family resettled among the Dutch of Flatbush. A year later she was married to James Mowatt, a prosperous New York lawyer, many years older than herself. Ill health sent the young bride on a long European voyage. Soon she and her husband were enjoying the continental theater, an important item for her later career. Meanwhile, on this side of the Atlantic had come the financial crash of 1837. By 1840 James Mowatt had lost his fortune.

As necessity had driven Charlotte Cushman to acting, so threat of poverty turned Anna Cora Mowatt into a dramatist. She was still only 26 years old when she wrote *Fashion*. The comedy was so successful that it was presented simultaneously in New York and Philadelphia. Then the handsome young author set herself up as a leading woman, enacting the standard heroines of the period. Her aging husband served as her manager until his death in 1851. The widow carried on by herself a few years longer till, in 1854, she married William F. Ritchie, editor of the *Richmond* (Va.) *Inquirer,* and prepared to retire into the anonymity of the correct Virginia matron. She never set foot upon the stage again.

No outstanding artistic merit is claimed for Mrs. Mowatt's *Fashion,* but it remains an interesting social document. In it all city women were given over to vanity. City men of business were defaulters. Foreigners, without exception, were scoundrels. The high-minded hero was a Cattaraugus County farmer. The supremely virtuous heroine was considered fatally compromised because, from the best of motives, she stepped into a darkened room to speak to a man. As a reflection of the mental attitude of the period this has significance, for *Fashion* gained a big popular following. More surprising, *Fashion* still survives on the boards. It was revived successfully by the Provincetown Players in 1920 as a period piece, and ever since then has been accepted on the little theater circuit throughout the country. A hundred years ago Anna Cora Mowatt, a self-taught dramatist, wrote a thoroughly playable play.

The social stigma of a stage career, even a successful one, is illustrated by the last phase of Mrs. Mowatt's life. When Mr. Ritchie brought his distinguished bride home to Richmond, the woman who was to be "Marion Harland" of later cookbook fame, was still Mary Virginia Hawes, daughter of a well-to-do merchant there. The town, she afterwards related, was thrown into a turmoil by this marriage of a leading citizen to a member of an outlawed profession (Chapter Note 3). The crucial point was whether to call, or not to call.

This particular actress, it was admitted, had been born and bred a lady. Her personal life was above suspicion. Yet she had been behind the footlights. Controversy boiled, and especially within the Hawes household, for Mr. Ritchie had suggested that Mr. Hawes's daughter might enjoy meeting Mrs. Ritchie. It was a delicate moment, for Miss Mary Virginia had just published a first novel, anonymously of course, and Mr. Ritchie's columns were very influential. So Mr. Hawes dodged the issue. His daughter, he explained, was about to leave town to visit relatives in the North.

In that interval Miss Hawes's second novel appeared over the *nom de plume* of Marion Harland, and received a most favorable review in the *Richmond Inquirer*. Common decency required that the young authoress pay a thank-you call. It happened that the lady from the stage was not at home. "I recall with a blush of shame," confessed the daughter of Richmond 50 years after the event, "how relieved I was that a card should represent me." Little by little, though, local ironbound conventions were stretched to include the new Mrs. Ritchie, whose only crime was to have earned an honest living in the theater.

THE BACKGROUND FOR ART

Oddly enough the next notable female practitioner of the arts was a sculptor. By logic one might have looked for a painter, since water colors had been a ladylike accomplishment since the Revolution. Indeed, there had been a few feminine portraitists, usually in miniature, in the colonial period. The chief surviving name is Henrietta Johnston of Charleston, South Carolina, who was doing portraits there shortly after 1700. But she, as well as her craft, had been imported from England. There was a lapse of more than a century before any American-born woman reached professional status.

Perhaps the first practical application of female craftsmanship in the new republic is that revealed by a curious advertisement printed in the *Salem* (Mass.) *Register* of 1808. It read: "Miss Honeywell, a young lady born without hands, and with only three toes on one foot; who is not so much a subject of wonder and admiration for her great ingenuity and elegance in embroidering flowers fit for framing and cutting with rich variety and taste gentlemen's watch-papers . . . as for the peculiar felicity of her disposition and her entertaining style of conversation . . . resulting in an admiration of the unparalleled good sense and cheerful resignation of this

Young Lady, to her peculiar lot . . . She threads her needle and ties the knot. N.B. large flowers, fancy pieces, watch-papers, etc. for sale by the young lady at the above mentioned place."

Admission was twenty-five cents, with children at half price. The young lady without hands was commercially on view from 9 to 12, 2 to 5, and 7 to 9. Nothing more is known of this attempt to combine the trade of the side-show with the art of the scissors. Only the old newspaper notice survives.

Meanwhile, throughout the settled regions of the new republic, there stirred the first halting efforts of women in the graphic arts. Usually the workers were anonymous, and the accepted media were needlework designs, funeral mementos and such like in pencil sketches or embroidery. Surviving examples of this "seminary art" now have their day of glory as museum pieces.

Rarer still were the women who made themselves into self-taught portraitists. Such a one was Ruth Bascom (1772–1841), widow of a Dartmouth professor and wife of a clergyman in the Deerfield and Ashby sections of Massachusetts. Starting with the cutting of silhouettes, Mrs. Bascom progressed to portraits in pastels, beginning (1819) with likenesses of her own nieces and nephews. Completely self-taught, she never learned to do a full-face, and when confronted with such items as spectacles, she cut them out of gilt paper and affixed them to her compositions (Chapter Note 4).

Less aspiring, but more proficient in technique were early craft-workers who made an art of lady's band-boxes. At least one woman among them has become a collector's item in our own day. She was Hannah Davis of New Hampshire, who thought well enough of her own wares to paste a printed label inside the cover: "Women's Wooden Band-Boxes Manufactured by Hannah Davis, Easy Jaffray, New Hampshire."

They were made of thin bass-wood, both light and strong, and were lined with old newspapers. Hannah, one suspects, was thrifty. The whole creation was then covered with wall-paper, which was standard, but through those long New Hampshire winters, Hannah used only flower-designs. Come spring, her boxes were loaded into farm-wagons and driven down to the mills at Lowell. There they were sold to the "loom ladies" though Hannah's own label discards the lady, and comes out flat-footed for "women." Her wares were also peddled to the female operatives of the old textile plants at Nashua and Manchester.

Now more than a hundred years afterwards, the boxes themselves testify to the soundness of their making. One salutes Hannah, but an "assist" may be due to her father, who according to antiquarian research, was an early maker of cheese-boxes. Thus one visualizes those old New England farms making winters both profitable and busy by turning the home kitchen into a small factory. Some farmers produced chairs or chair parts. The Davises concentrated on cheese-boxes.

The rest is speculation. Did Hannah fashion all those boxes that bore her label, or did she have other farm-girls to help her? Who constructed the first model, Hannah or her father? Who thought of the mill-girls as customers? Who did the marketing, Hannah or Farmer Davis? No one knows. But the facts themselves provide a little glimpse into a woman's craft that paid its way in the Forties.

In higher art forms, the first women to master professional techniques of painting were the numerous daughters of Charles Willson Peale and his brother James, both pioneers of American art. The Peale progeny learned their craft right in their home studio. In the rising generation were Margaretta Angelica, Anna, Sara, and Maria, all of whom wielded the brush in family style, from still life to portraiture. In 1819 Andrew Jackson "sat" to Anna Peale, while, in 1825, the visiting Lafayette permitted Miss Sara Peale to take his likeness.

But these ladies of the Peale family remain exceptional. Even recent research can unearth very few women among American primitives, and only a few women's names appear on Belnap's roster of early artists and craftsmen of Essex County, Massachusetts. There was Sarah Allen who did portraits in 1820. Hannah Crowninshield was "a talented amateur." Mary Ward (born 1800) also did portraits, while fifteen years later, Mary Derby had a studio of her own on Blaney Street in Salem, Massachusetts. This makes her the first American woman on record to have her own studio. (Her canvasses are preserved in the Essex Museum.)

Altogether, of 85 painters on Belnap's list, eight were women. Of 37 engravers, we have only Ophelia Akin, married to John Akin, who stood high in the craft. Of Ophelia, we know merely that she engraved a certificate of membership for the Newburyport Orphan Asylum. Among 30 "daguerrians" not one was a woman. Of 30 listed sculptors and carvers, there was exactly one woman, Louisa Lander, who went to Rome in 1855 (Chapter Note 7).

Such was Salem in Salem's golden era. From this background came Sophia Peabody, the gifted amateur who drew illustrations for Hawthorne's *Twice Told Tales,* and then married the author. Some of her anonymous copies of paintings at the Boston Athenaeum were actually sold. That was when her younger brothers had been expelled, in debt, from Harvard, and the Peabodys were pressed for money.

But the artist gladly concealed herself, a shrinking semi-invalid, in the family background recently reconstructed in Mrs. Tharp's story of the Peabody sisters. Their mother had her own private school in Salem. At fifteen the delicate Sophia was put to studying drawing to become her mother's art teacher. The Peabodys might sometimes be poor, but they were always genteel. Pupils were rebuked for being "unfeminine and indelicate." The young drawing teacher was admonished to read only those poets "with whom no one has found fault and which are perfectly moral." Then Sophia met the gifted Hawthorne and sketched herself into a long engagement. They were finally married in 1842 when Sophia was 33 years old (Chapter Note 5).

ENTER HARRIET HOSMER

A complete reversal of all this was Harriet Hosmer, the first American woman artist to attain international rank (Chapter Note 7). She was a most unexpected personality to emerge from the sober village of Watertown, Massachusetts, where she was born in 1830. A recognized sculptor at twenty-three, Harriet swam, skated, shot, climbed trees, rode to hounds and often swung a four-and-a-half-pound sculptor's mallet from eight to ten hours daily. Gone was Sophia Peabody's neurotic self effacement. Harriet tossed her curls back from her forehead, and had them cut short behind. Altogether, she was anything else but an early Boston model.

Equally arresting was Harriet's father, who educated his child almost completely according to principles that would be advocated much later by John Dewey. Harriet Hosmer was the daughter of a village physician whose wife and older child had died of tuberculosis. Dr. Hosmer then set out to develop the frail physique of his one surviving child (Chapter Note 6).

While other little girls were learning their catechism or dutifully stitching samplers, Harriet was given a thorough drill in all the sports, and hardly any formal schooling. She hunted, stuffed her trophies and mounted them. She found a clay pit on her father's land, and began modeling all her favorite dogs and horses, or the wild creatures she had shot. At length she was sent away to school. For several years her educational record was the list of places from which she was expelled. Finally, in despair, Dr. Hosmer appealed to Mrs. Sedgwick of the famous school at Lenox. She wrote back, "I like wild colts."

So to Lenox went Harriet Hosmer at sixteen. Mrs. Sedgwick supplied her with abundance of horse-flesh, and let her put in her spare time modeling the hands and feet of her classmates. For three years Harriet absorbed some amount of book learning. Then she announced her intention of becoming a sculptor. She went home, joined an artist's studio in Boston, walking the fourteen miles to and from her class. Next she determined to study anatomy. Since the Boston Medical School would not accept a woman, she went all the way to St. Louis to find one that would. Neither faculty nor students there welcomed her, "but to the credit of the members of the college, she suffered no annoyance from them." This degree of chivalry was enhanced by the lady's reputation as a dead shot.

All this became a little difficult for Dr. Hosmer. As the price of his victory, Daughter Harriet was now only too splendidly free of flouted conventions. From St. Louis, alone and unescorted, she rode down the river to explore New Orleans. Then she took the boat trip north to the Falls of St. Anthony, where, on a bet with the steamboat captain, she scaled the supposedly unscalable cliffs. After that she blew in on the Dakotah Indians, to smoke a peace pipe with them—a rather Amazonian exploit for 1850.

Back once more in Watertown, Massachusetts, she found a studio awaiting her, built by her devoted father. There she produced her first statue, "Hesper," which gained an immediate success in

Boston. Thereupon Harriet determined to go to Rome. Once more Dr. Hosmer was ready to back her. The year 1852 found her working in Rome, modeling from the antique. By the Summer of 1855 she had carved three "classic" statues, and a "Beatrice Cenci." All four were exhibited both in Europe and America, and were enthusiastically received.

FAME AND FORTUNE FOR HARRIET

But the country doctor had given till he could give no more. From Watertown came an urgent call for retrenchment. For the first time in her independent career Harriet Hosmer had to consider money. Luckily, she had reached a point where she could turn her talents to financial account. The classic statues were followed by a smaller and delightful "Puck" which won commendation from British royalty and was quickly sold. Even dukes placed orders for copies. Commissions for elaborate tombs and fountains were to follow.

When Miss Hosmer returned to her own country in 1857, she was its foremost sculptor, and as such was awarded the commission for the Benton statue in St. Louis. Critics today may not repeat the plaudits of the '50's, when Hawthorne sang her praise, but in her own day Harriet Hosmer was an achievement.

Her amazing success raises several questions. How much of it was genius, and how much of it was due to Dr. Hosmer's nurture? Without his generous backing, could her talent have been made effective? Could a woman, at that time and in this country, have earned her living while making herself into a sculptor? There are no fixed answers to these queries, but as Harriet's own Victorian biographer puts it, "A child of nature, she became a daughter of fame."

THE FIRST PRIMA DONNAS

The year 1842 saw the birth of two great American stars of opera, Clara Louise Kellogg and Annie Louise Cary.

Technically, the palm for priority might go to Maria Dolores Benedicta Nau, a famous European stage soprano, born in New York City in 1818. Or to Eliza Ostinelli Biscaccianti, born in Boston,

1824. But both of those singers only happened to be born here. Their parents were members of opera troupes from overseas. Little Maria Dolores returned speedily to Europe with her family, and had no further connection with this country except to tour here in 1854. Eliza Ostinelli was also soon removed to study in Italy. There she married the Marquis Biscaccianti; as Madame Biscaccianti she reaped a swift harvest in early San Francisco. Finally, the Adelaide Philips whom Jennie Lind "discovered" here was the daughter of an English theatrical family on tour.

So the Kellogg and the Cary remain the first strictly American ladies of opera put forth by the new world. Clara Louise, the soprano, was born in Sumterville, South Carolina, and Annie Louise, the contralto, in Kennebec County, Maine. One remained an aristocrat all her days. The other was a fine, hearty country girl with a golden flute in her throat. As a soprano, Miss Kellogg was more necessary to operatic history. Her rival had to rest content with the few notable contralto roles, building fame and fortune through concert and oratorio. Both made money, married happily and retired to enjoy their hard-earned gains, oddly enough, both in the state of Connecticut. Miss Kellogg took refuge at New Hartford, and Miss Cary in a house hedged about with rambler roses, just off the green in Norwalk.

CLARA LOUISE KELLOGG

Though southern born, Miss Kellogg's people were transplanted New Englanders, her father, a man of means and culture, serving temporarily as principal of the Sumterville academy. The family had always a musical bent. A maternal grandmother named Lydia Atwood, left a young widow, had supported herself and three children by going about Connecticut setting up looms and teaching thorough bass. That harmonic shorthand was in demand where printed music was scarce. Lydia Atwood must have been one of the earliest American women to master thorough bass, since she dates back nearly to Andrew Law, the pioneer music master of New England.

Lydia's granddaughter was marked as a musical prodigy from the start. At ten months she was imitating her colored nurse's crooning. At three she was trying the piano. Apparently she always sang, teaching herself to use a banjo accompaniment by copying the Negro players she had watched. When the family returned to its northern setting, they often went into New York to hear good music. With all her gift, Clara Louise might have remained just another talented amateur except for the panic of 1857 in which her father went bankrupt. Then she was taken to sing for Colonel Henry Stebbins, wealthy director of the Academy of Music, who arranged for her musical education along with his own daughters.

Admittedly now Clara was headed for opera, a goal that required courage from a girl still immersed in a strict Puritan background. Instead of expecting girl friends in New York to flock to her debut, Clara Kellogg called them together to warn them of her impending social disgrace. She would not expect them to "know" her any more, she explained, or even speak to her, should they meet her on the street.

Her first role was Gilda in *Rigoletto*. She had studied the part musically, months on end, but she was not permitted to learn what the story was about. Clara's mother took care of that. (Evidently young ladies of the 1850's accepted parental authority much more meekly than they do in the 1950's.) Mrs. Kellogg, though a good musician herself and devoted to her daughter's talent, so distrusted the stage that the young prima donna was not even allowed to talk with the artists among whom she sang. Also there was an uncle who still wanted to make a decent milliner out of Clara. Whenever they met, he would greet his niece by chanting "Broad is the road that leads to Hell." Years later the prima donna, still unforgiven, paid for the uncle's funeral.

On February 21, 1861 Clara Louise, aged 19, height five feet four, faced her first audience at the Academy of Music in New York. Charlotte Cushman, good and generous, was there to hail the appearance of this first American-taught prima donna. Afterwards, when Miss Kellogg had become world-famous, she returned the compliment by going to the theater where Miss Cushman was Queen Katherine, in *Henry VIII,* to sing the off-stage music to which the Spanish queen was to die. By a slight anachronism, the selection was "Angels Ever Bright and Fair" from Gounod's *Faust*. But the tribute was genuine and personal. It was never reported to the press of the period.

Clara Louise's long career is part of musical history. But some incidents in it illuminate the customs of the country. The general public still regarded opera as demoralizing. Admittedly many of the books of the opera were hardly suitable reading for the well brought up young person. Boston ruled out *Rigoletto*. The new *Faust* was considered "frightfully daring." For an entire year directors of the old Academy of Music in Brooklyn refused to have their audience contaminated by *Traviata*. This opposition was made so public that when the production was finally allowed, the whole town turned out to see it. "Every clergyman within travelling distance was in the house," said Miss Kellogg. And in spite of parental vigilance, romantic young ladies wrote letters to the leading Italian tenor. Harvard students "suped" for the opera when it came to Boston. It was Clara Louise Kellogg who created for this country the role of Marguerite in *Faust*. For this occasion Mrs. Kellogg allowed her daughter, then 25, to read Goethe's immortal tragedy.

In all her work the young opera star found the handicaps of the republic's "crude and primitive theaters" almost unsurmountable. Stage convention required that the women's roles be costumed in hoop-skirts regardless of part or period. Madame La Grange, a French soprano, carried this so far as to go to bed in a hoop-skirt in the sleepwalking scene in *La Sonnambula*.

As was the case with Charlotte Cushman, the Civil War drove the American prima donna to try her fortune abroad. Local producers had done their best. They had put on *Daughter of the Regiment,* interspersed with "Yankee Doodle" and "Hail, Columbia." They even introduced "The Star Spangled Banner" into *The Barber of Seville*. But all in vain. Classical music was out for the duration. So Miss Kellogg carried her career across the Atlantic, where the great Campanini proclaimed that her voice had "absolutely perfect tone."

But all this time the famous singer remained under the watchful eye of her mother. "I led a deadly dull and virtuous life of necessity," she afterwards declared. She was still not permitted to chat with any man in the theater, nor in any way to mingle with the artists among whom she worked. Miss Kellogg may have conquered Europe, but it was years before she achieved her own personal freedom.

THE LADY FROM MAINE

Very different was Annie Louise Cary, first American Amneris in *Aida* and, after that, the first American Ortrud in *Lohengrin*. A plain down-easter from the state of Maine, she studied in Boston and then in Milan. Her debut was made abroad, where she remained all through the Civil War. Not till 1870 did she return to her native land to reap the financial reward of her European acclaim.

Fate bestowed on Miss Cary a sunny personality. At the peak of her fame she remained "democratic and unconventional." For those long Western trips she went armed with her knitting bag. Out there hotels and theaters were usually thick with dirt, and like the good Maine Yankee that she was, Annie Louise could not abide dirt. The prima donna would send for porters and chambermaids, pails and scrubbing brushes. Also, when she felt it necessary, she would demonstrate on hands and knees what clean meant in Kennebec county.

To post-Civil War decades belong Miss Kellogg's intelligent effort to produce grand opera in English, and also her far less creditable feud with her rival prima donna. Since both Annie Louise and Clara Louise were great box-office attractions, a joint operatic tour was arranged by a management not too well versed in the ways of opera stars. Trouble began over travel accommodations. Miss Kellogg, always anxious about draughts, demanded that their special car be kept snugly heated. For the vigorous Miss Cary nothing was as good as fresh air. By Chicago the feud reached its climax.

There the soprano accused the contralto of ruining the cadenza of an opera duet. Though personally affable, Miss Cary had professional pride. The fault, she maintained, had been Miss Kellogg's. Even Chicago critics disagreed as to what had happened to the fateful cadenza, but all the reading public soon learned of the quarrel. For the rest of the tour, Clara Louise never "knew" Annie Louise socially.

Both rivals terminated their stage careers with equally successful marriages. Clara Louise Kellogg became Madame Carl Strokosh, her husband being the nephew of the famous opera impressario. Annie Louise Cary contented herself with a plain American bank president and became Mrs. C. M. Raymond of Cincinnati.

The Civil War interrupted serious musical growth in the United States, but the two famous opera singers had done their work. After them no one questioned the right of an American girl to go as far as her voice would take her. If stage careers were still rare, the close of the 1860's saw the rise of the professional choir soloist. Another field, and a well paid one, had been opened to this country's women (Chapter Note 8).

Meanwhile, from three thousand miles to the west came a new version of the success story, with the rise of the child-star, Lotta Crabtree. Not concerned with high art, Lotta's dancing and mimicry laid the foundation for one of the most amazing fortunes to be earned and kept in the American theater. When Lotta retired in 1891, still at the height of her drawing power, she was popularly supposed to be a millionaire. Sensational newspapers suggested that she might even be worth a million and a half, possibly two millions. Following her death in 1924 as a semi-recluse of 77, the surrogate's figures were startling. Her alleged fortune had not shrunk, as so many fortunes do. It had grown to five million.

Lotta's fame belonged to the California gold rush. It was at the raw and violent mining camp at Rabbit Creek that the tiny dancer—red-haired and black-eyed—made her first public appearance. Entertainment-starved miners threw gold nuggets at her lively feet, and Lotta's mother gathered the treasure in her apron. This was more money than the Crabtree family had ever seen before. And once Mary Ann Crabtree found gold raining down, she never let it go.

The Lotta story started in New York where John Crabtree kept an unprofitable bookstall on Nassau Street. His wife, Mary Ann, went on working in her family's upholstery business, making satin draperies for the carriage trade. In 1851 John Crabtree joined the gold rush. In '53 he sent for his wife and their little girl. No one knows who paid for their passage via Panama. At San Francisco a letter from John bade them come up the river to Grass Valley where fortune awaited them. Later it developed that the fortune was to be gained by Mary Ann's keeping a miners' boarding house in Grass Valley. Her handsome husband hadn't done so well at washing gold.

Yet romance gleamed in Grass Valley. There it was said that the little Lotta, only six and small for her age, encountered Lola Montez, renowned dancing adventuress. Lola, Irish-born, of good family, had won and lost two husbands, to become the publicly acknowledged "best friend" of old Ludwig of Bavaria, who made her Countess of Landsfeld. Driven out by a revolution, with unerring instinct the Countess headed for California, to capitalize on herself in the theaters of early San Francisco. There, too, she quickly acquired a third husband, Patrick Purdy Hull, owner of a San Francisco newspaper.

No one knows why the Hulls went up the river to Grass Valley. Possibly the élite of San Francisco hadn't approved of her play, *Lola Montez in Bavaria*. In Grass Valley the newly married pair acquired a dwelling close by the boarding house where Mary Ann Crabtree was supporting her family and rocking the cradle of a new baby, a boy.

Romantic tradition credits Lola Montez with having taught the little Lotta to dance. That story appeared years afterward when Lotta had conquered New York as well as California. It may or may not have been true, but it was a good story. Certainly the fame of Lola Montez meant something to the hard worked Mary Ann. Meanwhile the Countess had quarreled with her third husband, and departed for a widely advertised tour of Australia.

By this time John Crabtree had another fortune in prospect, farther away in the mountains. There was a newer, richer camp high up in the Sierras at Rabbit Creek. The fortune materialized into another boarding house, to which came an Italian musician. Like many another goldseeker, he hadn't prospered with pick and shovel. Instead he began putting on crude shows for the miners.

In much later years Lotta herself credited this Signor Bona with teaching her to sing and dance. She added that she had learned her soft-shoe technique from a nameless Negro slave that someone had brought to Placerville; the little girl had watched him on her mining camp circuit. From him she had also learned to play the banjo sufficiently to add blackface mimicry to her repertoire. In the profession such sketches were called Topsies. This Signor Bona is a documented figure. Under a stage name of Mart Taylor he organized the rough and ready mining camp tours that laid the foundation of the Crabtree fortune. As always, Lotta's mother went along, protecting her child, playing the cymbals and gathering in the nuggets. Before long John Crabtree faded out of the picture, not to rejoin the family group till his daughter had become a famous comedienne in the East.

Next Mary Ann Crabtree began her fight to get the little Lotta into the legitimate theater already flourishing in San Francisco. That too was rough going, with Mrs. Crabtree frisking her gifted child in and out of bar-rooms and auctions—anywhere that she might be paid to dance. At length, in 1856, she had a small part in a real play, performed in a tiny upstairs theater in Petaluma. Lotta's first theater appearance in San Francisco (1857) was followed by more of those hard but remunerative camp tours. It was in 1864 that Mrs. Crabtree bought Lotta her first silk dress and set out for a New York opening.

But those California sketches weren't good enough for Broadway, though again they coined money on extended road trips west to Chicago and St. Louis. On this swing around, the redoubtable mother came in contact with an English manager who arranged for her the sketches from Dickens, *Little Nell* and *The Marchioness,* with which Lotta charmed both Boston and New York in the season of '66–'67.

All these years Mary Ann Crabtree had kept her daughter and her daughter's earnings under close guard, training herself to become a good judge of investments. That skill, too, the mother passed on, and as with everything else that Lotta had been taught, she profited by the teaching. But the mother's hold remained so absolute that even after Mrs. Crabtree's death Lotta lived a secluded life outside of the theater. Her real friends were her pets, dogs and horses. When she died many years later, her fortune was willed to charities, the largest shares to Humane societies.

Those five millions and their destination precipitated a notorious lawsuit. A woman in California announced herself as Lotta's "secret" daughter. When that wouldn't work, the claimant took legal steps as the daughter of Lotta's long-dead brother, by a common-law marriage in some obscure mining town. Not only was the case thrown out of court, but the judge also ordered charges brought against the instigators. Lotta's will was upheld, and to this day her millions work for the protection of dumb animals.

1 Abby Hutchinson, the contralto of the Singing Hutchinsons, has one still live connection with our own day. She was the author of a gospel hymn "Kind Words Can Never Die," which is claimed as the original source of the army song "Old Soldiers Never Die." Sister Abby's hymn had several verses, with chorus, passing from Kind Words, to Childhood, to Sweet Thoughts, and culminating with Our Souls.

The turning of this hymn into a barracks ballad was transatlantic. Around 1870 the catchy tune reached England where it was worked into a song for the old soldiers' home in Chelsea. In the First World War British troops were singing the tune to words of which sister Abby would never have approved. Meanwhile, on this side of the water, the old hymn is said to have become a West Point song around 1900. Through all these chances and changes sister Abby's rhythmic creation has been preserved.

2 An interesting souvenir of Charlotte Cushman's stay in Albany is a long poem that she wrote on the Shakers of Watervliet, which was published in the old *Knickerbocker Magazine*. The Shakers were founded by an English woman, "Mother Ann" Lee, in 1776, with celibacy as one of their chief tenets.

Below is an extract from Miss Cushman's long poem.

> *Mysterious worshippers!*
> *Are you indeed the things you seem to be,*
> *Of earth, yet of its iron influence free—*
>
> *Have you forgot your youth . . .*
> *When all looked fair to fancy's ardent eye . . .*
> *You too! What early blight*
> *Has withered your fond hopes, that ye thus stand,*
> *A group of sisters 'mong this monkish band . . .*
> *and your pale brows*
> *Bear not the tracery of emotion deep—*
> *Ye seem too cold and passionless to weep.*

3 There seems to have been a time-lag of about twenty years between North and South on the social acceptance of an actress. In the North caste lines were broken by the triumph of Fanny Kemble, brought to this country by her father after her London success. Miss Fanny soon became a prized dinner guest in the best New York houses.

A more striking instance, though less publicized, was that of Priscilla Cooper who married the oldest son of President John Tyler. Her father, Thomas A. Cooper, was a scholarly interpreter of Shakespearian roles, some critics ranking him higher as a student than as an actor. He toured this country, 1820–1830, and was especially well liked in New York, where he married the daughter of a judge. Their child was this Priscilla who played small parts in her father's company previous to her marriage to the young Tyler. As the President's daughter-in-law, she was received with him at the White House in the interval before President Tyler's second marriage. The young Mrs. Tyler seems to have severed all connection with the stage, and shared her husband's misfortunes during the Civil War. Her acceptance in Virginia antedates Mrs. Ritchie's experience by fifteen years, but Mrs. Ritchie had been known far and wide as an actress. Priscilla Cooper's short career was obscure.

4   More is known of Mrs. Bascom than of any other early "lady limner" because she kept a diary which came down in her family, and her profile portraits have been preserved in the museums of Ashby and Leicester, Massachusetts. Folk art research has also unearthed a few more names from this largely anonymous period. A graveside water color, for instance, in the Colonial Williamsburg collection, has been identified as the work of Belinda Savage. Then Deborah Throop of West Brookfield, New York, at the age of fifteen and self-taught, began painting primitive portraits and miniatures. Jane Swisshelm in her early marriage essayed painting, to give it up because it interfered with the housework. Her self-portrait is owned by the Pennsylvania Historical Society. Eliza Taylor, an "eldress" of the Shakers, composed elaborate drawings presenting the Shaker doctrines graphically.

5   The pioneer educational work of Elizabeth Peabody (Sophia's oldest sister), who had been in schoolteaching most of her life, did not come until after the Civil War, and so is beyond the scope of this study. It was in 1867 that she visited Germany to investigate the methods of Froebel. On her return in 1870 she established in Brooklyn this country's first kindergarten. Born in 1804, Miss Peabody was then past today's accepted retirement age. Only, in 1870 she didn't know it.

6   At about the time that Dr. Hosmer was evolving his system of athletics for his young daughter, record shows the existence of an American girl acrobat. One Aaron Turner, a Connecticut shoemaker, began exhibiting a team of homemade acrobats, his two sons and a daughter. The

Turner daughter did not remain long in that profession. She married G. T. Bailey, "the first man to exhibit a hippopotamus in the United States." Aaron Turner's venture is remembered chiefly because, in 1835, he engaged a young fellow down on his luck, to be the cashier for his show. The young man was Phineas Barnum, soon to be a magic name in the world of early entertainment.

7   Harriet Hosmer retains sculptural priority over Louisa Lander by a slight margin. It was in 1855 that Miss Hosmer began exhibiting in Rome, although she had exhibited in Boston about two years before that. Miss Lander's best known work was a portrait bust of Chief Justice Shaw at one time placed in the Harvard Library, and a head of Nathaniel Hawthorne done in Rome, 1858–60. Emma Stebbins, to whom Charlotte Cushman sat for her portrait bust, belongs to the Civil War period. In 1867 she executed a statue of Columbus which was presented to New York City in 1869 by a wealthy donor, and then forgotten. After many years it was rescued from obscurity to be the center of Columbus Park in the lower east side of Manhattan.

8   Adah Isaacs Menken is not included as an early blooming artist since her personality erupted during the Civil War. It was then that she startled American playgoers by the nearest approach to nudity seen upon the boards till that time. The occasion was her ride on a live horse in the old drama *Mazeppa*. Her marital record is equally striking.

Originally Adelaide McCord, she was born sometime around 1837, somewhere around New Orleans. After a first marriage she became Adah Isaacs Menken, a name that she clung to throughout the vicissitudes of three other marriages. Divorcing Mr. Menken, she removed to New York where she married a prize-fighter, John C. Heenan. Under pressure of great poverty she persuaded a theater manager in New York to let her do the "live" Mazeppa, clad in tights and strapped to the back of a real horse. It was a sensational feat for the '60's.

She was still "Mazeppa" when she was arrested in Baltimore as a Confederate spy in 1864. By this time she had divorced Heenan, the prize-fighter, to marry a plain citizen of New Jersey named Newell, the briefest of all her marriages. Divorcing Newell, she married Captain James Barkley, a professional gambler. Then she left the United States to mingle in the bohemian circles of London and Paris. She died suddenly, with Swinburne writing a final tribute to her beauty and magnetism.

CHAPTER EIGHT

Beyond the Mississippi

$\mathcal{B}_Y$ 1850 that huge territory west of the Mississippi gained by the Louisiana Purchase was the republic's new frontier. Although Louisiana state had been admitted in 1812, and Missouri in 1821, the plains further north were still sparsely peopled. Only Iowa was to achieve statehood before 1850 (Chapter Note 1).

Yet, for all its newness, this region was the stepping-off point into a greater unknown. Through almost unbroken prairie went trails into more distant wilds—the cattle regions of the southwest, the early emigrant routes to Oregon and California. Across this wide waste would pass the country's largest and strangest exodus, the Mormons seeking a refuge within the bastion of the Rockies. By 1847, the Latter-day Saints were laying out the truck farms that would later furnish supplies to goldseekers on their way to California.

This new frontier claimed farmers, traders and adventurers from both North and South, besides a growing element of emigration from overseas. Once more old Indian wars were reenacted, but in new terms. Instead of the mountain valleys of Kentucky and Tennessee, the battlegrounds were the plains of the buffalo hunter. Instead of a blockhouse for defense, there was a circle of wagons set end to end, with women, children and cattle in the middle. Instead of a cunning ambush nearby, there might be a warning glimpse of mounted men on some distant rise of ground, or a moving cloud of dust on a far horizon.

This enormous trans-Mississippi expanse offered the greatest variety of people and customs. North of opulent Louisiana were raw trading towns coming into being at river crossings where emigrants must wait on the weather and replenish stores. That which is now Kansas City was Westport on the Missouri. St. Joseph was the farthest west for river boats, while the fur outpost of St. Louis still retained a French flavor.

Here men were too busy laying out farms and towns to make note of how people lived. The women, especially, were taken for granted. Rarely did anyone record women doing this or that. Still more rarely was there a woman of sufficient importance to compel notice. The women of this time and place must be recovered from scanty and scattered mention.

TWO WOMEN OF FORT SNELLING

The first documented women in what became Minnesota are found in army annals. That was part of the traditional pattern of western expansion: first an isolated army post, then settlers who could rely on it for a minimum of protection. So at Fort Snelling there were two pioneering army women whose husbands served there before any real fort had been built. The post was then called St. Anthony.

The tale will be fragmentary, with gaps suffered in the lapse of time. But the women were very real. First was Charlotte Clark, whose husband was commissary at St. Anthony from 1819 till 1827. Her memories of that grim assignment were of the long winter's cold with recurring shortages of provisions. For white female society she had only a girl of sixteen, the recent bride of a soldier. Yet Mrs. Clark established a Sunday school at the post, probably for Indian children, since there were no white children at hand.

Then to St. Anthony came Abigail Snelling, for whose engineer husband the Fort was later named. She was a woman of the very old army, antedating even Margaret Taylor (the wife of "Old

Zach") who covered much of this territory twenty years later (Chapter Note 1). Abigail was born about 1797–8, and born into the army. Her father, a Lieutenant Colonel Hunt, had been assigned to Mackinac when it was chiefly an Indian trading station. As a child Abigail remembered their Scots regimental surgeon, whose shrewd Indian wife conducted a fur-trading business of her own. On its proceeds the doctor sent his half-white daughters to distant Montreal for the best schooling there.

After Mackinac Colonel Hunt was shifted to Missouri. There Abigail went to her first school, a French convent at St. Louis. Her father, meanwhile, presided over the river post to which Lewis and Clark returned from their famous expedition. In 1809 both Colonel Hunt and his wife died. Young Abigail was returned to grandparents in Massachusetts who placed her in a boarding school in Salem. After this brief contact with New England's golden age, she once more joined the army. This was at Detroit where she had an older brother, and the time was just previous to the opening of the War of 1812. There, at fifteen, Abigail Hunt married a young Captain Snelling, from "Tippecanoe's" troops. There, too, she witnessed the humiliating surrender of Detroit without a shot fired; her own wedding ceremony was in progress as the British drew up for assault. The service was hastily concluded. As a bride of two weeks Abigail elected to share her husband's captivity in Montreal. Afterwards officers were shipped en parole to Boston where her first child was born, she being not yet sixteen.

After the signing of the peace treaty the young couple had a respite at Governor's Island in New York harbor, and at Plattsburg on Lake Champlain. Then Snelling was ordered to the upper Mississippi. En route the family stopped at St. Louis, where one of the children died. From St. Louis to Prairie du Chien, the trip took three weeks. There, from regimental blockhouses, Abigail could watch Indian traders by day, and by night listen to the howling of the wolves. Abigail's fifth child was born at this post in September 1819. Her room was "papered and carpeted with buffalo robes . . . warm and comfortable."

Then the Snellings joined the Clarks at St. Anthony. There, for two years, the troops were kept busy felling logs while Captain Snelling drew plans for a real fort. It was to be diamond shaped, with barracks of logs and stone and "a neat stone building for officers' quarters," the whole to be surrounded with high stone walls. Altogether, construction took two years, but the army women, possibly tired of tents lined with buffalo robes, moved into their new stone quarters before they were completed. In this far wilderness Abigail Snelling buried a year-old baby.

The fort was inspected and greatly praised by General Scott, who ordered it named for its army-captain architect. That was in 1825, and there the records leave Abigail. It is known only that Captain Snelling died somewhere out in the West, and that his widow, still young, remarried herself out of the army.

AN AUTHOR SEES MINNESOTA

When Frederika Bremer crossed the Mississippi in 1850 to visit the newest Swedish settlements, she was the first woman to report on women in the northern plains region. She reached Minnesota 25 years after the building of Fort Snelling, but St. Paul was less than two years old, and a fur-trading center.

"Here the Indians come till the city swarms with them," wrote the novelist. "The Indian women are less painted and I like their appearance better than that of the men. They have a kind smile, but they are evidently merely their husbands' beasts of burden."

She was taken to "a very respectable Indian hut." There, for a moment, she felt the call of the wild. Recalling gaslit drawing rooms of New York and Boston, the wigwam seemed a happier world. "There they sat at their ease without stays or anxiety to charm. But again I thought me of the life of an Indian woman, serving a husband whom they have seldom chosen themselves, who merely regards them as servants or as a cock regards the hens around him. . . ." Then the fate of an Indian woman seemed tragic. Yet she was told of squaws married to white men, who waited for their children to grow up, and then went back to the wilds, "sickened of their easier lot."

Dividing her attention between the Swedish colonists and the Indians, Miss Bremer made no mention of Harriet Bishop, one of the first Yankee women to reach Minnesota. She was a schoolmarm with a mission. A pupil of Miss Catharine Beecher, Harriet Bishop crossed the Mississippi in 1847, two years before the region was set up as a territory. Undismayed by the primitive conditions, she opened a school in St. Paul, beginning with two white and five Indian children as her first pupils. She was also firm for Temperance, and had the church bells rung in triumph when, in 1852, the new territory passed a strong antiliquor law. (It was afterwards pronounced unconstitutional.)

With her sketchy account of Minnesota Miss Bremer's tour was nearing its end. From Keokuk—pictured as a rough mixture of squatters, Indians, Mormons, Scandinavians, "adventurers, gamblers and thieves"—the author boarded a Mississippi River boat on the first lap of her long journey home. On the steamer she had one last encounter with that phenomenon of the new world, the New England schoolteacher off to the great open spaces. This time she met two young sisters all the way from Vermont, bound for the deep South. There they expected to take over the management of a ladies' seminary. The Yankee girls were quite alone on the vessel, Miss Bremer noted, but seemed well able to look out for themselves.

A RADICAL IN MINNESOTA

Five years after Miss Bremer's hasty report, there came to Minnesota an American woman able to give an account of the experiences of an independent female in the Northwest. This was Jane Swisshelm, Horace Greeley's "Sister Jane," previously known as a venturesome antislavery editor in western Pennsylvania (Chapter Note 2). Her new observation post was St. Cloud, up the river from Minneapolis and about 50 miles southeast of what this century calls Sinclair Lewis's Sauk Center. Like *Main Street's* heroine three generations later, Jane found the path of rebellion far from smooth.

In 1855, separated from her husband, she and her only child joined a married sister in distant Minnesota. Jane had planned on her own little cottage by the lake, with just enough land to feed two. But the shifting of Fort Snelling's troopers to embattled Kansas brought down Indian raids on the outlying settlements. Jane and her little girl then retreated to St. Cloud where the mother once more turned to printer's ink for a livelihood. She started a weekly newspaper which she named *The Visiter* after her abolition journal.

Soon the editor found herself in conflict with the territory's political boss, General Sylvanus Lowry. Lowry, a slave-owning Tennessean, demanded the *Visiter's* support for President Buchanan. Brisk verbal skirmishes followed. In the course of these the editor printed an unflattering description of a frontier belle, easily identified as the wife of Lowry's attorney. This belle was "a large, thick-skinned, coarse, sensual-featured, loud-mouthed, double-fisted dame," wrote the lady-editor. Shortly afterwards a so-called Committee of Vigilance broke into her office, destroyed Jane's press and scattered her type into the street.

The citizenry of St. Cloud resented this attack. A mass meeting was called at which the editor was asked to state her case. This was the first time that Jane Swisshelm ever spoke in public. She named Lowry and his attorney as wreckers of her office, whereupon a mob outside began to hurl stones and to shoot at random. But the men of St. Cloud refused to be intimidated. The meeting voted to purchase a new press and new type for *The Visiter*.

In another two months Jane was back in the fray. To avoid a libel suit, her paper was re-named *The Democrat,* but the editor began campaigning for the new Republican party. Thereupon the Democrats of St. Cloud burned Mrs. Swisshelm in effigy. To cap the climax, the Sioux Indians then staged another revolt. The editor was soon giving shelter to some forty women and children fleeing massacre. "We kept large kettles of boiling water ready as one means of defense," she wrote later.

What with lecturing and editing, Jane held out till 1863, when she was offered a clerkship in Washington in the War Department. She never returned to Minnesota (Chapter Note 2).

IN PROSPEROUS IOWA

But border warfare was not the whole story of the Plains. There were small fortunes to be made in the cities springing up along the rivers. Particularly was this true in Iowa where an impressive degree of urban comfort had been reached by 1850. The year before the state auditor reported ownership of 28,000 horses, 5298 pleasure carriages, 3112 watches and 32 pianos. It was Iowa that saw the transformation of Amelia Bloomer, symbol of women's rights, into a decorous matron of Council Bluffs. That town claimed 3000 inhabitants in the '50's, some still living in their first log houses, others having attained finished frame dwellings. Everyone believed in the town's future. So also did Dexter Bloomer, husband of the lady in trouserines.

THE BLOOMER GOES WEST

In 1853 this notable pair decided to quit Seneca Falls for the new regions. Possibly Amelia had wearied of being a symbol. Possibly the loyal Dexter had had his fill of reform. Anyway, the Bloomers sold out of Seneca Falls.

They paused for a year in Ohio where Dexter bought *The Western Home Visiter* for his wife to edit while he explored commercial possibilities further on. So with one hand Amelia was deputy on the *W.H.V.* while with the other she cultivated her own *Lily*. There, in Ohio, Mrs. Bloomer took one more forward step. She introduced a woman typesetter. Where such a scarce article was to be found in rural Ohio of 1853 history does not tell. But when the male staff refused to accept a female colleague, the owners cleared out all the men typesetters (probably bibulous), and replaced them with strictly teetotal ladies. Three men were retained for heavy printshop chores. Industrially, Amelia Bloomer in Ohio was a good two generations ahead of her time. Also, when she resolved to sell *The Lily,* there was a woman writer ready to venture her all as an editor (Chapter Note 3).

Soon the prosperous pioneers from Seneca Falls were on their way further west by river steamers. But not unheralded. At St. Joseph, Missouri, where they waited for an upstream boat, enterprising citizens spotted the Bloomer (a bit conspicuous in the Missouri landscape of 1855), and hauled her off to make a speech. It was loudly acclaimed in the local paper.

Further welcome followed when the couple finally landed at Council Bluffs. Amelia was haled, not as a radical, but as the embodiment of far-off Eastern culture. Three days later she was elected president of the women's club of the Congregational church.

(Up to that time, she had been an Episcopalian.) Soon she was speaking for the local Methodists as well. Now Amelia deserted the bloomer, advocating in its stead the fashionable new whale-boned hoop skirts.

Dexter Bloomer meanwhile opened a law office specializing in farm questions. The couple began to revel in domesticity—adopting two children to bring up in their new home. Less and less the first lady of Council Bluffs exercised her pen, though she did go on lecturing, sometimes on Women's Enfranchisement, more often on Temperance. Once Amelia demanded (and received) the same fee as that given to Horace Mann the week before. This thriving new West wanted culture and was willing to pay for it. Amelia, late radical, had become the leading conservative hostess of Council Bluffs, her homemade jellies taking prizes at the new county fairs. The Bloomers lived to celebrate their golden wedding in Iowa.

IT HAPPENED IN KANSAS

There was nothing urbane, or even mildly comfortable about pioneering in Kansas or Nebraska. In both these territories, settling was delayed by greater distance, and also by early exploration reports which consigned the region to "The Great American Desert." With abundant fertile land elsewhere, a great American desert did not attract farmers. Until Kansas became a political issue, the area was left chiefly to the Indians—those numerous tribes given refuge there following removal from more favored areas. With the Indians came Indian missions. By 1837 Methodists, Baptists, Quakers, Catholics and Presbyterians all had stations there, along with Indian traders. When the territory was organized in 1852, there were not more than 800 whites in Kansas.

The first named woman in Kansas belonged to the missions. Her record is fragmentary but worth preserving. She was Eleanor Richardson, a volunteer teacher at the Ottowa mission station. There she met and married Jotham Meeker, who had come in 1833 and had made a linguist of himself. It was said that he could speak and translate in ten different Indian tongues. It is known only that Mrs. Meeker had three children out there, and assisted her husband in printing his translations of mission literature. While civil war ravaged Kansas, this devoted couple lived out their scholarly lives in peace.

But violence filled the air. With the passage of the Kansas-Nebraska bill (1854) "free soilers" and "slavers" began pouring across the borders, North and South. Each group was determined to win the state, by force if necessary. Pioneer farms and villages became only too truly "bleeding." One has only to mention John Brown and Pottawatomie Creek to recall years of cruel reprisals. Lawrence, founded in 1854 by "abolition money," was first raided then pillaged two years later.

That date was May, 1856. The same year brought an episode that reveals the temper of early women settlers. Someone opened a "liquor den" near the threatened citadel. One can only guess that to these war-torn women, this was one thing too much. They resorted to direct action, attacking the den with hatchets, hammers and even large axes. Their leader was Mrs. Helen Hutchinson who came from Randolph, Vermont. Two generations before Carrie Nation, Helen Hutchinson poured the offending liquids into the soil of Kansas (Chapter Note 4).

MISSOURI BACKGROUND

Crossing the boundary line south into Missouri brings a marked change. This was an older region. Settlement had begun while Louisiana was still French and St. Louis was a trading station of the Chouteau fur company. When Americans arrived, they were mostly southerners, the famous compromise of 1820 accepting Missouri as slave territory. The settlement pattern was the southern plantation, frontier style, while, during the '40's, the fur-trading post on the river mushroomed into a city of 30,000.

Missouri has a woman narrator. She was that Jessie Benton Frémont whose secret marriage to a penniless exploring map maker in 1841 had set all Washington agog.

St. Louis was home for Jessie Benton, though she had been born in Virginia (1824). Her father, the notable Missouri senator, Thomas Hart Benton, had come to St. Louis from Andrew Jackson's army at New Orleans. Benton's prowess at law and politics

215

produced a spacious home that stood "among its great trees, in a square of its own." Like all early St. Louis, the Benton mansion was in French style, built around a courtyard with separate wings for a family's married sons and daughters.

In Jessie's childhood the French flavor was fading fast, but she could remember its older people as French Catholics and Royalists. "Languages, customs and prejudices," she was sure, "were all French." The young people were "sallow-faced, tawny-haired, black-eyed . . . On the border of an immense and unexplored Indian country," hunters, traders and caravans from Sante Fé were seen in the streets. There were also French peasant women with white caps and sabots, red petticoats and blue or yellow kerchiefs crossed over their white bodices. But even then pear orchards were being cut up into town lots and American business-men were marrying French girls.

Jessie's schooling was French, the senator decreeing that his daughters should speak both French and Spanish. That first school was kept by Monsieur Savary, a resigned soul who struggled daily with some thirty girls from six to sixteen. The little Bentons were escorted by their mother's maid past gardens in which French ladies in negligee were always ready to chat. At the Savary home-academy there was no discipline, but as a reward for good conduct pupils were permitted to assist Madame Savary in the making of fine preserves. "I do not recall anything of lessons," the pupil set down many years later, "but I was taught to hem handkerchiefs." The gentle Monsieur Savary was a victim of the bad cholera year when the Benton children watched drays loaded with coffins go jolting through the streets.

From this easygoing establishment the Benton daughters were graduated into the Convent Sacré Coeur, conducted by five sisters, "accomplished French ladies . . . of gentle refined man-ners." At this stage the girls were taken on trips to New Orleans where they reveled in Louisiana elegance, including dinner tables set out with gold and crystal. Fruits and ices were served while young slaves dressed in white cooled the company with huge fans of peacocks' feathers. Compared with New Orleans, St. Louis was just a village where everyone knew everyone. When the Sena-tor's household went to Washington, it was a two weeks' journey.

They returned regularly every other year to the French mansion with its screened galleries, where life was "light and gay" (Chapter Note 5).

It was to St. Louis that Jessie returned with her mother and her baby, to see Frémont off on his most famous exploration— the expedition that mapped routes to Oregon, then back through the southern Sierras and the old Spanish Santa Fé trail (1843). In the old Benton mansion Jessie held back a Washington dispatch ordering his recall, while she sent her husband a private message urging him to go on. Here, too, she set out a supper table nightly for eight months, expecting the explorer's return, and filled the anxious days by translating the Bernal Diaz diary for her father. In St. Louis Frémont, his mission accomplished, dictated to Jessie his famous report on mountain routes and rivers. This, printed later, was to become the bible of the covered wagon.

Later involvements carried both Frémonts out to California (see Chapter IX) and also into politics. But the Civil War brought them back to Missouri, with Frémont in command of the western department. When Jessie visited there for the last time, she found everything changed. Orchards had been erased. Gardens had disappeared. German had replaced French as a second language, and there were ugly square meeting houses near the old Cathedral. "St. Louis," this was Jessie's parting word, "was now a large city."

SILENCE OVER ARKANSAS

Arkansas, further South, supplies almost no traces of early women. Although Arkansas Post was founded by the French in 1686, the 100 years that followed brought less than 200 settlers. Marsh fevers in the lowlands retarded growth until after the War of 1812, when voyagers began ascending the rivers in search of good land for raising cotton and tobacco.

The names of the men are on record, but there is no mention of any wives. A French group near this first American settlement in western Arkansas had married women from the neighboring Cherokees. By 1834 small steamboats trading along the Arkansas river were selling calico. Since the gentlemen of Arkansas then arrayed themselves in full suits of deerskin, the presence of feminine consumers may be argued. Also one old diary speaks of riding 50 miles for a dance, which again infers a dancing partner.

The one woman in Arkansas annals previous to statehood in 1836 was Tiana, the Indian mate of Sam Houston before he went to fame and Texas. Houston had been elected a young governor of Tennessee in 1827. In 1829 he married, his wife leaving him very shortly afterwards. The cause of the rupture is still unknown, but Houston resigned and took refuge from gossip by joining his boyhood friends, the Cherokees, then located in Arkansas. Tiana was described by the whites as "goodlooking for an Indian." The union lasted till her death several years later. Then Andrew Jackson sent Houston into Texas on an Indian treaty mission. The rest is history.

SOME LOUISIANA LADIES

To Frederika Bremer New Orleans of 1850 was just another large city. If she felt anything of its French origin, it was not confided to her journal, which tells of the week she spent there while waiting for a river-boat.

It was on Christmas morning that a steam packet set her down in New Orleans. Dutifully she went forth to church—a Protestant one—to be rewarded only with what she called a dry and soulless sermon. Beyond this her notes were sociological. She attended several slave auctions and saw a woman and child sold for 750 dollars. Their appearance gave "every evidence of good treatment," the auctioneer boasting of this "uncommonly superior woman and her child."

Next Miss Bremer made a round of prisons to visit "women accused of capital offenses." "A lady charged with the murder of her husband from jealousy" seemed particularly bold and proud. With others, "their dress spoke of circumstances far removed from poverty but their countenances . . . of violent and evil passion." In one prison she found Negro women sequestered there by owners in danger of bankruptcy. One young girl had been so confined for two years. Finally the Swedish traveler took in a colored revival service. It was, she stated succinctly, "a tornado."

In that week, between boats, Miss Bremer made no attempt to go beyond the city itself. She saw nothing of the plantations back from the river which still held happily to their Creole ways. Cotton and sugar had built splendid mansions with imported furnishings, handwrought ironwork, damask hangings, china and glass brought from France. Survivors of this world remain today, architectural treasures of a long-gone past. For the life that went on in those houses in the '50's, a glimpse comes from the diary of Lestant Prudhomme, a law student who kept a journal in English to practice the language that he must later use in court.

Unconsciously the youth pictured an old Creole household with its big happy family and numerous visiting relatives. The young ladies in the journal, all charming, attended a convent school. Accompanied by governesses, they had their daguerreotypes taken, and also bought lottery tickets. On Holy Thursday when the Stabat Mater was sung, the young ladies assisted by the young gentlemen of the neighborhood, took up a special church collection.

Incidentally, these Louisiana plantations were happy hunting grounds for Northern-schooled governesses, who obtained there the highest pay given anywhere for teaching in the old republic. Salaries ranging from 700 to 1000 dollars a year are on record, while not a few of the governesses married themselves into comfortable establishments. Others saved their money to start schools of their own. Earlier, Lucy the Pennsylvania wife of Audubon, supported the family by teaching in Louisiana while her husband pursued his art. Here, too, one finds more music reported than in other sections of the country. People played the piano, the flute, the violin, even the drums. There were "comic and innocent songs," and the ladies expected to journey to New Orleans to hear Jenny Lind.

In Prudhomme's diary the girls, mostly cousins, were expected home from the convent, on vacation, so the youth busied himself making feather fans to present to them. Then the family all went to Natitoches for the circus. Later he reported that his girl cousins had been reproached by the nuns for having danced the waltz at home. At this rebuke, "the little doves" had been bathed in tears. Occasionally a more prosaic note is sounded. "After breakfast," states the journal, "my mother occupied some servants cleaning under my room." It had become infested with fleas from the family cats and dogs. Small pecan brushes, he noted, were used for this cleansing.

There was much fine food in this world, much family affection and many easy tears. A thunderstorm was greeted with "screams, fainting fits and great excitement indoors," so much so that Aunt Theophile must resign her keys and take to her bed. When the diarist left for Natitoches only fifteen miles distant, to start his law studies, his mother and sisters wept, while the boy was "in an agony of grief." When word came that Aunt Hupp's son had died in a distant city, all the relatives assembled to break the news to her. She, poor soul, straightway fainted. Then she continued fainting and collapsing for weeks, while the entire household went into deep mourning. By March, though Aunt Hupp remained prostrated, her nephew reported her as resigned.

THE LALAURIE MYSTERY

It is noticeable that there is no mention of the extraordinary Madame Lalaurie in the pages of either Jessie Benton Frémont or of Frederika Bremer. It was not the kind of story that would have been told to a child in the '40's, and by the time of Miss Bremer's visit, another ten years later, one suspects that New Orleans was constructively forgetting the ghastly revelations of the 10th of April, 1834.

On that date a fire broke out in one of the finest houses on the Rue Royale, that belonging to Dr. and Mrs. Louis Lalaurie. Of the best Creole background with a dash of Irish thrown in, Delphine Lalaurie was a ranking beauty and hostess of the still Gallic city. Not a young beauty, though, for Madame had been twice widowed before she married Dr. Lalaurie, a quiet man of middle age. Near neighbors had begun to talk among themselves after the death of a young colored girl, one of the Lalaurie slaves, who fell or jumped from an upper window into the courtyard. This episode was not imagined, since there is record of a fine imposed on Madame for involvement in the accident.

In the course of fire-fighting on this April 10th, neighbors insisted on breaking into a closed-off top storey of the stately mansion. There there were found seven slaves, young and old men and women, chained and bearing evidence of mutilation. The police were sent for. In the long delay before their arrival, mobs formed outside. Suddenly the door of the carriage house opened, and the Lalaurie coachman, a young mulatto, drove the carriage through the crowd, supposedly with both Madame and her doctor husband concealed within. By the time the police appeared, the mob was surging through the mansion, wrecking its expensive furnishings.

This much is fact, duly reported by four New Orleans newspapers of the following day, April 11. Later when the rescued captives had recovered sufficiently to tell their stories, nothing of a horror-thriller was lacking. Reduced to a minimum, it became evident that the handsome Delphine Lalaurie had become the victim of a terrible insanity. This is the basis of the legend that has made a "haunted house" of this fine surviving example of French Empire architecture. But quickly friends and relatives of the Lalauries began hiding the disgrace or referring to it as the work of "enemies."

Their tactics might well have succeeded except that Harriet Martineau read those New Orleans newspapers and included the story in her *Retrospect of Western Travel,* published in London in 1838. When George W. Cable retold the tale in one of his sketches in 1881, he was accused of having made it up.

Many unanswered questions remain. Rumor made both husband and wife escape in that carriage to Mobile, and thence to France. Rumor later reported having seen either the doctor or his wife in some small French town. But nothing of their afterlife is actually known. This in turn reaches the heart of the mystery. Granted Madame's insanity, why did her husband, himself a physician, conceal her affliction, and by such concealment, permit her perverted practices? And why did the young butler-coachman, himself a slave, join with the Lalauries against victims? Finally, if Dr. Lalaurie was not in the fleeing coach along with his wife, what did become of him? Not even modern research has been able to provide the answers.

DEEP IN THE PAST OF TEXAS

To quit Louisiana for the uncharted wilderness of Texas is to step into a far harsher world. Early Texas had no place for little doves or fainting females.

Records show that women were reckoned on in Austin's venture on the Brazos (1826), but they remain anonymous. At that time Texas was a Mexican province, and Austin's grant gave him permission to settle 900 families. A bid was made for farmers' wives by offering over 4,000 acres, at a purchase price approximating 200 dollars, to each married settler. This bait drew some couples, for along with sawmills and cotton gins, Austin also erected schools. Altogether by 1834, his San Felipe project held some 750 families. With the Texan war of independence intervening, further account of these adventurous wives and mothers is lost. In general, the settlers were Southerners (Austin came from Missouri via Arkansas) who were allowed to bring their slaves as indentured servants.

It seems astonishing that with the older southwestern states so thinly populated, farming families were willing to remove still farther, and into a foreign country. But the financial crash of '37 had been preceded by withdrawal of credit and currency shortage in the West. Besides enormous stretches of land at a minimum cost, Austin's settlers were protected against collection of any debts left behind them. Altogether, migration to Texas could attract harried farmers of the southern river states. As for their wives, willing or unwilling, they went along.

When Texas was admitted to the Union in 1846, it was the country's wildest open space. The few women who emerge from its past were hardy. No shrinking female could survive there. Once more the enemy was the red man. Take the episode of Weathersford where a white woman had been killed by Indians. Avenging neighbors then attacked the Indians, taking nine scalps in retaliation. These grisly trophies were brought back to Weathersford and hung from a rope around which a jubilant citizenry did a war-dance. White women joined the men in this ceremony, in which the ladies (says a record) "stomped" as vigorously as the men.

To the '50's belongs Elizabeth Crockett, statued symbol of the women pioneers. Nearly twenty years after the Alamo the widow of David Crockett came to Texas, along with her son, in the traditional covered wagon. Texas, in tribute to Crockett's memory, had awarded her a large farm about 30 miles west of Fort Worth. "The old Crockett house" of today's legend was a log cabin. Strictly speaking, Elizabeth Crockett's pioneering becomes a bit academic since she was past 65 when she arrived. Her own life had been spent in Carolina and Tennessee, and she brought her china teapot along with her into the wilds. She spent the last six years of her life on the Crockett farm, where she died in January, 1860. An idealized figure of her crowns the monument erected in 1913 to "Pioneer Woman." On it she is shown as a young and vigorous matron, shielding her eyes with upraised hand and hopefully peering West.

AUGUSTA JANE EVANS OF TEXAS

This frontier also had its literary lady, for Texas was the childhood home of the novelist, Augusta Jane Evans. Born in Georgia "of good family," Augusta Jane was brought west in 1847. The family made brief stops in both Houston and Galveston before her father settled himself in the San Antonio section as an early sheep-raiser there. This was in the Mexican War period, when the region swarmed with roving soldiery from both camps, a perilous background for the eight Evans children. There were no schools. Any teaching had to come from the mother. When this oldest girl was fifteen, she was sent to Mobile, Alabama, for two years of formal education.

While still at school there, and at the age of seventeen, Augusta Jane wrote her first novel. It was also the first novel of Texas, and was called *Inez, A Tale of the Alamo*. It was published anonymously in 1855. Doubtless it would have achieved only oblivion except that four years later, this selftaught author produced her famous *Beulah*. For several decades, this was to be a best seller, read from coast to coast (Chapter Note 6).

BELIEVE IT OR NOT

For real blood and thunder, take some women of western Texas who reached there just after the early victories of the Mexican War. Two family groups, the Benhams with a child of seven, and the Braxtons with two sons of fifteen and eighteen respectively, left the Red River Valley of Louisiana for the valley of the Pecos. No mention is made of their motives in emigrating, or even their given names, though it is explained that they followed the Red River Valley, west. But to reach the Pecos they must cross the Llano Estacado, a hot, treeless plain, almost a desert.

The group cut down luggage to necessities, the chief of which was water for two days. Towards evening of the second day, with 40 miles still to go, their remaining water-cask burst. On the third day, their horses and mules gave out. In this horrible plight they were set upon by Mexican guerillas who robbed the travelers and cut the throats of their mules. The two women were seized, leaving the men and boys to die of hunger and thirst.

The gang had a hideout on the Pecos, about four hours distant. There the women were locked in an upper storey while their six captors celebrated with a drinking bout. Under cover of its commotion the women wrenched the bars off the window, climbed out and reached the stables without being discovered. There they found six fresh horses, and hamstrung the rest. (How they secured a knife for that bloody business, the record does not tell.)

Each woman mounted a horse, riding astride, and leading two more horses. Riding all night, at sunrise they came to the spot where the men and boys lay stretched out on the sand, awaiting death. How the women found the trail in the dark also remains unexplained, but with fresh horses and fresh hope, men, women and children reached the Pecos safely.

There they purchased an abandoned adobe house, together with land for grazing and farming. The house was a Texas version of a frontier "station." Its adobe walls were pierced with loopholes, its doors of double-oak planking were bulletproof. The structure enclosed an open courtyard for the safekeeping of horses and cattle. The two families felt secure enough to remain after government troops had been withdrawn from the neighborhood. They were able to add to their numbers three Irish sheep herders, who might have been ex-soldiers.

The next year, the place was attacked by twelve Mexicans

among whom the women recognized their former captors. A stout resistance was put up, but Mr. Braxton was killed by an unlucky shot through a loophole. In pioneer tradition the women kept loading the guns for the men to fire. Hearing footsteps overhead, Mrs. Benham seized a hatchet and a revolver, and made her way into the loft. Three Mexicans had already forced an entrance there. She shot one and clove the skull of another. The third fled.

The marauders next resorted to the old Indian trick of firing the roof with blazing arrows. The two women carried buckets and fought the flames. When water gave out, Mrs. Braxton stripped her husband's blood-soaked coat from his dead body, and used the bloody clothing to beat out the fire. By nightfall the attackers withdrew, having lost half their number. A later recall of troops reduced the section to comparative safety. By 1848 the Widow Braxton was a widow no longer. She married an ex-soldier named Whitley.

It might seem that Mrs. Braxton-Whitley had had enough adventure to last her the rest of her life. But during the '50's Whitley learned of a rich placer deposit discovered by a discharged soldier-comrade. The mine was across the line, in what is now Arizona. This time, says the record, the frontier woman was reluctant to set forth, but the spirit of '49 was in the air. Eventually the couple sold all they possessed to equip a party of three.

The former comrade was able to guide the others to the site of the rich placer deposit. But returning with their treasure brought disaster. In some canyon of the Colorado Trooper Crossman fell down a precipice to his death, along with two mules. Now, with thirst by day and bitter cold at night, Whitley went insane and, on reaching the Mohave river, drank himself to death. Ten days later a ragged ghost of a woman crawled into a mountain settlement where she was nursed back to health.

A year later the widow's cache of gold dust was found buried under the carcass of the last mule. This was twenty miles distant from the settlement that Mrs. Whitley had finally reached alone and on foot. The annals conclude that she "had a larger share of nerve and hardihood than usually falls to the lot of her sex." But no one bothered to tell what the twice-widowed border heroine did with her 30,000 dollars.

ACROSS THE PLAINS

The 1850's west of the Mississippi had their crowning symbol of adventure in the covered wagon. The wide plains, still unsettled, served as a passage area for prairie schooners beating their way towards a somewhat golden west. After '49 the trickle of voyagers became a swelling stream.

There were two chief assembly points for this migration. In the north it was Council Bluffs in Iowa, with Trader's Point (that would become Omaha) on the opposite shore. Further south was Independence, Missouri. If a man were solicitous for wife or young children, he might send them by boat as far as St. Joseph, to shorten the land journey. But the bulk of emigrants gathered at Council Bluffs and Independence where wagons sorted themselves into companies for the safety of numbers.

At these junction points voyagers waited for word that the rivers were past their spring floods, and that grass had started on the prairies to give fodder for cattle. Many wagonloads were wholly masculine and family parties could be told by sight of cows yoked among the oxen. On the long march, after morning milking, any surplus went into leather buckets slung under the wagons. By nightfall continuous jolting had turned the contents into butter and buttermilk for the evening meal. Family wagons, too, started out with eggs packed in pails of cornmeal.

Both jumping-off points provided wheelwrights and blacksmiths for wagon repair, and rough banks for traders who sold oxen and mules to the travelers. Independence in the '50's was a swarming confusion of cattle, merchandise and wagons, with drinking, gambling and brawling on the side. Not all female migrants were ladies. The diary of Lavinia Porter describes groups from Arkansas and Tennessee where men and women fought with horsewhips and cudgels. The literate Lavinia found the language of these women "unbearable." Also, they dipped snuff.

Once the prairie schooners started rolling west, casualties began. Disease came first, usually dysentery. Then there were the children thrown from pitching seats to be crushed under heavy wheels. Most wagons lacked brakes. A woman's diary of 1855 noted that brakes were still so "newfangled" that only one wagon in their entire train was so equipped. At the bad river crossings—the Kaw, the Vermillion, the Platte, the Big Blue—there were drownings. There were stampedes of cattle in which less agile women and children were likely victims. Trail burials were hasty and usually without coffin, though one forehanded woman carried a metal coffin with her in her wagon. (They finally buried her in it, up in the mountains.)

As the emigrants reached the treeless stretches, family wagons began discarding their iron stoves for want of fuel. Hoop skirts, umbrellas and surplus clothing were dumped beside the trail. Books followed, though a Bible or a dictionary might be kept. When food began to give out, supplies were augmented with buffalo meat, each wagon train having its hunters. At first, they ate it fresh-roasted, but later everyone was down to jerked meat. On Sundays the cattle were given a day of rest, while men greased harness and women cooked and washed. Often some wagon would house a preacher who would make his way from group to group, ready with his Sunday sermon.

But hardships or no, the tide of travel rose. At Fort Laramie, in the Summer of '51, a count showed 37,171 men to 803 women and 1,094 children. These emigrants had passed in nearly 9,000 wagons, drawn by 30,000 oxen and 7,400 mules. The check also listed 5,700 cows.

Out in the Black Hills some nameless woman climbed to the crest of a red stone mountain, and scrawled upon it, "Remember me in mercy, O Lord." Then the nameless woman went on to whatever fate awaited her.

ON TO THE GREAT SALT LAKE

Of all the wagon trains crossing the Plains, the largest carried the famous Mormon exodus of 1847. In the '30's the brethren had had trouble in Ohio. Later they had been driven out of Missouri. Now, with the two Smiths shot dead in Carthage jail, the charter to their community in Illinois had been revoked. So the call had been issued for the Latter-day Saints to assemble at Kanesville (near Council Bluffs) under a new leader, Brigham Young. One who did not heed the call was Emma, Joseph Smith's widow, known to have opposed violently his secret revelation of polygamy in 1843. Emma Smith remained in Nauvoo, to become a successful hotelkeeper there, respected by her "gentile" neighbors (Chapter Note 7).

But more than 4,000 gathered at Kanesville. Their wagons were strong and well provisioned. En route the young men hired out to frontier farmers for pay in crops. The mass migration was long and laborious, but it had been well planned. Its size warded off Indian attack. Finally they "toiled up the well-nigh inaccessible heights of the Wahsatch of Utah range," a climb of four miles, for a first view of their promised land.

It was the gold rush that brought prosperity to Deseret, with the Mormons in a strategic location for selling provisions to other wayfarers. By 1850 Salt Lake City, with a population of 5,000, was divided into large squares by broad streets laid out at right angles. Two small canals brought pure water from the mountains "to every man's door," for use in house and garden. They also built a huge place of worship called The Bowery, in which the rough trunks of trees served as pillars. The great luxury of early Salt Lake City was its warm-water baths, fed by local hot springs. This refinement was allotted four days a week to men, and two days a week to the women. Still those early Mormon matrons did have hot-water baths.

The city might lack tallow for candles, but it looked good to the emigrants of the '50's who detoured there for rest and reprovisioning. To some wearied women the adobe houses were so welcome that they went no further. "Oh, the luxury of a house, a house!" one woman's diary exclaims.

Lucy Cook with her husband and baby stayed all one winter in Salt Lake, and wrote home a description of it in 1852. "It seemed such a treat to see houses again, and to hear chickens crowing . . . We camped opposite a boarding house and Pa wishing to give us a treat ordered dinner for our family, and oh, when we sat down to the table . . . never did victuals look more tempting."

After scanty dried meat on the trail the travelers had beef and chicken, green peas, potatoes, cheese, bread, butter and tea. "Then it all looked so clean," Lucy went on, "and the house so trim and neat . . . So unused were we to chairs that on entering the parlor we all dropped down to the floor and sat thus till one remarked the situation and we forthwith rose and took chairs." Over the winter

Lucy found their Mormon neighbors hospitable and kind, "though we understood enough to be guarded in our speech . . . there seems to be a strict surveillance kept on all outsiders."

THE HANDCART BRIGADE

Later in the '50's came the epic of Mormon women—the famous handcart brigade. Salt Lake City had been drawing converts from abroad as well as from this country, with many converts from rural England. In general, these bands were ably led, but in 1856 nearly 2,000 converts poured into Missouri by rail and steamer. Wagons were in waiting, but not enough. Some 600 men and women were provided only with handcarts to carry their belongings thousands of miles across the Plains.

"The train was stringing out two or three miles" says an eye-witness account of the wanderers approaching the Rockies. "There were old men pulling and tugging their carts, sometimes loaded with a sick wife or children . . . women pulling along sick husbands, little children six to eight struggling through mud and snow."

Word of their plight had reached Salt Lake, and a relief wagon-train was sent out, which met the harried wayfarers at Devils Gate Fort in the mountains. Then heavy snow fell, and some 1,200 were trapped there, half of them belonging to the "handcart brigade." A hard winter set in. Provisions were scarce and the converts near exhaustion. The death toll rose day by day, "the men dying faster than the women and children," states the record. Eventually the survivors reached Salt Lake City.

A hundred years later, the "handcart brigade" is still remembered. To be descended from it ranks with Mayflower ancestry. "Oh, you must meet Mrs. So-and-so," the inquirer is told. "Her grandmother was a handcarter."

NOTES FOR CHAPTER EIGHT

1 The briefest summary of this region's growth is the admission dates of the states concerned: Louisiana, 1812; Missouri, 1821; Arkansas, 1836; Texas, 1845; Iowa, 1846; Minnesota, 1858; Kansas, 1861, and Nebraska, 1867. It must be remembered that when Zachary Taylor was an obscure officer, his wife followed him to army posts from what became Minnesota, south to Louisiana. An account of her experience is contained in the author's *First First Ladies,* and so is not repeated here.

2 After 1866 Mrs. Swisshelm retired to western Pennsylvania to a cottage that came to her from the Swisshelm estate. She died there in 1880.

Her spelling of "Visiter" represents the older usage laid down in Dr. Johnson's dictionary. Noah Webster's American classic was not in print till 1841. In regions like western Pennsylvania, the older usage prevailed some while longer.

There was another woman associated with an early trans-Mississippi journal. Near Sauk Rapids William H. Wood and his wife Elisa from Loudon, New Hampshire, founded *The New Era.* But Mrs. Wood was only her husband's assistant, whereas Jane Swisshelm was her "Visiter."

3 One regrets to record the demise of Amelia Bloomer's famous *Lily* at the hands of the woman who bought the magazine when Mrs. Bloomer left for Iowa. The purchaser was Mrs. Mary Birdsall, who had been writing a "ladies column" for an Indiana farm journal. But writing and editing proved different trades. Without Amelia's skillful hand, the prosperous *Lily* drooped and died.

4 Nebraska as a settled region hardly enters pre-Civil War reckoning. Trading posts had been located there from 1800 on, with a first white settler reported in 1807. Army stations followed, but there was no post office till 1849. By furnishing a northern overland route for California, the territory gained importance and more inhabitants. In 1861 there was a population of 30,000 scattered over the vast open plains. Not a few of these settlers had started for California, only to be turned back by the formidable barrier of the Rockies.

5   Although the Bentons were southerners living in a slave state, Senator Benton was a "free soil" expansionist. The servants in his house were free persons of color, children of former slaves who had worked out their purchase money as indentured servants in Ohio and Illinois.

6   Augusta Jane Evans, whose *Beulah* sold so prosperously, ran a hospital for Confederate soldiers in Mobile during the Civil War. In 1868 she married L. M. Wilson of Mobile. The next year she published her perennially popular *St. Elmo.*

7   Emma Hale Smith, Joseph Smith's widow, had been one of the prophet's first converts and had helped him in transcribing *The Book of Mormon,* and in the founding of the earlier Mormon communities. It was while Nauvoo was prospering that Smith had the vision that was to add polygamy to the previous Mormon tenets. That was in 1843. Tradition has it that Emma reacted so strongly to this new dispensation that it was kept under cover in the upper circles. It was not promulgated publicly till 1852 in Salt Lake City.

CHAPTER NINE

Go West, Young Woman

*B*UT the great adventure of the '50's was California or Oregon, that name covering the huge territory later cut up into several states. It was adventure back into the primitive. When weary women from across the Plains entered those strange mountain valleys, these latter were more remote, more isolated than any part of the entire globe is now. This new world was completely without communication as today knows communication—by airplane, telegraph, telephone and radio. Even the New York *Tribune's* dispatches from West Coast seaports were carefully labeled "one month later."

It was of course the discovery of gold at Sutter's mill that centered attention on California, drawing hordes of adventurers of all nations, male and female, but mostly male. They came around the Horn or over the Panama Isthmus or up from Mexico, as well as overland through both northern and southern mountain passes (Chapter Note 1).

Reliable estimates claim 42,000 overland arrivals in 1849, in addition to 33,000 by ship and some 9,000 via Mexico. Thus, on the shores of the Pacific, the old drama of the frontier was restaged on a vast and picturesque scale. The overwhelming wealth of the mines, the exotic Spanish background added melodrama to the scene. Decidedly, though, the gold rush was a man's world. In its mushroom towns women and children formed only 8% of the population, while in the mining regions the proportion dwindled to 2%.

THE FIRST OVERLAND PIONEERS

There were also a very few Americans who had already come to California to farm. The first of such groups arrived in 1842. That rash contingent started with 69 men, women and children who left Kansas early in May. Using furtrapper guides, the party reached the famous old Fort Hall almost intact. Half the group voted to winter there, but 32 bold spirits chose to push on, with Benjamin Kelsey of Iowa as "captain." With him were his wife and little daughter. This Nancy Kelsey was the first American woman to appear by name in the overland story.

Well advised as to route, the Kelsey-Bidwell party reached Salt Lake suffering only minor water shortages. Beyond there they abandoned their wagons for ox-packs. Struggling through dreadful rocks Nancy Kelsey saw the Humboldt River four years before explorer Frémont was to give it that name. Now carted provisions were gone, and the men had to begin killing the oxen. Tradition has it that Nancy carried her little girl up the steep Sierra trail. In a bad canyon the men had to haul water to keep their few remaining animals alive. Finally, with four men pushing and four pulling, they got their mules through the canyon. They slaughtered their last ox, and began to eat crows. But Nancy then saw her first big sequoia tree. They had reached the San Joaquin valley with its wild grapes and antelopes. The date was November 1, 1842.

Four years later brought the settler's revolt against Mexico. Tradition also gives Nancy a part in this, asserting that the first Bear Flag was made from her white petticoat. Another local account derives the flag from a red petticoat belonging to the wife of a sailor known there as Dirty Smith. Official state history ignores both petticoats. According to Josiah Royce of California and Harvard, the flag-raising was centered around William A. Todd from Kentucky, a nephew of the Mary Todd Lincoln who would be the First Lady of the Civil War.

LADIES OF YERBA BUENA

But even before the Bear Flag, names of a few women occur in early records. The first American baby at the sleepy little trading post that was to become San Francisco was Rosalia Leese, born April 15, 1838. Her father, Jacob Leese, had built the first waterfront commission house there two years previously. By 1844 the settlement could boast perhaps twelve houses and 50 permanent residents. When a shipload of 200 Mormon converts reached the Golden Gate, the population of Yerba Buena was doubled. This produced the town's first hotel, the old Portsmouth House, which was staffed by three women from the Mormon contingent. Mrs. Mercy Narrimer, a widow, was the housekeeper. Lucy Nutting was the waitress and Sarah Kettleman the cook. Two Mormon carpenters made the hotel's tables, benches and bedsteads. By 1847 Yerba Buena was officially San Francisco, and only too soon the hotel's treasured cook had become the wife of Dr. Elbert P. Jones.

WOMEN OF THE DONNER STORY

The famous pioneering tragedy of the northern Sierras enacted by the Donner group also belongs to pre-gold rush history. The families who made its annals of heroism and horror came as prospective farmers and traders, with women and children outnumbering the men.

The party started out from Independence, Missouri, in the spring of 1846, well provided with oxen, cows and mules. George Donner, aged 63, was a man of means carrying in his wagons goods to sell and money for trading in the old Spanish California. With him was his young wife Tamsen, their children and the family of his brother Jacob. In the group were also: Patrick Breen from Iowa with wife and five children; James J. Reed, wife, mother-in-law and four children; the Widow Murphy from Tennessee with her daughters and sons-in-law, and five people come recently all the way from Germany. The party started out cheerfully with music and singing. One notes especially the seventy-year-old mother of Mrs. Reed. She could not be left behind, so rode along in a rocking chair placed for her in a special wagon. She died, still in her rocking chair, and was buried "on the bank of the Big Blue . . . the emigrants moved on."

This death was the only casualty all the way to Fort Bridger in Wyoming, a famous early trading post presided over by Trapper Bridger and his Indian wife. At this point the emigrants learned of a route, via the Humboldt, 200 miles shorter than the trail by way of Fort Hall. The group then split, George Donner becoming captain of those wishing to try the cutoff. When going became too difficult, they turned back, meanwhile having lost valuable weeks. By September 1st, they reached Salt Lake, where three more weeks were spent mending wagons. Resuming the journey on short rations, James Reed, co-leader with Donner, lost his oxen from thirst.

Then at Gravelly Ford, on October 5th, Reed and one Snyder came to blows. Reed had reproved Snyder for beating an ox pulling uphill. Mrs. Reed (so the record tells) rushed between the two men, receiving a blow on the head from Snyder's heavy whip-stock. Reed came at Snyder with a knife, stabbing him to death. The party buried the victim, then sat as a court. Reed was sentenced to banishment into the wilderness without food or arms, practically a death sentence.

But come night, Mrs. Reed managed to send off her young daughter Virginia, then eleven years old, to bring her father his gun and a supply of ammunition. This must have been prearranged, for the child returned safely to camp, her mission accomplished. Now Mrs. Reed and her children had neither oxen to carry them nor a man to fend for them, but the Donners shared rations with Reed's supposed widow.

Disasters multiplied. In the Humboldt Sink cattle were turned out to graze unguarded, and Indians stole twenty of them. After that, all who could must walk. The death toll rose. At the Truckee crossing, the starving emigrants received provisions sent out to them from Sutter's Fort by Indian guides. Then they rested three days, the final error that was to precipitate disaster.

Arrived at the mountain pass, they found five feet of snow. By Truckee Lake, the five feet had become ten. (To this day, this Sierra pass, now called Donner, has the deepest snowfall in the United

States.) Disorder and consternation prevailed, but it was agreed to kill all animals and preserve their meat. Two log cabins were built near an old one found standing along the pass. Hoping to find fish, the Donner family erected their shelter up a creek. Snowed in at the Pass there were in all 43 men, fifteen women and 43 children, their ages not given in the old chronicles.

On December 16th, the group called the Forlorn Hope set out, nine men, five women and a boy of thirteen, all who could use improvised snow shoes. The party was given six days scanty rations from the common store. The Forlorn Hope crossed the summit, and had eaten their last morsel of food when a fresh storm broke. It held them back a week, and horror began. On January 4, a man died and was eaten, though his wife refused to touch his flesh. William Eddy shot a deer, making food for two days. Then a man saw two Indians on the trail, and shot them. Their flesh, too, was eaten. Soon eight men were dead and a ninth had gone mad. Only William Eddy remained. Far inside his pack he had found a small parcel of meat with a note from his wife, bidding him eat it, keep himself alive and bring back help for her and their children. It was William Eddy, his life preserved by his wife's sacrifice, who finally stumbled into an Indian encampment barely able to tell his story. The Indians half-carried him to Sutter's Fort.

Now a relief party set out, each man packing 50 pounds of food on his back. In all, there were four relief parties, an achievement in itself since most of California's able-bodied men were off in the Bear Flag army. The five women of the Forlorn Hope were alive when help reached them but died before reaching the Fort. Survivors in the cabins were down to boiled ox-hide, but twenty-one emaciated people were brought out, all who could stand the trip. About February 23, rescuers and rescued were caught in another snow storm, in which several of the weakened survivors died. Of necessity, the strong went on, to send back help. The Breen family with five children and an ailing father were left behind in a crude shelter, with what fuel and food could be spared.

This became the Starving Camp. It was also a place of miracles. Mrs. Breen kept the children alive on snow and sugar, and gathered wood for the fire. The sick husband fell to eating flesh from bodies lying frozen in the snow. But Mrs. Breen "would rather have the children die . . . she never did eat of the bodies." Each day's fire dropped their shelter deeper into the snow-pack. As they huddled helpless at the bottom, she believed their last hour was near. Together they repeated the Litany. Then she crawled up to the surface to keep her watch for help. Only half conscious, she heard the words, "There is Mrs. Breen alive, anyhow." Relief had come.

VIRGINIA'S FATHER REAPPEARS

By another miracle, this second relief group was led by James Reed who had been banished into the wilderness at Gravelly Ford. He had come through his ordeal alive, and was now back to rescue his family. This he did. Two Reed children, Mary and Isaac, were with the Breens. Mrs. Reed, Virginia and Martha Jane were still alive at the Lake cabins, though they had only boiled ox-hide to feed on since December 23. "Trembling forms of women and little children, men reduced to skeletons . . . The relief party wept," says an old chronicle.

Once .more family groups must be broken, to take out the strongest, those who could still walk. Several relief men carried children on their backs. Among these were Eliza and Leanna Donner, children of George and Tamsen. Jacob Donner had died weeks before. Survivors too feeble to be moved were left to strengthen themselves on the food packed through the drifts, awaiting a later rescue.

This third attempt brought out young Mary Donner, and three of the Graves children, all carried, since they could not walk. But Tamsen Donner chose to stay with her husband. His death was imminent, but with another snowstorm threatening, the relief men dared not linger. Tamsen kept her vigil alone, wrapped her dead in a sheet, then laid herself down to perish beside him.

There was a fourth relief party, the last of Sutter's manpower. These men were recruited only by hope of finding the Donner gold, and immortal heroism ended in scandalous recriminations. Behind these lurked the tale of buried Donner treasure, rumors of which have persisted into the present.

SURVIVING WOMEN

In all, 45 of the fated group were found alive, some to survive for only a brief interval. Three "Donner children" have left records. Virginia Reed—the same child who brought the gun to her father through a wilderness night—wrote to relatives back home. This, the first word of the Sierra tragedy to reach the East, was dated May 1847. Virginia was twelve years old at the time. She grew up, married and in 1891, (when she was 56) wrote her recollections for the old *Century Magazine*. Her sister, Martha Jane, also grew up and was married in 1856 at Santa Cruz. Her wedding dress of white satin and lace is viewed each year by the thousands who now visit the Sutter's Fort Museum comfortably by car. The two orphaned daughters of Tamsen Donner were kept by Captain Sutter till homes could be found for them. In 1856 Eliza, the older daughter, was a pupil at St. Catherine's at Benicia. Later she married, and much later, when close to 80, she published her account of the tragedy (Chapter Note 2).

California was speedily admitted as a state in September, 1850. Emphasis then swung from the wide acreage of the coastal regions where Monterey was capital, to the more northern trading port with its huge harbor, and to a still newer town up the river. Sacramento, where the first building rose in 1849, became almost overnight a business center for the sprawling camps along the Feather and American rivers. At the southern end of the mother lode were the placer mines of Mariposa. Yet the Donners were not entirely forgotten in the rush for gold. That earlier catastrophe saved the lives of thousands who were to cross the mountains in '49 and the early '50's. Now army relief teams were ready to help the adventurers over the mountains, while Mormon stations along the route both sold and gave succor.

SOME WOMEN OF THE GOLD RUSH

Because of their scarcity, the few women to reach this Land of Promise became news. Brief mentions testify to the presence of a wife, mother or daughter in some mining camp. For instance, Moor's

Flat was so named because he was the first man to bring his wife into the gold fields. Then, on an emigrant train of '49, "Mr. Rhynierson and wife" had a child born to them on the Virgin River. The girl baby was named Virginia for the stream that provided the party with much needed water. When the same group reached the mines, a "Mrs. Erksom" tried out shortening from "a very fat bear," with which she made "some pretty good pies." The miners were glad to pay a dollar or even two dollars apiece for them. At the end of the year this thrifty couple had amassed sufficient cash to leave the diggings for a farm of their own in the Santa Clara valley. Then at Placerville there was the wife of James Caples who turned to pie baking when her husband was invalided by the hardships of gold digging.

To such printed records should be added the mute evidence of exhibits at the Sutter's Fort museum. Take the blue and white bedquilt woven in Ohio in 1842. A decade later it had reached Sacramento. Or the china doll head that came unscathed overland in 1849, or the touching tiny doll treasured all the way from Michigan. More elegant is a wedding dress of white satin brought by a Massachusetts bride in 1850, also the two upstanding soup tureens which arrived via the brig *La Grange* (Chapter Note 3).

Most of these items speak for well guided wagons that reached their destinations with only bearable hardship. Yet route cutoffs still lured the slow-moving prairie schooner. Scantily marked trails that sufficed for Indians and hardened mountain men would prove lethal to family groups from eastern farming regions. "We were green but we learned fast" is a revealing comment from an old trail diary.

THE DEATH VALLEY SAGA

One of the best authenticated tales of hairbreadth escape gave Death Valley its name. The story starts in the winter of '48–'49 when news of the gold strike reached Asabel Bennett, a frontier farmer living ten miles beyond Madison, Wisconsin. Probably California sounded very attractive in the depth of a Wisconsin winter. Anyway, Farmer Bennett organized a small party including his wife and three children, and a young hunter. Heading west, other groups joined them to give the safety of greater numbers. Apparently all went well until they neared Salt Lake City. There a Mormon guide was hired at 10 dollars per wagon, to take them through to San Bernardino. Unfortunately, at this juncture, someone obtained a new map with a cutoff warranted to save hundreds of miles. The party now split up, about half choosing to follow the guide, the rest to follow the new route. Thus, by strictly democratic process, these latter voted themselves into a fine slice of hell.

They were: "A. Bennett, wife and children . . . J. B. Arcane, wife and child" . . . "the Rev. J. W. Brier and family," besides some wholly masculine wagons. Water ran short, and Bennett's young hunter tried to persuade his employer to turn back to the guided route. Sarah Bennett added tearful pleas. Mrs. Arcane was "in heart-rending distress." Four children were crying for water, but there was not a drop to give them, nor would any be reached before the next day. "The mothers were nearly crazy . . . For the love of gold they had left homes where hunger had never come." But a scout came back with canteens of water, and the march went on.

Reaching camps with water, the party would linger several days to recuperate, but soon they began slaughtering their weakest oxen for food. On Christmas day the young hunter visited the Brier wagon, to discover the "Rev. gentleman cooly delivering a lecture on education to his two boys . . . with starvation staring us in the face."

The leaders now resolved to turn wagons into ox-packs, while the two scouts were to push on through the dreadful valley to the settlements for help. Once more gaunt oxen were killed and their meat dried, while the women made a knap-sack apiece out of the hides, for the scouts. They followed the young men as far as they dared, begging them to bring back food for the hungry children. (The Bennetts' were George, Melissa and Martha, the Arcane's boy was Charlie.)

Through incredible defiles the young men forced their way till, on the first of January, 1850, from a hill top, they could see green country ahead. Soon kindly people from the Spanish ranches were giving them food. Again it was tough going to get back to the wagons where Sarah Bennett fell on her knees, clinging to the young hunter "like a maniac." To bring the party out, everything was abandoned except food, water, blankets, a cup apiece and one camp kettle. Women and children were mounted on the strongest of the surviving oxen, the youngsters in riding bags made from "hickory shirts." Mrs. Arcane, "from a city," arrayed herself in her best hat trimmed with flowing ribbons. The children tired quickly in their riding pockets. Mrs. Bennett, now walking, tried to carry her baby, "but she is too heavy for her strength." The men took turns carrying the youngest. "The women reached camp so tired they were nearly dead . . . and slept as they were." Waking at length with swollen eyes and uncombed hair, they were told that they were finally through Death Valley. "But the women won't believe it."

By coaxing and cajoling, making rough hide sandals to cover the women's blistered feet, the scouts herded them on to "the Falls." There the oxen must be let down by ropes. The men carried the youngsters while the women "can scarcely stand." Beyond this point they thirsted again, cut their hide footgear on more rocks. "The women contracted an intense dislike to this region, and said they never wanted to see it again," states the hunter's old record.

Finally, having left camp at daybreak to climb a snow pass "a mile or two down we came to a bubbling brook." A scout shot a stray yearling. As the women cut off meat to roast, he heard them exclaim, "See the fat! Only see how nice it is." But the next morning Sarah Bennett was sick from her rich meal. Wet to the waist, the travelers must wade a stream, but the women preferred that to the desert. Even little Charlie began to recover from the body rash that had kept him crying day and night. Then one day from a hillside they saw "a green meadow of a hundred acres." They had come through alive to tell the tale. Soon a good lady came out of a ranch house, saying "mucha pobre." Thus, at long last, Sarah Bennett and the nameless Mrs. Arcane who loved city finery, slept once more under a roof.

After that Mr. Arcane traded his remaining oxen for a horse to carry his wife and son to the nearest seaport. His one other asset, his spy glass, he gave in gratitude to the young scout. So, penniless but hopeful, they rode away. "Mrs. Arcane could hardly speak." The Arcanes later became residents of Santa Cruz.

The Bennetts headed for Los Angeles. "Mrs. Bennett's dress

hardly reached her knees, the children dirty and ragged." They passed a camp of immigrants who had kept to the older route, and heard a man exclaim, "My God, it's Bennett." Sarah Bennett disappeared within a tent. "She emerged with her face washed clean, her hair combed and wearing a clean new dress."

Remarkably, too, the "Rev. Brier, wife and children," also survived. At an early stage of the desert ordeal a group of "Jayhawkers," well organized Illinois frontiersmen, crossed the Bennetts' trail. The Briers, fortunately for them, had followed the Jayhawkers. Mrs. Brier, small and brisk, was (according to scout William Manly) "the best man of the party." She built fires, cooked the food, put packs on the oxen, "and did all sorts of work when the father was too tired . . . which was almost all the time." The Bennett men had nothing but scorn for the invalid preacher, but when an ox was killed, "they would take the liver to Mrs. Brier for herself and the children."

A few weeks after the Death Valley group had come through, young William Manly, the scout, found the Rev. Mr. Brier snuggly ensconced, managing a boarding house for well-to-do immigrants who had come by the South Pass. Manly did not see Mrs. Brier. Perhaps she was functioning in the kitchen.

For Sarah Bennett the story had no happy ending. At San José, in 1857, "she had a new baby and died of consumption the following day." Asabel Bennett gave away the new baby to a friendly woman, sold his farm on the Salinas, and, with one child, headed for Utah. There he "married a Mormon woman, growing poorer all the while."

AGAIN JESSIE BENTON FRÉMONT

The first woman of the great world to reach gold rush California was Jessie Benton Frémont, who has also been encountered in Washington and St. Louis. Conflicting orders during Frémont's brief military governorship of California had resulted in a court-martial, his resignation from the army, and a decision to turn rancher in the region back from Monterey. Now he planned to explore the southern mountain passes while his wife and young daughter journeyed from New York by steamer and the Isthmus, to join him in California. So it happened that Mrs. Frémont arrived in Panama along with the earliest of the gold-seekers. (A still younger daughter had died shortly before her far western venture.)

Rough as she found the Panama crossing, her was hardly typical. She had a maid of sorts with her, and semiofficial standing with the railway surveying company, as well as the escort of the Governor of Kentucky, who was her brother-in-law. Even at that it was a terrifying experience for a sheltered woman. At Chagrés, "if it had not been for pure shame," she later confessed, "I would have turned back to New York." Where ordinary voyagers were poled up the river by canoe, the Frémont party was provided with "a company whaleboat with a responsible crew." At Gorgona some twenty miles of mule-track lay ahead, with numerous fords and no bridges. Aghast at the "small, badly fed, ungroomed wretched little creatures" usually hired for the journey, Jessie obtained the loan of a fine mule, from the "company."

Arrived at Panama City, she saw fever-ridden gold seekers lying helpless on the beaches, but an official introduction took the Frémont party to a "house with fine old servants." There, ill and exhausted, the explorer's wife took to her bed. Later the *S.S. Panama* which had come around the Horn, made room for Jessie and her child, in spite of some 400 gold rushers being already crowded into accommodations designed for 80. There was a stop for fresh water at San Diego, where Jessie received word of Frémont's safety.

Then the ship went on to San Francisco. The town had by her account "only three or four regularly built houses," the swarm of newcomers being camped in tents along the waterfront. While she awaited her husband's arrival the senator's daughter obtained use of a house "with fine carpets, fine furniture, but no housemaid." Carpenters at San Francisco, she noted marveling, were getting sixteen dollars a day. Two weeks later Frémont joined her bringing word of the gold strike on their own landholdings, a discovery that turned them into millionaires.

Even this new-found wealth would not supply in California the domestic comforts of St. Louis. To find a housemaid in Monterey, Jessie was obliged to take a woman suspected (unjustly, it later proved) of belonging to a shipload of ex-convicts from Sidney. Their cook had fled from a man-of-war. Fresh provisions were always running out, to be replaced by uninviting canned goods.

Later they made a home in San Francisco that was soon to be destroyed by the fire of 1851. By that time, too, Jessie had a young son. Now politics took her to Washington with Frémont as senator from the new state. Her tour of Europe ('52–'53) was followed by a St. Louis interval in which another child was born and died. The Frémonts then returned, briefly, to San Francisco, this being the occasion when she obtained a custom house appointment for the young and penniless Bret Harte. The Free Soil candidacy of '56 again called both Frémonts east. Not for 30 years would California again be home for Jessie Frémont (Chapter Note 4).

WOMEN OF EARLY SACRAMENTO

Meanwhile, up the river from San Francisco, gold was pouring into that new town of Sacramento from the mining camps. The city itself had been laid out on paper in 1849. Its first directory published a year later furnishes direct evidence that some women had already reached this outpost. The population was given as "6280, white and colored, male and female." Of these, only twelve women appear in the directory by names and addresses. There were also 70 doctors and 60 lawyers, who may or may not have had unlisted wives.

Most of the population lodged in 56 small hotels. The American House advertised "Rest for the Weary and Storage for Trunks." At the Quincy House Mrs. Sarah Steinagal was manager. Among 40 listed boarding houses, six had women proprietors. Mrs. Hein of 67 3rd Street was a dressmaker. Margaret Burk of 21 5th Street was designated as "washer," two men also being put in that category. (Laundry was a rare and costly service.) Mrs. H. Dodson was accorded a residential status on H street. "Miss Margaret Lolor," without listed occupation, could be found on K street, while Fanny Smith, with no designation whatsoever, had quarters at the Palace Hotel. Miss Juliette Vines was accredited to the Jenny Lind House, elsewhere noted as a saloon. By record alone, these women either might or might not have represented the "undesirable" element that found its way so quickly to the gold regions.

Besides these individual names there must have been some everyday wives and mothers, since both Presbyterian and Methodist churches (organized in 1849) advertised their Sabbath schools.

Also James Rodgers kept a "Boarding and Day School" at the Methodist church. In another year there was listed a Roman Catholic church and an "African M.E. for the Colored Race," this last suggesting colored "help" in hotels and boarding houses.

The term hotel, however, should be redefined. Take the account of Luzena Wilson who came, with her husband, in September of the gold rush year. Mr. Wilson sold his oxen to buy "a hotel on K street." Here is Luzena's description: "a long room dimly lighted by dripping tallow candles stuck in whiskey bottles—bunks built from floor to ceiling on either side." In the corner, opposite the bar, some men were quarreling over a card game, while a cracked fiddle gave out enough of "Money Musk" to set a half-dozen men to dancing. "Some men lay sick in their bunks, and out of one stared the white face of a corpse. They had forgotten even to cover the still features with the edge of a blanket," Luzena Wilson remembered, many years later.

TWO SUCCESS STORIES

It was a rough world but one in which money was quickly made and quickly spent. Take for instance the tale of Florinda Washburn, a spinster who traveled overland with a group in the '50's. Her age is not given, but by profession she was a milliner. Furthermore, she had accumulated enough to finance her own wagon and the services of "a strapping youth" to drive it. She was to feed him all the way to the diggings, but once there, he was to give her half of his first year's earnings. Florinda evidently had an eye to business. Her prairie schooner contained the makings of a millinery shop to be set up in the Land of Golden Promise. In it also was a heavy old-fashioned tailor's "goose" for pressing straw. When hauling became tough, Florinda Washburn stuck to the tools of her trade. She even carried the heavy iron herself to spare the oxen. At length, through deadly heat, they toiled across "Destruction Valley" to the Carson River. Without a word, Florinda bore her "goose" to the shores of the stream. There she sank it, perhaps as a thank-offering for her own survival. The record does not tell.

Arrived at the mines, the strapping youth didn't do too well. Florinda never made much out of her bargain with him, but her millinery shop soon prospered mightily. She was later rated as a woman of wealth.

The Krohs of Stockton, too, were a success story. The "Rev. Kroh," a missionary from Cincinnati, had pushed his way overland in 1849 to become the first minister of Stockton. In '51 his wife and daughters came on, via the Isthmus, then up the river from San Francisco. There they had had to remain aboard ship because at that date there was no accommodation in town for women alone. On *The American Eagle,* going upstream, the Kroh ladies were the only women passengers. Once in Stockton—and here a German musical background is suggested—the six daughters began giving porch concerts. So delighted were the entertainment-starved residents that the merchants of Stockton imported a fine Chickering piano for the young ladies all the way from Boston. This was the first piano in town. Of the six daughters, Margaret later found place in California annals as "vocalist and teacher of music" at the very early Young Ladies Seminary of Benicia.

"DAME SHIRLEY" WRITES HOME

For a woman's account of the gold fields, there are the notable Dame Shirley letters, written by Louise A. K. S. Clappe, a graduate of Mt. Holyoke, formerly of Connecticut but, in 1851, a resident of Rich's Bar on the North Fork of the Feather River. (Bars in mountain streams were likely spots for gold digging, and so supplied names to various mining ventures—Bidwell's Bar, Rich's Bar, etc.) Louise Amelia was the wife of Dr. Fayette Clappe who had left San Francisco for the mountains to recover his health. The narrative begins when Dr. Clappe returned to escort his wife to the diggings. Her first letter opens: "I am bound, Molly, by my promise to give you a true picture of mining life and its peculiar temptations." Admittedly, this correspondence was a literary effort. For that purpose Louise Amelia turned herself into Dame Shirley, and also kept copies of her missives. They were printed later in *The California Monthly Magazine.*

Beyond the river the Clappes' journey was by muleback over a route where ranch houses furnished overnight lodgings. Soon the saddle turned, Dame Shirley fell. Then the riders lost their way, arriving at Marysville very late and very hungry. Luckily the doctor could round up a meal of hot oysters, potatoes and coffee. The next day (September 1, 1851) they set out in a springless wagon for Bidwell's Bar. The doctor's wife was enchanted with the mountain scenery. "I am a regular nomad," Dame Shirley proclaimed. From the jerking wagon she saw Indian women gathering flower seeds "which mixed with pounded acorns and grasshoppers forms the bread of these miserable people." The women were naked except for "a quantity of grass bound round their waists." On their backs they carried wonderfully woven baskets, kept in place by leather thongs across the forehead. Now the travelers approached a very steep hill. The driver called Louise Amelia "the fust woman that ever rode over that hill without hollering." It was fear, not courage, the writer confesses, that kept her quiet.

Between Bidwell's Bar and Berry Creek they lost their way again, this time in territory where a week before, Indians had murdered a Frenchman and his wife. Safe but exhausted they reached a lodging, a place called the Wild Yankee's. Encountering another "herd" of Indians, Dame Shirley was struck with "the extreme beauty of the limbs of Indian women." Their faces, though, were hideous, their blankets dirty. One young girl of about sixteen looked "like a dark beautiful spirit," but her cotton chemise was "disgustingly dirty." The Clappes missed their trail again, camped overnight, and had breakfast at Pleasant Valley ranch—"a filthy uncomfortable flea-haunted shanty standing amid majestic solitudes."

The Empire Hotel at Rich Bar was the only two-storied building in town, and boasted three glass windows, a luxury unknown elsewhere. "A huge shingle palace," it had been erected by gamblers for their womenkind, but local law and order had banished them, and turned the premises into a hotel. Walls were covered with red calico, a characteristic of gold rush housing, and on the street level was a bar.

The bar had "a really elegant mirror," a background for decanters and jars of brandied fruit. Nearby, a table covered with green cloth was flanked by rough benches for prospective players of monte. That was all. The rear of the room was a shop that handled velveteen, leather, flannel, hams, preserved meats, oysters and groceries. Four steps up brought Dame Shirley to the parlor furnished with a long and narrow sofa and a looking glass. The few small bedrooms were lined with purple calico. Doors of blue drilling hung on leather hinges. "Nothing more awkward and unworkmanlike" could be imagined, but it had cost the owner 8,000 dollars. Everything had been "packed" from Marysville at 40 cents a pound.

LADIES OF RICH BAR

The hotelkeeper had come overland in '49. His wife was only twenty-five but already her complexion was "a dark and permanent yellow." She was cooking supper while nearby her two-weeks-old baby was cradled in a champagne basket. The mother had had no medical attention, beyond the help of a neighbor woman who had left directly the baby was born. The infant had not been washed or dressed for two days.

There were three other women in town, including a girl from Indiana who had packed 50 pounds of flour on her back "and walked down that awful hill" when the road was blocked with snow. One couple with three young children called their log cabin hotel the Miner's Home. In it the tiny Mrs. B. was bartender.

Through the middle of the camp, wrote Dame Shirley, "runs the street, thickly planted with tenements—round tents, square tents, plank hovels and log cabins . . . and one formed of pine boughs covered with shirts." In this street Dr. Clappe set up his office, a floorless tent-cabin ten feet long and furnished with just a bench. His medical library was six volumes, assisted by "a respectable array of medicines."

In September there was a mining-camp funeral. Little Mrs. B., sick four days, had died of peritonitis. The body rested on two butter tubs covered with a sheet. The green cloth from the hotel's monte table served as a coffin cover. Mr. B. held "a sickly babe of ten months, moaning for its mother." Beside him stood the little girl of six, for whom someone had run together a new calico dress that trailed to the ground. There was an extempore prayer, and a procession to a hillside burying place. "All the gold on Rich Bar could do no more," Dame Shirley moralized.

Profanity, she wrote her sister, prevailed in California. She had heard more at Rich Bar than in all the years of her life. The miners didn't swear in front of a woman, but their lusty oaths went right through thin cloth partitions. In spite of its blasphemy, the literary lady found mining camp profanity "grotesquely sublime."

Not all, however, went by chivalry. A miner described "a woman of the right sort . . . Why, she earnt her old man $900 in nine weeks, clear of all expenses, by washing! Such women ain't common, I tell you," the miner regretted. "If they were a man might marry and make money by the operation." The going price for washing linen handkerchiefs in San Francisco, Dame Shirley reminded her sister, had been 8 dollars a dozen.

HOME AT INDIAN BAR

A little later Dr. Clappe removed to Indian Bar where they could have a log cabin of their own. It was twenty feet square, its ceilings made elegant with white cloth, and its walls hung with rosy chintz. Chintz also curtained off their bedroom, for which they made a dressing table by mounting a trunk on two empty claret cases. Another trunk provided a washstand, which was supplied by a pail of water brought daily from the river. Later they contrived a window for their living room out of bottle glass.

Still, the Clappe cabin was a model of elegance to Indian Bar. They had a mattress and bed linen brought on from Marysville, and, a real treasure in a mining camp, Dame Shirley's books. She listed a Bible, a prayer book, Shakespeare, Coleridge, Keats, Shelley and Lowell's "Fable for Critics," which must have sounded very unreal in the high Sierras. Breakfasts and suppers Dame Shirley cooked in their cabin fireplace, but their dinners were brought in by the cook from the local hotel.

Indian Bar, larger than Rich's, had a polyglot population. People there spoke French, Italian, German, Kanaka and some East Indian Spanish. Most of these foreigners Dame Shirley rated as "degraded," though she did have a good word for a young Kanaka wife, "a pretty little woman of fifteen," who had walked all the way from Sacramento. Americans there included "better class mechanics," sailors, farmers, a few store clerks, one lawyer and the ever present gamblers. Death from knife fights and shooting duels were common. One "new lady" who had arrived clad in the latest Eastern fashions, fainted when her husband got himself involved in a bar-room brawl.

There were also newcomers, overland. "The poor women arrive haggard, burnt to the color of a hazel nut." Usually there had been tragic deaths along the trail. One woman had been left with nine children, including a baby. The oldest child, a boy of fifteen, was now wearing his father's clothes. "She owned nothing in the world but her team," Dame Shirley set down. At stopping points the widow washed clothes to feed her children. At that, she had to "allowance her young ones on eating, no butter and very little bread." One very neat immigrant woman had washed every Saturday, all the way across the Plains. "Immigrant women deserve high praise," Dame Shirley conceded, "for having adopted the Bloomer dress, frightful as it is on all other occasions."

THE VANDERBECK-BANFIELD LETTERS

Much more spontaneous and heartfelt than Dame Shirley's are the letters that Mary Banfield wrote from San Francisco at about the same date. These letters (Chapter Note 5), now in the archives of the New York Historical Society, are a family saga that shows San Francisco when that small settlement found itself a gateway to swift fortune. There John Banfield, a skilled workman, planned to turn his trade into needed capital, and then return east. Home was "Green Point" in Brooklyn, where Vanderbecks, Haddens, and Banfields made a closely intermarried clan.

First to reach California was Abraham Vanderbeck, stepfather of the young Banfields who were to follow. But Abraham never reached the Diggings. Apparently, he was one of the many Forty-Niners who found only an unmarked grave in the mountains. Undeterred by his fate, a year later John and Mary Banfield were on their way. They chose the Panama route, for they had their little Louisa with them. Her age is not given, but she stood "3 feet 1½ inches" and weighed over 40 pounds. Also there was a new baby expected, whose arrival was chronicled some months later.

Mary's first letter, written at Chagrés, September 1851, voiced indignation at their steamship accommodations. "Anybody that you know is coming tell them to come in the first cabin or not at all, for such living as it is here in this cabin! Tin plates, tin cups, iron knives and forks which have never been cleaned since we started, hard bread, herb tea of some kind, I don't know what, tainted beef, oh it is awful . . . I have not been to the table but once, one of the stewards smuggles me enough to eat from the other cabin for six shillings a day . . . The ship rolls so that it is impossible to write almost. I wish we was to San Francisco. . . ."

Her husband had planned to take first cabin from Panama on, but had underestimated the cost of those few miles across the Isthmus. "Saturday morning we took mules to Panama," Mary Banfield related, "and such a ride as we had was a caution . . . and if you know anybody that is coming tell them to come the Nicaragua route. It wants anybody to be made of money to travel this. Ten cents for a cup of coffee, ten for two pilot biscuits, 30 or 40 cents to lie down on a cot, no bed on it, two dollars a day for board and a great favor to get it at that price for there is so many passengers. Hundred dollars apiece in the steerage from here to San Francisco but we have found plenty of friends who will lend us to get through . . . Since I got over my seasickness I can eat all that comes to me, things I never thought I could be hungry enough to eat . . . Louisa says she don't like this excursion . . . it is too long."

A final blow was the ship's running on a rock in the fog 25 miles outside of the Golden Gate. But all 200 men passengers were set pumping, and the steamer was kept afloat till rescue came.

IN GOLDEN SAN FRANCISCO

By October '51 the Banfields were at the Railway House, at 100 dollars a month. There'd been two married couples to a room in their first boarding house, where "an old man of 55–60 bothered her."

Soon Mary's husband was getting "a shanty to go housekeeping." They expected to "live comfortable on ten dollars a week . . . They have the largest vegetables that I ever saw, cabbages weighing 28 pounds, tomatoes large as a saucer . . . Beef from 12 to twenty cents a pound, pork 18–20, flour ten dollars a barrel. I like this place first rate," Mary assured her mother (Prudence Vanderbeck), "all but the sand . . . It is as noisy as New York, and as for dress

. . . every day you see hardly anything but silk and satin. Common hats trimmed very plain is 8 dollars, four cent ribbons home here 25 cents, the same for a spool of cotton, fifty cents for twelve hairpins . . ."

Back country in the mountains the Diggings still poured out their golden flood. "One day last week," so Mary tells, "a fellow came down from the mines and stopped here. Wanted a pocket handkerchief hemmed. I done it. He gave me fifty cents for it. I wish I had plenty such jobs. I saw a woman today says her and her daughter never earns less than a hundred dollars a week washing . . ." The Banfields were beginning to worry about the expected baby, for "doctor's bills is from 25 to 50 for a job." Nurses are very scarce. "I heard of one who charges $55. for ten days," Mary concludes, "so you see this is a great place for money."

John Banfield's letter of February 10th announced "daughter born 7th Feb 23 minutes before 7 in the morning Mary is quite smart and able to eat her allowance . . . and I am the nurse. A lady acquaintance from Alabama comes every day to dress the child and all the neighbors send in goodies so we are getting along right well . . . The gal weighs 9½ pounds and 20 inches tall . . . and has a nice head of black hair."

Father Banfield had his hands full. "Mary have took her gin sling and I have killed a rooster for soup tomorrow . . . finished my day's work by washing shitten diapers and making bread." But he apparently believed in babies. "We have plenty lady neighbors and very clever" (this to his mother-in-law) "all first rate and all good breeders. Our next door lady got a gal last week and four or five every day on the lookout, and one lady in the valley . . . has had four pair and ready again—maybe two more—only 27 years old. Hurrah for California!"

The wife's letter, dated February 28, was less triumphant. To her mother she confessed that John had been disappointed because the new baby wasn't a son. She had been sick and homesick. "Oh for somebody to talk to, oh for a chance to go to one of our prayer meetings . . . Oh how many thousand times I have wished for you when I was sick . . . here alone it was anything but pleasant . . . Prudy will be three weeks old to-morrow. Today I took a walk . . . The things in the garden look first rate."

By March Mary was "up to work again," and through with homesickness. They had been doing well financially. John had finished paying for the house, and when work was slow in San Francisco, he could always get high rates in Sacramento, where good carpenters were in demand.

Then came the crucial statement. "I have not regretted as yet that I came out here, nor do I think I shall. If you have not sold the stair carpet and oil cloth, ship it round the Horn for it is so dear here, and 16 stair rods. If I have got to stay here, I may as well have things a little like home." The transplanting had been accomplished. The Banfields were in California to stay. The year 1870 leaves them with a farm of their own in Sonomo County, and a family of eight living children.

AS TOLD BY SARAH ROYCE

One of Dame Shirley's letters noted: "Immigration this year contained many intelligent and truly elegant persons."

Such a one was Sarah Royce, the English-born mother of Josiah Royce, later to become a confrére of William James at Harvard. These Royces, a young married couple with one child, left a New York state farm in April '49. They had their own modest capital, which they hoped to increase at the Diggings, then to invest in home and business in California. Sarah Royce kept a diary of her trip (Chapter Note 6).

They were the last family to clear the Sierra passes in the gold rush year, and at the end of October reached Hangtown. This was a mining camp known to protect its gold dust by the abrupt stringing up of thieves. To a literate woman, from an ordered community, this was a shocking business. Yet the same men who had taken the law into their own hands were very gentle with Sarah Royce's little girl, a child at the Diggings being a rarity. Sarah saw men in rough mining clothes, carrying pick and shovel, whom she would later know as "cultured gentlemen." The only other woman in the camp was what she called "a plain person from the western states, acquainted only with country life." Soon this plain person was being paid 100 dollars a month to cook in one of the camp boarding places. When next Sarah saw her, "her hair was dressed in a very youthful fashion; she wore a new gown with full trimmings." It was easy, the diarist speculated, for the homeliest woman to become a mining-camp belle.

But the Royces were set for a business venture in Sacramento. The flooding river, however, swept their hopes away and carried the Easterners downstream to San Francisco. They arrived in January 1850. Like the Banfields, they encountered makeshift living at fabulous prices. The Montgomery House, called one of the best, had one stove only and that in the bar. Canvas walls and muslin partitions divided the upper storey into bedrooms, two and a-half feet by six. Sarah Royce called them berths.

The minister of a newly organized church found lodgings for the Royces. Sarah describes the services at this early church, with its congregation almost entirely masculine. The six or eight women present, "dressed with the unassuming neatness common among Christian ladies at the East," were treated with enormous respect.

After the devastating fire of May, 1850, an evening benefit was arranged by the ladies of the city's four new churches. All the town's best and most respectable gathered. "There entered a man prominent for wealth and business power," so Sarah Royce recalled, "bearing upon his arm a splendidly dressed woman, well known . . . as the disreputable companion of her wealthy escort." Did the ladies of San Francisco hesitate? Were they quelled by wealth and power? Not for a moment. The man was informed that the lady managers declined to receive "one who stood in the relation occupied by his companion." The couple was "respectfully requested to withdraw. The which they did. "The foundations of morality and civilization," said Sarah, "were upheld."

MEET MISS ATKINS

At this juncture there arrived on the scene the first woman to become a personage in California's educational upbuilding. She was Miss Mary Atkins—much later to become Mrs. John Lynch—a schoolmarm with a taste for travel. Born in 1817 on a prosperous Ohio farm, she had taught in western New York, had gone to Oberlin College in the class of 1845 and for two years had been assistant principal of Oberlin's "academy department." After that she had gone to the Hughes high school of Cincinnati "at an unusually high salary for a woman," states the record.

Miss Atkins reached California in 1854. On a steamer plying between Panama and San Francisco a leading citizen of that town beheld two ladies clad in bloomers. They were Miss Atkins and her traveling companion, Miss Pellet. The startled gentleman learned that Miss Atkins purposed founding a high-principled school for young ladies. Kindly but patronizing, Major Sherman warned the ladies that something more conservative in costume would be required by California's first families. Evidently Miss Atkins took heed. Those bloomers were never seen again, while the equally trousered Miss Pellet slated to lecture on temperance, simply fades out of the picture. But Miss Atkins, with her fine pedagogical background, was soon received in the best circles.

And with good reason. In 1852 monied fathers who did not want to send their daughters back East for schooling, had started a Young Ladies Seminary at Benicia, up the bay from San Francisco. In those two years the "Y.L.S." had operated with a never-ending set of troubles, including an annual deficit. But worse than that was the recurring matrimonial menace. Miss Lord, the first lady principal, imported from New England, married within a year. Miss Jemima Hudson, her successor, lasted even more briefly. By 1854 seven out of nine directors had resigned.

At this crucial moment came Miss Atkins. She was swiftly appointed lady principal. In another year, doubtless with relief, the trustees "sold" the school to her. Now it was Miss Atkins who had to fight the war of weddings. Between 1852 and 1865, of 45 assistant teachers, only fourteen remained longer than a year. The lady principal herself nobly "postponed matrimony" till her 52nd year.

THE "Y.L.S." OF BENICIA

The first catalogue issued by Miss Atkins announced that her "teachers deem it of the highest importance that all ladies should be able to spell correctly, to read naturally, to write legibly, and to converse intelligently." To this end, there must be "unremitting attention to orthography, reading, writing, English grammar and the history of the U.S." Beyond this foundation were "ornamental branches," such as piano and guitar, drawing, crayoning, water coloring and ornamental needlework.

Parents were warned against "unnecessary indulgence in spending money" as well as boxes of sweets from home. The school would provide "regular daily gymnastics" and "ample facilities for bathing"—not further specified. Although the Seminary proclaimed itself nonsectarian, "on Sundays the pupils must attend church with the Principal." This Presbyterian church building had been framed in Massachusetts and shipped around the Horn (Chapter Note 1). At services Miss Atkins's young charges were seated in the gallery "beyond the gaze of young men."

Such protected schooling came high for 1850. Board and tuition was 340 dollars, with 100 dollars extra for music, 40 for modern languages, 60 for drawing, and 80 for water colors. As Mary Banfield wrote of San Francisco, "This is a great place for money." The Y.L.S. prospered. Its first class to be graduated had pupils from San Francisco, Sacramento, Stockton, Santa Barbara and San Bernardino. The management, however, was still harried by the matrimonial menace. Writing home in 1856, Miss Atkins referred to her establishment as "The Young Ladies Courting School."

Already Miss Mary herself had become a tradition, accredited with the traditional romance. It was said that she came to California a blighted being. Her fiancé, an engineer on the Panama railroad construction, had died there of fever, and she had gone devotedly to mark his grave. Family letters to and from Ohio make no mention of any young man in Panama. Still Miss Atkins proved quite capable of keeping her own secrets. In 1856, regardless of the Presbyterian flavor of her school, she herself joined the little old Episcopal church at Benicia. She managed to keep this theological defection from the ears of a disapproving family for two years.

MISS ATKINS SEES HAWAII

Overwork drove the lady principal to a sabbatical year in 1863. She turned this into a tour of Hawaii, Japan, China and Siam, quite a swing-around for a lady in the hoop skirt era. She sailed in

November on the brig *Advance,* keeping a diary of her travels. She was the only passenger on the little trading ship except the owner's fourteen-year-old son, Charlie Hare. By November 11 Miss Mary wrote herself down as seasick and half frozen, though, as the seas grew calmer, she revived sufficiently to teach the captain to play backgammon. By the end of the month she was sightseeing with Charlie in Honolulu. They heard Lincoln's Emancipation Proclamation read out in church to a congregation of seamen and whaling masters. The service was closed with the singing of *The Star Spangled Banner.*

When the *Advance* set sail in December, the schoolteacher began studying a history of Japan. By the end of the month she was thoroughly wearied with the boy Charlie. He was (says the diary) "boorish and uncultivated . . . I wonder if all boys are like him." Day by day Miss Atkins set down the latitude and longitude, even while they rode out a typhoon. In Yedo Bay, on January 26, the captain learned that the Confederate raider *Alabama* was cruising the China seas. The *Advance* left Yokohama on February 16, with the schoolteacher's entries growing constantly shorter. On March 2 they reached the Yangtse Kiang. Miss Atkins wrote firmly, "Thus ends my trip to Shanghai." And that was that. What she saw in Siam, or what she thought of it, remains unknown.

The good brig *Advance* brought the lady principal safely to San Francisco in September, 1864. By the following summer she was once more presiding over the graduating exercises of her school. A visitor there reported "a class of gymnasts dressed in bloomer costume and bearing dumbbells," who performed intricate evolutions to music. There were also "musical selections" by the young ladies, "interspersed with papers." But when a Miss Bell read the fourth one of those essays (it was on Cypress Trees), attending relatives began to disappear in the direction of the refreshment tables.

Success or no, Miss Atkins was growing weary. In October of 1865 she sold her seminary to two missionary teachers just come stateside from Hawaii, and celebrated her release with a trip to Vancouver Island. The next year found Miss Atkins obtaining a passport to visit Europe, tradition sending her to the Paris Exposition. Once more back in her native Ohio, on March 28, 1869 she became the second wife of an Oberlin graduate, John Lynch. Soon Mr. and Mrs. Lynch were engaged in the "reconstruction" of Louisiana, with headquarters at New Orleans till 1876. Mrs. Lynch died six years later, in semiretirement at Santa Barbara.

This first schoolmistress of California provides a link with the future, for the missionary couple who bought the "Y.L.S." at Benicia were Cyrus and Susan Mills of the later Mills Seminary. Susan Mills added two "science courses" to old Benicia, teaching them herself in the mornings, then retiring to the kitchen to provide the fourteen pies needed for the boarding pupils' dinners. In 1870 the Mills' erected their own Seminary "in the suburbs of Oakland." That main building is still in use today as part of Mills College.

CONCEPCIÓN ARGÜELLO OF FACT AND FICTION

The old Seminary at Benicia also links back to the one famous woman of Spanish California, Dona Maria de la Concepción Argüello. When Mary Atkins came to Benicia Dona Concepción was the mother superior of St. Catherine's convent there, the first religious house for women in California. (It had been founded in 1851 at Monterey, but removed to Benicia when that little river town became the state's interim capital.) In 1857 "Sister Domenica" was buried in the convent grounds. Apart from romanticised accounts by Bret Harte and Gertrude Atherton, documented record reveals the original Spanish background, long before the Yankees came. Sister Domenica "never acquired a knowledge of English," says an old convent letter.

She was born at Yerba Buena in 1791, one of the nine children of José Argüello of the Rancho de las Pulgas, a little matter of 35,000 acres. Later Don José was to be the acting governor of both upper and lower California.

Romance touched her when, as a girl of fifteen, in her father's house, she met Count Nikolai Rezánof. This young Russian nobleman had come to Yerba Buena from Alaska to buy provisions for the Czar's starving colonies up North. Such trade agreements had to be approved at long distance by the Viceroy in Mexico. Not till May was the young count's errand completed. Then he left, bound all the way to St. Petersburg to obtain the Czar's consent to his marriage with this beautiful young Spaniard. Also, there must be a dispensation from the Pope. Rezánof never returned, rumors of his death filtering back to Yerba Buena.

Then Senorita Maria joined the Third Order of Saint Francis in the World "to teach native Californians and Indians the truths of our holy faith." Tradition has Dona Concepción traveling the length of California on her vocation. Church papers, however, connect her chiefly with the Mission Soledad, "thousands of acres of barren brown plain," thirty miles south of Monterey near the Salinas River.

Not till 1842 did Dona Concepción learn the facts of Rezánof's death, through a visiting explorer. The count had been thrown from his horse in the long journey across Siberia. Bret Harte (Chapter Note 7) presents a dramatized version of this episode, poets rarely adhering strictly to history. Eight years later, when three Dominican sisters arrived to found Santa Catalina at Monterey, Dona Concepción applied and was accepted. Shortly Santa Catalina at Monterey became Saint Catherine's at Benicia. There, in April, 1852, "Sister Domenica" made her perpetual vows. She died December 1857, as the convent's first mother superior. To the poor of old California she was La Beata. A memorial of her stands today in her convent garden.

ON TO OREGON

From the time of Lewis and Clark the Oregon trail was fairly well established in terms of trappers, traders and fur company "forts" (Chapter Note 8). The advent of white women in these most distant parts came nearly a generation later, and centered around the early Indian missions, which proved a fresh challenge to the indomitable Yankee schoolmarm.

The first mission in the field was the Jason Lee Methodist on the Willamette, opened in 1834, while the huge region was still under joint British-American authority. In that year Lee is recorded as having held the first Protestant service between the Rockies and the Pacific at the old trading post of Fort Hall. Lee apparently came overland with a "fur company," and then pushed on. To his mission on the Willamette a sailing ship brought Chloe Aurelia Clark, the very first schoolteacher to venture so far west so early. All known of her is that while all of Jason Lee's three wives succumbed in the course of his missionary career, Chloe Aurelia survived. Later she married William Willson, the founder of Salem, Oregon.

The year 1835 saw a Presbyterian mission added to the field, and, by 1836, the Board of Foreign Missions dispatched Dr. Marcus Whitman, a physician of eight years' experience, to open stations on the northern overland trail. This venture was the most ambitious in the region, and because of its tragic ending, it is also the best documented. After a year among Oregon tribes, Whitman returned east to marry Narcissa Prentiss (March, 1836) who had also volunteered for the far west. Along with the Whitmans went "the Rev. H. H. Spalding and wife," also a lay assistant. Narcissa Whitman and Eliza Spalding are accepted as the first white women to traverse the old Lewis and Clark route.

The clerical venture was well organized, with wagons, cattle and two Indian boys to manage the cattle. The group traveled with an American Fur Company contingent as far as Green River. Beyond that the Hudson Bay Fur Company sped them on to the Columbia. But to ladies of a churchly bringing-up, there were hours of extreme discomfort if not actual danger. They were utterly dependent on the good will of the mountain men, yet both women were appalled at their blasphemous speech. It was almost enough to shake one's faith. Yet these same blasphemers fabricated the crude skiffs which put the women across the Riviere Boisee, and otherwise saw to their safety.

By September, 1837, the missionaries reached the junction of the Walla Walla River with the Columbia. There, in a river loop of 300 acres, Whitman located his station, Wailatpu—"The Place of the Rye Grass." This site is near the present city of Walla Walla. The Spalding mission was miles back in the Idaho mountains, in the region of what is now Lewiston. Both missions were to stress farming for men converts and domestic crafts for the women. The Whitmans also included a school for whatever children might be available.

WOMEN OF GOD IN THE WILDERNESS

Of Eliza Spalding old reports give only tantalizing glimpses. She came of Ohio farming people, and had been a country school-teacher. She had married her husband while he was completing his missionary training, and there was a child on the way when she started that long hard journey to Oregon. She could hardly sit a horse. Yet she reached her remote station, and both she and the baby survived. Except for Dr. Whitman who covered long wilderness miles to officiate at the birth, their only companions were Indians. This courageous and enduring woman was dark and not very good looking. Also, she was either shy or taciturn. Nevertheless, Eliza Spalding was successful in handling the Indian women, and in teaching them to weave. Indeed, the red men liked this plain quiet woman so well that, eleven years later, she and her children were spared when the Whitmans were massacred at the Wailatpu Mission, on Nov. 29, 1847.

Narcissa Whitman was younger, very blond, and at her best, little short of beautiful. Daughter of a prosperous upstate New York family, she had been sheltered and well schooled. Her letters home, which took months in delivery, show the wilderness life. Her nearest white neighbor was the hospitable keeper of a Hudson Bay outpost on the Columbia that was garrisoned by twelve men. There were also the trader's Indian wife and their six children. Narcissa wrote of the wife as "a native female that promises to be much society for me. She is learning to speak the English language quite fast." It was this Indian woman who later was nurse for Dr. Whitman when Narcissa's child was born.

Narcissa's house was built of adobe with wooden doors and window frames. Beds were made of "boards nailed to the side of the house, sink fashion." As for food, though the plantation was soon supplying vegetables, for meat they were frequently reduced to horse-flesh. "This will make you pity us," Narcissa warned her mother. "I do not prefer it to other meat, but can eat it very well when we have nothing else." Altogether, the Whitman station consumed 23 wild horses in three years. Meanwhile both missions prospered, teaching and farming. Additional missionaries came on, bringing wives with them, so that another station was opened at Spokane.

BACKGROUND TO TRAGEDY

Yet this peaceful interval brought sorrow to the Whitmans in the death of their two-year-old daughter, a blond baby, whose fair color was a source of wonder to the Indians. The child got away from her Indian nurse and fell into the river, drowning before help could reach her. After this, Narcissa Whitman's health began to fail.

Meanwhile each year brought a trickle of Oregon settlers to whom the mission stations were havens of rest, and also sources of food supplies for the depleted wagon trains. Some way or other, Wailatpu always managed to feed the immigrant trains. The stations "gave the valley the cheerful and busy air of civilization," says an old diary. Or so it seemed to the wayworn travelers.

Unfortunately sectarian rivalry was developing in the mission field. It was spurred on by renegade whites bent on driving out the missionaries, so that the traders could regain their hold on the Indians. In 1842 the Mission Board ordered the closing down of controversial posts. To protest this Whitman made his famous "winter ride" to Boston. Narcissa meanwhile went to Fort Vancouver for medical care during his absence.

Congress then had before it the Linn Land Bill, with its bait of free land for western settlers. Anticipating its passage, some 900 prospective Oregonians had assembled in Missouri, waiting word of the bill's passage before setting out across the plains. This was called "the Great Migration," and because of it, the Mission Board permitted Whitman to retain his outpost.

MASSACRE AND AFTERMATH

In the wake of increasing white migration rumors of Indian discontent began to reach the missionaries. But the immediate cause of the Whitman disaster was the outbreak of a deadly form of measles. Dr. Whitman's medicine was seen to save the whites, while Indian children went on dying. In November, 1847, the Cayuse Indians fell on Wailatpu, killing both Whitmans "and twelve other persons."

That term included several part-Indian children, whose white fathers had placed them at Wailatpu for schooling. Little Helen Meek, child of a notable mountain guide, died of terror. Captain Bridger's Mary Ann was captured and held for ransom, only to die a little later. But a few escaped to carry the news to the Hudson Bay fur post. Not long afterwards a French priest, newly come to a Canadian mountain mission, happened in on the scene of the slaughter and "gave the mutilated bodies a Christian burial."

The Oregon settlers, though few, started a war of revenge, and sent to Washington for help. Their messenger was Joseph Meek whose child had died at Wailatpu. His success with Congress belongs to political history. For old Oregon it should be noted that he had married, in succession, three Indian wives.

An uneasy peace now prevailed in the Oregon valleys. The boundary dispute with Great Britain had been adjusted. Settlement was resumed, but few women came. Although a special "donation" bill allotted as much free land for a farmer's wife as it did for the farmer, the gold strike in California proved a stronger magnet. Embittered Oregonians accused their rivals of intercepting family wagons in the mountains, and diverting families into California. Unattached women, coming by sea, were only too apt to leave ship at the Golden Gate.

Nor did the Rogue River Indian war of 1853 tend to attract the ladies. In 1854 a hardy Oregon woman tavern keeper wrote to a niece in the middle-west advising her against coming out to the coast. Women there were so scarce, she warned, that settlers would be likely to seize her by force. (Or maybe the letter writer didn't want that niece in her tavern!) A Californian, visiting Salem at about the same time, reported the Oregon outlook as grim and churchly. Its struggling communities, he complained, were New England all over again. He missed that vivid mingling of races and tongues that gave San Francisco its gaily cosmopolitan flavor. Certainly settling remained slow. By 1860 all of Oregon territory could claim only 60,000 in population, as against the 375,000 counted in California.

THE INCREDIBLE MERCER GIRLS

Such was the situation when, in 1861, a Yankee carpenter named Asa Mercer hit upon a novel scheme to relieve the woman shortage. Asa had come out to the Puget Sound region to join a brother who was a pioneer judge in Seattle. Like every other newcomer, he quickly noticed the scarcity of women. But he stood ready to do something about it.

Knowing that the Civil War had begun to cut cotton supplies to the Lowell Mills, Asa returned east to round up idle lady operatives, offering them positions as schoolteachers in Seattle. Eleven misses were willing to undertake the trip. Within a few months of their arrival, one had died, but the other ten were married, 320 acres to each lady's husband. Fate has preserved the names of these mettlesome weavers. They were Georgia and Josephine Pearson, Annie May Adams, Kate Stickney, Lizzie Ordway, Kate Stevens and "the Misses Cheney," all straight New England names. Then there were Maria Murphy and Sarah Gallagher, suggesting an early Irish infiltration from Boston.

So successful was Mercer's first attempt that he agreed to provide a second and larger contingent of unemployed from the Lowell looms. From this point on the originator began to build up trouble. There was a matter of contracts with prospective bridegrooms. On 300 dollars being advanced for her travel expenses, Mercer pledged to produce "a wife of good moral character and reputation." In and around Lowell he was able to recruit some 300 "orphans of the war."

Mercer then began negotiating with the government for use of a troopship for the ladies' mission. That bright idea brought difficulties and delays that ate into the sums advanced by Seattle swains. Meanwhile the New York *Herald* got wind of the affair and printed a lurid story accusing Mercer of preparing to supply girls for the waterfront dives out on the Pacific Coast. Not surprisingly, many of the 300 volunteers began to lose their nerve or were warned away by their relatives. At length less than 200 embarked (January 1866) in a hired ship, the *Continental*, with Mercer himself concealed in a coal bunker.

Among this second delegation of "Mercer girls," as the *Herald* had called them, was Flora Pearson, whose two older sisters had gone out in the first contingent and were now happily married in Oregon. It was Flora who wrote home the story of the expedition's rugged passage. Like the Argonauts who had earlier set sail for California, the Mercer girls found the ship unbelievably dirty. (It had been a troop transport.) Also, the food was bad and far from plentiful. But like the good Yankees that they were, the Mercer girls turned to and scrubbed their own walls and decks. Tiring of salt beef and poor tea, they invaded the cook's galley and did a bit of provisioning for themselves.

Altogether it was a pretty unpleasant passage of 96 days around the Horn and into the Golden Gate. There worse was to follow. When the *Continental* reached San Francisco, it was learned that the ship was to be sold on the spot, leaving the girls to walk to Oregon if they wished. The money advanced for the "Mercer girls" had merely paid for the ship's removal from the Atlantic to the Pacific, adding to the profits of a speculative sale.

Mercer was now at his wits' end—no ship, no money and angry suitors awaiting him in Oregon. The best he could do was to forward a few girls at a time on any Seattle-bound boat whose captain was generously disposed. That was slow work. Meanwhile the number of volunteers was shrinking, since marriageable young ladies were also in demand in California. By summer Asa and his remaining protégées reached Seattle, and marrying began. Just how Mercer settled with swains who had paid in their 300 dollars and got nothing, is not told. But he evidently escaped jail, for the last note is a happy one. Mercer himself married one of "the girls."

Special thanks are given to the Bancroft section of the University of California Library (Berkeley); to the Library of the State Museum at Sacramento, and to Miss Katherine V. Newsome, for use of the unpublished Vanderbeck-Banfield letters, now in the New York Historical Society.

1 In the gold rush period, actual buildings sometimes came from afar, owing to shortage of manpower and machinery on the Pacific coast. Structures of the early Protestant churches were literally framed in New England, disassembled, and then shipped around the Horn. Other structures came by sail from Hawaii, or even from distant China where labor was cheap and materials were plenty.

The East started promptly to go after the Pacific coast trade. Advertisements in the New York *Tribune* of '49 and '50 offered "passports for California," also "portable iron houses," egg powders, condensed coffee, "California Gold Vests," complete with scales and jewelers' weights, besides a patented "gold washer." At 349 Broadway there was a "California Miners' Depot" where such goods could be bought for shipment around the Horn.

2 In recalling the Donner tragedy of 1847, readers are reminded that in January 1952, a hundred and five years later, a "luxury" train to the Pacific Coast was trapped by deep snow in this same pass. In spite of ample motorized rescue equipment, it took relief crews three days to remove the marooned passengers. It was another three days before the train could be pushed through the defile. Curiously reflecting the past, Mexican track workers packed fuel and food on their backs to provide the stranded passengers with two hot meals daily while the temperature hovered around zero. As soon as motorized units opened up a passage on the state highway, these track workers trampled with their feet a rough passage from the highway to the train, by which the passengers reached the rescue equipment. The only fatalities in this modernized version of the Donner story were among the rescue workers.

3 Popular ballads of the period also give the gold rush picture. One was called "The Fools of '49."

They bought their ships, came round the Horn, in the fall of '49
The poor, the old and rotten scows were advertised to sail
From New Orleans with passengers, but they must pump and bail;
The ships were crowded more than full, and some hung on behind,
And others dived off from the wharf and swam till they were blind.
With rusty pork and stinking beef, and wormy rotten bread,
And captains too that never were up as high as the mainmast head.
The steerage passengers would rave and swear they'd paid their passage
And wanted something more to eat besides Bologna sausage . . .

Women appear in ballads such as "The California Bloomer."

Miss Ella she is twenty-nine
Has taken two degrees,
And torn her shirttail off behind
So she can show her knees.

Miss Ella is a gallus nag,
Miss Ella she is neat,
Her eyes look like a saffron bag,
And Lord, what awful feet!

Miss Ella has a claim, they say,
She works it all the while.
She creviced round the other day
Panned out a little pile.

She'll get it all after a while,
If patiently she waits
I'll leave her when I make a pile,
And vamose for the States.

4   Following the "Frémont and Jessie" presidential campaign of '56—
the first in which the charm of a candidate's wife was publicly utilized—
the defeated candidate made New York his legal residence, with a town
house and a summer place up the Hudson. In 1857 the youngest child,
a frail boy, was born.

Complete financial disaster overtook Frémont in the crash of
railroad properties during the "decade of scandals." Mrs. Frémont then
began writing for Bonner's *Ledger* sketches of travel and recollection
which won immediate popularity. Meanwhile Frémont put in a claim
for their San Francisco property—Black Point near the Golden Gate—
which had been taken over by the army during the Civil War. The claim
seemed to lose itself in a mass of governmental procedure. In 1878
Frémont gladly accepted three years' governorship of Arizona territory.
The claim procedure dragged on, but Frémont was restored to army rank
and pension. He died in New York, 1890.

The widow returned to Los Angeles to a house presented by the women of Southern California. In 1885 Josiah Royce entered into a long correspondence with Mrs. Frémont, with regard to her husband's part in the seizure of California from Mexico. Apparently Royce assumed that Frémont himself was too ill to attend to this. The correspondence is in the Huntington Library. Jessie Benton Frémont died in 1902.

5   The Vanderbeck-Banfield letters quoted here have a history. Written "home" to Greenpoint in Brooklyn, the letters were kept in the family for nearly a hundred years. Then, at the time of the California gold rush centenary, a descendant of the Banfields presented the letters to the New York Historical Society.

6   *The Frontier Diary* by Sarah Royce (Yale University Press, 1932) is not the original diary that Sarah Royce kept on her journey from Council Bluffs to San Francisco, but her own revision of the original. During the '70's, when her distinguished son Josiah was working on his history of California, he asked his mother for material. Apparently the original manuscript was then in existence. Now, some 30 years after the facts, she rewrote her journal in more literary form, adding to it and sometimes quoting her first-hand notes. Her religious experiences crossing the Plains make touching reading. The publication of the revised manuscript was more than 80 years after her journey.

7   Bret Harte's version of the Argüello story begins:

> *Forty years on wall and bastion swept the idle breeze.*

Then

> *Sir George Simpson, famous traveler and guest . . .*
> *At a costly banquet sat.*

At this feast in Governor Argüello's House, the English explorer is asked if anything has ever been heard of Count Rezánof. The visitor announces:

> *He died forty years ago this day—*
> *Died while speeding home to Russia,*
> *Falling from a fractious horse—*
> *Left a sweetheart, too, they tell me.*

At the rear of the hall he sees:

> *A trembling figure rising.*
> *Two black eyes in darkened orbits*

Gleamed beneath the nun's white hood. . . .

"Lives she yet?" Sir George repeated

As Concha drew closer yet her nun's attire.

"Señor, pardon, she died, too." . . .

Gertrude Atherton based an early novel *Rezánof* on this story.

8   No account of American women in Oregon should omit their predecessor—Sacajawea, Indian wife of a Canadian guide for the Lewis and Clark expedition, 1803–06. She is the best documented Indian woman in our history. After the explorers reached the end of navigation in the Dakotas, she, as interpreter, helped to persuade Indians of the region to furnish the horses so needed for crossing the great divide to the head waters of the Columbia river.

The daughter of a Shoshone chief in Idaho, Sacajawea was born around 1787, and as a girl was captured by another tribe in the recurring pattern of tribal warfare. She and another Indian girl were sold to a French trader among the Mandans—Toussaint Charbonneau. He promptly married both girls by Indian rites. This slightly irregular family was at Fort Mandan when the Lewis and Clark expedition wintered there, 1804–05, and there her first child, a boy, was born, February 11, 1805. Two months later, with Jean Baptiste strapped to her back, the young mother was off with her husband on the great adventure, chosen because of her previous knowledge of the territory and peoples through which they must pass.

Later on William Clark made a pet of the little boy, nicknaming him Pomp. The mother's name he shortened to Janey. Clark apparently manifested interest in the child's future, for, in 1809, the parents brought him to Clark in St. Louis, where the explorer was now Indian Agent and Territorial Governor of Missouri.

Charbonneau then annexed himself and wife to an exploring unit of the big Missouri fur company that was headed by Manuel Lisa. At Fort Lisa, near what is now Omaha, Sacajawea had a little girl born in August, 1812, and named Lizette. Two months later Lisa's company clerk listed the mother's death "of a putrid fever . . . leaving a fine infant."

At this point documentation ceases. What the humane Clark did with the little orphan is unknown. He meanwhile had married a young lady of Virginia, who was to provide him with four children of his own. One legend maintains that Sacajawea didn't die, but tiring of white men's ways, returned to her own people in Idaho. Whatever the truth, her fame is secure. In years to come a river, a peak and a mountain pass have been named for the Indian woman, besides three official statues which may or may not have resembled her. One may also note that Governor Clark outlived three wives in early St. Louis.

EPILOGUE

THE YEAR WAS 1860, the year that had seen the election of Abraham Lincoln. With every week, threat of civil war came closer.

Here we leave this study of American women, for in the course of that bloody cleavage their capacities were to be clearly revealed. Women poured into Washington to be clerks, to be nurses, to work in the Freedmen's Bureau. In the South women who could manage plantations were managing hospitals while ladies put aside their fine needlework to keep their families clad and shod. Sheltering nightly in caves outside of Vicksburg, other women huddled and endured. In northern cities there were the ladies of the Sanitary Fairs. Mother Blickersdyke of the Shaker bonnet was working with the wounded and Clara Barton was running her own service of hospital supply. On both sides there were lady spies in hoop skirts. Everywhere there was grief to be borne. In the White House Mary Lincoln mourned her son. Varina Davis mourned hers in that other mansion in Richmond.

These and other Civil War figures most of us have already heard about. But readers who have followed the earlier trail of American women in this book—sometimes through decades of submersion, sometimes surmounting ingrained opposition—know that women like those of the Civil War were there all the time. Usually they were in the background and for the most part silent. Now war stresses demonstrated to their world what American women had been feeling and thinking ever since 1776.

So we give you these women of the past—the valiant, the timid, the wise, the foolish, the romantic and the practical. They are all a part of our American heritage, to be set down before the record has been too much blurred by the passage of time.

ACKNOWLEDGMENTS

The author wishes to make grateful acknowledgement of the use of unpublished material and records from the following organizations:

CHAPTER ONE	The Morgan Library
CHAPTER TWO	Boston Athenaeum Smith College Library—Sophia Smith Collection New York Public Library
CHAPTER THREE	The New York Historical Society The New York Public Library
CHAPTER FOUR	Smith College Library—Mott letters and Barton papers
CHAPTER FIVE	The New York Historical Society The New York Medical Society Library
CHAPTER SIX	Congressional Library, Washington, D.C. Cossett Library, Memphis Tenn. Smith College Library
CHAPTER SEVEN	New York Public Library—Theatre Section
CHAPTERS EIGHT AND NINE	Bancroft Library of the University of California California State Library, Sacramento The New York Historical Society The New York Public Library

BIBLIOGRAPHY — GENERAL

ADAMS, JAMES TRUSLOW *New England in the Republic*. Little Brown & Company, 1927
——— *The Adams Family*. Little Brown & Company, 1930
——— *The Living Jefferson*. Scribners, 1931

ADAMS, JOHN QUINCY *Diaries, 1794–1845.* Longmans Green, 1928

ALCOTT, WILLIAM A. *Young Woman's Guide to Excellence.* George W. Light, Boston, 1840

AMORY, CLEVELAND *The Proper Bostonians.* E. P. Dutton & Co., Inc., 1947

ARMSTRONG, MARGARET *Five Generations.* Harpers, 1930.

ARTHUR, T. S. *Stories for Parents.* Lippincott, Grambo & Co., 1851

BEARD, MARY R. *America Through Women's Eyes.* Macmillan, 1933

BOOTH, EDWARD TOWNSEND *Country Life in America as Lived by 10 Presidents.* Alfred Knopf, 1947

BRADFORD, GAMALIEL *Portraits of American Women.* Houghton Mifflin, 1919

———— *Wives.* Harpers, 1925

BROOKS, VAN WYCK *The Flowering of New England.* E. P. Dutton, 1936

BROWN, HARRIET CONNOR *Grandmother Brown's Hundred Years.* Little Brown & Co., 1929

BRUCE, H. ADDINGTON *Women in the Making of America.* Little Brown & Co., 1928

BURT, STRUTHERS *Philadelphia, Holy Experiment.* Doubleday, 1945

BUTTERFIELD, ROGER *The American Past.* Simon & Schuster, 1947

CALLENDER, JAMES H. *Yesterdays on Brooklyn Heights.* Privately printed, 1927

———— *Yesterdays in Little Old New York.* Privately printed, 1928

CARGILL, OSCAR *Intellectual America.* Macmillan, 1941

CARMER, CARL *The Hudson.* Farrar & Rinehart, 1939

COOPER, JAMES FENIMORE *Gleanings in Europe.* (Ed. by R. E. Spiller) Oxford University Press, 1906

DAVIS, VARINA HOWELL *Jefferson Davis, Ex-President of the C.S.A.* Belford, 1890

DEXTER, ELISABETH ANTHONY *Career Women of America 1776–1840.* Marshall Jones, 1950

DUNSHEE, KENNETH H. *As You Pass By.* Hastings House, 1952

FISH & WILSON *History of the United States.* American Book Company, 1934

GILMORE, INEZ HAYES *Angels and Amazons.* Doubleday Doran, 1933

HANAFORD, PHEBE A. *Daughters of America.* B. B. Russell, 1883

HANDLIN, OSCAR *This was America.* Harvard University Press, 1949

HAWTHORNE, NATHANIEL *American Note-Book.* James R. Osgood & Co., Boston 1874

HONE, PHILIP *Diary 1828–51.* Dodd Mead, 1879

HOWE, M. A. DE WOLF *The Articulate Sisters.* Harvard University Press, 1946

IRVING, WASHINGTON *Letters* (Ed. by Hellman). Putnam, 1915

LEECH, MARGARET *Reveille in Washington.* Harpers, 1941

LOGAN, MRS. JOHN A. *Women in American History.* Perry Nalle Publishing Co., Wilmington, Del., 1912

MARTINEAU, HARRIET *A Retrospect of Western Travel.* Saunders & Ottley, London, 1838

MEYER, ANNIE NATHAN *Women's Work in America.* Henry Holt, 1891

MIRSKY-NEVINS *The World of Eli Whitney.* Macmillan, 1952

NATIONAL EXPOSITION SOUVENIR *What America Owes to Women.* Charles Wells Moulton, 1893

NEVINS, ALLEN *American Social History as Recorded by British Travelers.* Henry Holt, 1923

RANDOLPH, SARAH N. *Domestic Life of Thomas Jefferson.* Cambridge Press (Reprint), 1939

ROBERTSON, ARCHIE *That Old-Time Religion.* Houghton Mifflin, 1950

RUSSELL, WILLIAM HOWARD *My Diary, North & South.* Burnham, 1863

SANDBURG & ANGLE *Mary Lincoln,* Harcourt Brace, 1932

STANTON-ANTHONY-GAGE *History of the Suffrage Movement.* Fowler & Wells, 1881

STEPHENS, MRS. ANN S. *Malaeska.* 1860

TATE, ALLEN *Jefferson Davis, Rise & Fall.* Minton Balch, 1929

THARP, LOUISE HALL *The Peabody Sisters of Salem.* Little Brown & Co., Boston, 1950

VAN DOREN, CARL *The Great Rehearsal.* Viking, 1948

WARFEL, H. R., GABRIEL, R. H., WILLIAMS, S. T. *The American Mind.* American Book Co., 1937

WHITTON, MARY ORMSBEE *First First Ladies.* Hastings House, 1948

WRIGHT, RICHARDSON *Forgotten Ladies.* J. B. Lippincott Co., 1928

BIBLIOGRAPHY—BY CHAPTERS

CHAPTER ONE

ALLAN, HERBERT S. *John Hancock.* Macmillan, 1948
BOBBÉ, DOROTHEA *Abigail Adams.* Minton, Balch & Co., 1929
BROWN, ALICE *Mercy Warren.* Scribners, 1896
CAIRNES, WILLIAM *Early American Writers, 1608–1800.* Macmillan, 1910
CARY, W. M. *Sally Cary.* Privately printed—De Vinne Press, N. Y., 1911
CRÉVECOEUR, ST. JOHN DE *Sketches of 18th Century America.* Yale University Press, 1925
CUSTIS, G. W. *Private Memoirs of Washington.* Moore, 1859
DESMOND, ALICE C. *Martha Washington.* Dodd Mead, 1942
DUKE, JANE TAYLOR *Kenmore and the Lewises.* Doubleday & Co., Inc., 1949
ELLET, ELIZABETH F. L. *Women of the American Revolution.* George W. Jacobs (Reprint), Philadelphia, 1900
———— *Domestic History of the American Revolution.* Baker & Scribners, 1851
———— *Court Circles of the Republic.* Denison, New York, 1869
FORBES, ESTHER *Paul Revere and the World He Lived In.* Houghton Mifflin, 1942
FREEMAN, DOUGLAS S. *George Washington.* Charles Scribner's Sons, 1948–1953
MALLOY, ROBERT *Charleston.* D. Appleton–Century Co., Inc., 1947
O'BRIEN, HARRIET E. *Paul Revere's Own Story.* Privately printed, Perry Walton, 1929
PALMER, CATHERINE B. *Appalachian Valley Pilgrimage.* National Geographic, July, 1949
SEAVER, JAMES E. *The Narrative of Mary Jemison.* J. D. Burns, Canandaigua, N.Y., 1829
WAMSEY, HENRY *An Expedition to the 'United States of North America' in the Summer of 1794.* G. & T. Wilkie, London, 1796
WARREN, MERCY *The Rise, Progress & Termination of the American Revolution.* Manning & Loring, 1804

WHARTON, ANNE H. *Colonial Days and Dames.* J. B. Lippincott, 1895

WOODBURY, ELLEN C. D. *Dorothy Quincy, Wife of John Hancock.* The Neale Publishing Co., Washington, 1905

CHAPTER TWO

ADAMS, ABIGAIL *New Letters, 1788–1801.* Houghton Mifflin, 1947

ASBURY, HERBERT *The French Quarter.* Alfred A. Knopf, 1936

BARNARD, EUNICE FULLER *Co-Eds Round Out a Century.* New York Times, October 3, 1937

BERNARD, JOHN *Retrospection of America 1797–1811.* Harpers (Reprint) 1887

BROOKS, VAN WYCK *The World of Washington Irving.* Dutton, 1944

————— *The Times of Whitman & Melville.* Dutton, 1947

CHASE, MARY ELLEN *Jonathan Fisher, Maine Parson.* The Macmillan Co., 1948

COOPER, JAMES FENIMORE *The Chain Bearer.* Collier, 1891

————— *Home as Found.* Collier, 1891

FARRAR, MRS. JOHN *The Young Woman's Friend.* Samuel & William Wood, New York, 1841

FEARON, HENRY *Narrative of 5000 Miles.* London, 1818

HOWE, HENRY *The Great West.* Reprinted, 1851

————— *Historical Collection of Ohio.* Henry Howe & Son, Columbus, O., 1891

IRVING, WASHINGTON *Tour of the Prairies.* G. P. Putnam, 1863

MC CLUNG, JOHN A. *Sketches of Western Adventure, 1755–94.* G. F. Tuttle, N.Y., 1858

ORMSBEE, THOMAS H. *Early American Furniture Makers.* T. Y. Crowell, 1930

QUINCY, JOSIAH *Figures of the Past.* Little Brown & Co., 1927

ROBERTS, KENNETH & ANNA *Journals of Moreau de St. Méry.* Doubleday, 1947

SCHLESINGER, ARTHUR M. *Learning How to Behave.* The Macmillan Co., 1947

SCHULTZ, CHRISTIAN *An Inland Voyage 1807–08.* New York, 1810

SMITH, MARGARET BAYARD *Forty Years of Washington Society.* Scribners (Reprint), 1906

STEELE, MRS. *Summer Journey in the West.* John S. Taylor & Co., N.Y., 1841

WHITE, TRYPHENA ELIZABETH *Journal, 1805.* Grafton Press, N.Y., 1905

CHAPTER THREE

ABBOTT, JOHN S. C. *The Child at Home*. American Tract Society, 1835
———— *The Mother at Home*. Harpers, 1852
AMES, MARY CLEMMER *Alice & Phoebe Cary*. Hurd, Houghton, Boston, 1874
BANTA, R. E. *The Ohio*. Rinehart & Co., N.Y., 1949
BASSETT, JOHN SPENCER *The Southern Plantation Overseer*. Smith College, 1925
CLEAVES, FREEMAN *Old Tippecanoe*. Scribners, 1939
COOPER, JAMES FENIMORE *Pioneers*. P. F. Collier, 1891
———— *Ways of the Hour*. P. F. Collier, 1891
DICKENS, CHARLES *American Notes*. Chapman & Hall, London, 1913
FOWLER, WM. W. *Women in the American Frontier*. S. S. Scranton & Co., Hartford, 1877
GREENWOOD, GRACE *Recollections of My Childhood*. Ticknor, Reed & Fields, Boston, 1854
GROSSMAN, JAMES *James Fenimore Cooper*. William Sloane Associates, 1949
HANSEN, HARRY *North of Manhattan*. Hastings House, 1950
IRVING, WASHINGTON *Bonneville's Adventures*. G. P. Putnam, 1863
KINZIE, MRS. JOHN H. *Early Days in the Northwest*. D. B. Cooke & Co., Chicago, 1857
MARRYAT, CAPTAIN *A Diary in America*. Cary & Hart, Philadelphia, 1839
MORREL, MARTHA MC BRIDE *Young Hickory*. E. P. Dutton, 1949
MUSCHAMP, E. A. *Audacious Audubon*. Brentano, 1929
NEVINS & THOMAS (Editors) *The Diary of John Templeton Strong*. The Macmillan Company, 1952
PORTER, SARAH HARVEY *Life & Times of Anne Royall*. Torch Press, Cedar Rapids, Iowa, 1909
PUTNAM, EMILY JAMES *The Lady*. Sturgis, 1910
ROYALL, ANNE NEWPORT *The Black Books. Pennsylvania. Letters from Alabama. The Southern Tour*. Washington, 1828, 1829, 1830, 1830–31
SAXON, LYLE *In Old Louisiana*. Century, 1929
SEITZ, DON C. *Horace Greeley*. Bobbs Merrill, 1926
———— *The James Gordon Bennetts, Father & Son*. Bobbs Merrill, 1926
SPRING, DR. GARDINER *Hints to Parents*. Taylor & Gould, 1835

TROLLOPE, FRANCES   *Domestic Manners of the Americans.* Harpers, 1838

TWAIN, MARK   *Life on the Mississippi.* Harper & Brothers, 1904

———— *Autobiography.* Harper & Brothers, 1924

WHEELER, CANDACE THURBER   *Yesterdays in a Busy Life.* Harper & Brothers, 1918

CHAPTERS FOUR AND FIVE

Note: Sources for these chapters are so frequently intermingled that their bibliography is given as a unit.

ALLEN, HERVEY   *Israfel—Edgar Allan Poe.* Farrar & Rinehart, 1934

ALLEN, WILLIAM   *American Biographical Dictionary, 1857.* John P. Jewett, Boston

ANON   *Eminent Women of the Age.* S. M. Betts, Hartford, 1868

ANON   *Life and Beauties of Fanny Fern.* H. Long & Brother, 1855

ANON   *Little Journeys to the Homes of Famous Women.* G. P. Putnam, 1897

ANON   *Our Famous Women.* A. D. Worthington & Co., Hartford, 1884

BELL, MARGARET   *Margaret Fuller.* Charles Boni, 1930

BOLTON, SARAH K.   *Lives of Girls Who Became Famous.* Thomas Y. Crowell, 1925

BRAINERD, EZRA   *Mrs. Emma Willard's Life & Work in Middlebury.* Middlebury College Bulletin, October 1918

CHILD, LYDIA MARIA   *Letters from New York.* Francis, 1855

CLEMENT, J.   *Noble Deeds of American Women.* George H. Derby & Co., Buffalo, 1852

CURTIS, A. W. AND C. S.   *Spirit of '76* (Satire). Little Brown, 1868

FINLEY, RUTH E.   *The Lady of Godey's.* J. B. Lippincott Co., 1931

GARRISON, WENDELL P. & FRANCIS J.   *William Lloyd Garrison.* The Century Company, N.Y., 1883

GODEY   *Lady's Book, 1838.*

GRISWOLD, RUFUS   *Gems from American Female Poets.* 1842

HARE, LLOYD C. M.   *Lucretia Mott.* American Historical Society, Inc., N.Y., 1937

HARRIS, SEALE   *J. Marion Sims, Woman's Surgeon.* The Macmillan Company, 1950

LOZIER, DR. A. W.   *In Memoriam, Clemence Lozier.* Privately printed

LOZIER, CLEMENCE   *Childbirth Made Easy.* R. G. Johnston, 1870

LUTZ, ALMA   *Emma Willard.* Houghton Mifflin, 1929

M'LAUGHLIN, KATHLEEN   *Co-Education Era Thrills Oberlin.* New York Times, October 7, 1937

NEW YORK TIMES, SUNDAY MAGAZINE *Original Bloomer Girl.* November 19, 1944

ROOF, KATHARINE METCALFE *Colonel William Smith & Lady.* Houghton Mifflin, 1929

ROURKE, CONSTANCE MAYFIELD *Trumpets of Jubilee.* Harcourt Brace, 1927

SLAUGHTER, ROSALIE *Woman Surgeon.* Frederick A. Stokes, 1937

STOWE, CHARLES *Life of Harriet Beecher Stowe.* Houghton Mifflin, 1911

STOWE, HARRIET BEECHER & CATHARINE BEECHER *The American Woman's Home.* J. B. Ford, 1869

STOWE, HARRIET BEECHER *Oldtown Folks.* Houghton Mifflin & Co., 1889

——— *My Wife & I.* J. B. Ford, 1872

THARP, LOUISE HALL *Until Victory.* Little Brown, 1953

THORPE, MARGARET FARRAND *Female Persuasion.* Yale University Press, 1949

TIFFANY, FRANCIS *Life of Dorothea Lynde Dix.* Houghton Mifflin, 1890

WELD, THEODORE *American Slavery as It Is.* American Anti-Slavery Society, 1834

WHITTON, MARY O. *At Home with Lucretia Mott,* American Scholar, Spring 1951

WILLARD, FRANCES & LIVERMORE, MARY A. *American Women, 1500 Biographies.* Mast, Crowell & Kirkpatrick, 1893

CHAPTER SIX

BROWN, LOUISE FARGO *Lucy Maynard Salmon.* Harpers, 1943

BREMER, FREDERIKA *Homes in the New World.* Harpers, 1853

BUCKMINSTER, HENRIETTA *Let My People Go.* Harpers, 1941

CONRAD, EARL *Harriet Tubman.* The Associated Publishers, Inc., Washington, D.C., 1943

DAKIN, EDWIN F. *Mrs. Eddy.* Scribners, 1929

EHRLICH, LEONARD *God's Angry Man.* Readers Club, 1941

ELLET, ELIZABETH F. L. *Queens of American Society.* Porter & Coates, Philadelphia, 1867

GARLAND, HAMLIN *A Daughter of the Middle Border.* Macmillan, 1921

GARWOOD, DARRELL *The Story of Kansas City.* W. W. Norton & Co., 1948

HELPER, HINTON ROWAN *The Impending Crisis.* A. B. Burdick, N.Y., 1860

HIGGINSON, THOMAS WENTWORTH *Letters & Journals 1846–1906*. Houghton Mifflin, 1921

HOLBROOK, STEWART H. *The Yankee Exodus*. Macmillan, 1950

KEMBLE, FANNY *Journals of a Residence on a Georgia Plantation, 1838–39*. Harpers, 1863

LEE, MARY *John Brown Amid the Mountains*. New York Times Sunday Magazine, October, 1929

LEWIS, LLOYD *Captain Sam Grant*. Little Brown, 1950

MC BEE, ALICE EATON *From Utopia to Florence*. Smith College Studies in History, Vol. XXXII, 1947

MERRY *Merry's Museum*. D. M. Macdonald, N.Y., 1848–49

MOTHER'S MAGAZINE 1859

MYGATT, TRACY D. *Julia Newberry's Sketch Book*. W. W. Norton, N.Y., 1934

NEAL, ALICE B. *Widow Bedott Papers*. J. C. Derby, 1856

NORDHOFF, CHARLES *Communistic Societies of the U.S.* Harper & Bros., 1875

RANDALL, RUTH PAINTER *Mary Lincoln*. Little Brown, Boston, 1953

SEITZ, DON C. *Uncommon Americans*. Bobbs Merrill, 1925

SMITH, MORTIMER *Ann Lynch's Salon*. The New Yorker, September, 1936

TATE, ALLEN *Jefferson Davis, Rise & Fall*. Minton Balch

WILTSE, CHARLES M. *John C. Calhoun 1840–1850*. Bobbs Merrill, 1951

WINSTON, ROBERT *Andrew Johnson, Plebian & Patriot*. Henry Holt, 1928

CHAPTER SEVEN

ANONYMOUS *Forgotten Statue*. New York Times, May 13, 1934

ARDITI, LUIGI *My Reminiscences*. Dodd Mead, 1896

ART & LIFE IN AMERICA Rinehart & Co., New York, 1949

BAKER, THEODORE *Biographical Dictionary of Musicians*. Scribners, 1900

BARNUM, P. T. *The Life of Phineas Barnum*. Redfield, 1855

BELKNAP, HENRY WYKOFF *Artists & Craftsmen of Essex County*. Essex Institute, Salem, Mass., 1927

BERMAN, ELEANOR D. *Thomas Jefferson Among the Arts*. Philosophical Library, N.Y., 1947

CAIRNS, WILLIAM *Early American Writers*. Macmillan, 1910

CLAPP, H. A. *Reminiscences of a Dramatic Critic*. Houghton Mifflin, 1902

CRAWFORD, MARY CAROLINE *The Romance of the American Theatre*. Little Brown, 1925

FAULKNER, JAMES *America's Old Masters*. Viking Press, 1939

FORD, ALICE *Folk Art*. Studio Publications, Inc.

HARLAND, MARION *Autobiography*. Harper & Brothers, 1910

HAWTHORNE, JULIAN *Nathaniel Hawthorne & His Wife*. Osgood, Boston, 1885

KELLOGG, CLARA LOUISE *Memories of an American Prima Donna*. Putnam, 1913

MOWATT, ANNA CORA *Autobiography of an Actress*. Ticknor, Fields, Boston 1854

ORMSBEE, HELEN *Backstage with Actors*. Thomas Y. Crowell & Co., 1938

QUINN, ARTHUR HOBSON *Representative American Plays*. The Century Company, 1917

ROURKE, CONSTANCE *Troupers of the Gold Coast*. Harcourt Brace, 1928

STEBBINS, EMMA *Charlotte Cushman, Her Letters & Memories*. Osgood & Company, 1878

THOMAS, ROSE FAY *Memoirs of Theodore Thomas*. Moffat, Yard & Co., 1911

UPTON, GEORGE *Musical Memories*. Mc Clurg, 1908

CHAPTERS EIGHT AND NINE

Note: Sources for this chapter are so frequently intermingled that the list here is given jointly.

ARGÜELLO, CONCEPIÓN Letters relating to: Bancroft Library, University of California, Berkeley

ATHERTON, GERTRUDE *Rezánov*. F. A. Stokes, 1915

ATKINS, MARY *Diary*. (Reprint) The Eucalyptus Press, Mills College, 1937

BAGLEY, CLARENCE *Early Catholic Missions in Old Oregon*. Lowman & Hanford Co., Seattle, 1932

BANCROFT, HUBERT HOWE *Retrospection*. The Bancroft Company, New York, 1915

BARTLETT, WM. C. *The Founder & Builder*. Culvery & Co. San Francisco, 1894

BIDWELL, GENERAL JOHN *Echoes of the Past*. (Reprint) Chico Advertiser, Chico, Cal., 1892

BOURNE, EDGAR *Legend of Marcus Whitman*. Chas. Scribner's Sons, 1901

CLAPPE, LOUISE AMELIA *The Shirley Letters from California.* T. C. Russell, San Francisco, 1922

DANA, RICHARD HENRY, JR. *Two Years Before the Mast.* 1840

DOBIE, J. FRANK *Coronado's Children.* Literary Guild, 1931

DOUTHIT, MARY OSBORN *A Souvenir of Western Women.* Portland, Oregon, 1905

DRURY, CLIFFORD MERRILL *Marcus Whitman, MD.* The Caxton Printers, Caldwell, Idaho, 1937

ELDRIDGE, ZOETH S. *The Beginnings of San Francisco.* Z. S. Eldridge, San Francisco, 1912

ENGLE, FLORA A. *The Story of the Mercer Expedition.* Washington Historical Quarterly, October, 1915

FOREIGN MISSION BOARD *Report on Early Labors in Oregon*

FRÉMONT, JESSIE BENTON *A Year of American Travel.* Harper & Brothers, 1878

———— *Letters to Josiah Royce.* Huntington & Bancroft Libraries

HOOVER-RENSCH *Historic Spots in California.* Stanford University Press, 1948

JAMES, E. O. *Notes on the History of Benicia Seminary.* (mss) Bancroft Library, Berkeley

KEEP, ROSALINDA *Fourscore Years.* Mills College, 1931

MILLS SEMINARY FOR YOUNG LADIES Franklin Printing House, San Francisco, 1871

MOODY, C. A. *Jessie Benton Frémont, a Study.* Outwest, Vol. XVIII

NEVINS, ALLEN *Frémont, A Biography.* Harpers, 1928

OUTWEST Vol. XVIII, Ed. by Charles F. Lummis, Outwest Co., Los Angeles, 1903

PADEN, IRENE D. *The Wake of the Prairie Schooner.* Macmillan, 1943

———— *Prairie Schooner Detours.* Macmillan, 1949

ROSS, NANCY WILSON *Westward the Women.* Alfred A. Knopf, 1945

ROYCE, SARAH *A Frontier Lady.* Yale University Press, 1932

SAXON, LYLE *Fabulous New Orleans.* The Century Co., 1928

TALLANT, ROBERT *The Romantic New Orleans.* E. P. Dutton & Co., Inc., 1950

VANDERBECK-BANFIELD LETTERS (Unpublished) New York Historical Society

WELLS & PETERSON *The 49'ers.* Doubleday & Co., 1949

WHITTON, MARY ORMSBEE *Some New Forty-Niner Letters.* American Scholar, Summer, 1953

Index

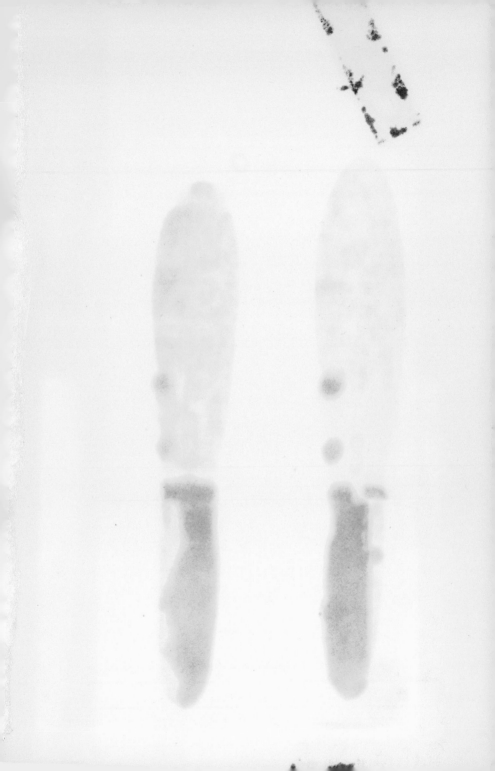

11/10/54

DATE DUE

GAYLORD   PRINTED IN U.S.A.